Battleg
N(

WALKING D-DAY

Battleground series:

Battleground Europe
NORMANDY

WALKING D-DAY

PAUL REED

Pen & Sword
MILITARY

First published in Great Britain in 2012
and reprinted in 2014 by
PEN & SWORD MILITARY
An imprint of
Pen & Sword Books Ltd
47 Church Street
Barnsley, South Yorkshire
S70 2AS

ISBN 978 1 84884 836 8

A CIP catalogue record for this book is
available from the British Library

Typeset in 10 pt Palatino by Factionpress

Printed and bound in Malta by Gutenberg Press Ltd

Pen & Sword Books Ltd incorporates the Imprints of Aviation, Atlas,
Family History, Fiction, Maritime, Military, Discovery, Politics, History,
Archaeology, Select, Wharncliffe Local History, Wharncliffe True Crime,
Military Classics, Wharncliffe Transport, Leo Cooper, The Praetorian Press,
Remember When, Seaforth Publishing and Frontline Publishing

For a complete list of Pen & Sword titles please contact
PEN & SWORD BOOKS LIMITED
47 Church Street, Barnsley, South Yorkshire, S70 2AS, England
E-mail: enquiries@pen-and-sword.co.uk
Website: www.pen-and-sword.co.uk

CONTENTS

PREFACE

On a summer afternoon many years ago I sat outside the Gondrée Café in the shadow of the original Pegasus Bridge. Having grown up on a diet of Airfix kits and Commando comics, it was a dream come true to be seeing where the actual events of D-Day unfolded. In those days the café was not as busy as it is now, and two old men sat with me, my only companions. One was my father, a veteran of the Italian campaign who had been good enough to bring me here, the other was a mystery. We sat for a while looking at him; there was something strangely familiar about the face. Seeing he was of a similar age my father asked him if he had served in the war; he confirmed he had. My father asked where. Here, he replied. My father explained that he thought he was a Normandy veteran but he had meant to elicit a response a little more specific than 'here'. He rose from his chair and walked over to us, his hand outstretched. 'I did mean *here*. Let me introduce myself . . . Major John Howard.'

And so began my passion for Normandy. I returned for both the fortieth and fiftieth anniversaries, and often in between, but as the 1970s crept into the 1980s and 1990s my fascination for the Second World War waned a little as I became more and more engrossed in an earlier conflict – the First World War. Living in France for a decade rekindled the interest and led to many family holidays exploring Normandy in the same way I had learned to 'read' a battlefield on the Somme and in Flanders, an invaluable schooling as it has proved.

And so this book. I had mistakenly believed that everything was known about the Second World War and that visitors were swamped with guidebooks. Then I realised, as I had done with the Somme two decades before, that there was no clear lead in walking the ground and that the War Diaries in The National Archives sat covered in dust, largely untouched. There was, after all, a tale to tell and a way to tell it.

While the fighting in Normandy was essentially a mobile war, it was still a conflict in which the 'Poor Bloody Infantry' marched into battle and saw the ground on their feet. And as such, and in many respects this is true of any battlefield, the best way to see it was, and is, to walk it. I can only hope the reader gets as much pleasure in seeing the D-Day coastline as I did in the research for this book, and takes time to remember those who paid the ultimate price to secure a foothold on that fateful day in 1944.

Paul Reed
Kent and Calvados
January 2012
www.dday1944.co.uk
www.twitter.com/sommecourt

Men of 101st Airborne receiving directions from a military policeman.

Canadians landing at Bernières-sur-Mer.

USER GUIDE

USING THE BOOK: While primarily aimed at those who want to walk the Normandy battlefields, each chapter is divided into a historical section and a section describing one or more walks. As such it can be easily used as a general guide to the D-Day beaches to be kept in your car, or in your pocket as a participant in a battlefield tour. It can also be read from the comfort of your armchair, but whatever, I hope it does inspire you to walk the ground at some point, as there is really no other battlefield experience like it.

THE WALKS: The scope of this book is aimed at the most common form of battlefield traveller – individuals or small groups in a car. Each walk is circular, so that a vehicle can be left in a given location, and returned to (usually) without having to walk back across the same route. However, the walks will suit anyone visiting the battlefields in coach parties, on foot alone or by bicycle or mountain bike. Car crime in France has risen in recent years and walkers should be aware of this when choosing somewhere to park their vehicle, and it is advisable never to leave valuables on display.

THE MAPS: The maps are based on field sketches by the author using IGN 1/25,000 maps as the base for map data. These IGN Blue series maps are easily available in Normandy at newsagents, supermarkets and in shops at sites like Arromanches. They are very useful to have on the walks. Digital versions of the maps are available for the iPhone and iPad from Memory Map (www.memory-map.co.uk) and from the App Store. Other versions for different models of smart phone and GPS device are also available. Routes can be downloaded from the author's website at www.dday1944.co.uk.

GETTING THERE: There are numerous routes into Normandy. From the UK ferries run from Portsmouth to Cherbourg and Caen (Ouistreham) throughout the year. A longer route is Dover–Calais and then down the motorway; from Calais it takes about 3½ hours to Caen. It is also possible to fly into Normandy to Caen-Carpiquet airfield (www.caen.aeroport.fr), or to Paris, from where a fast train (TGV) can be taken to Caen or Bayeux. Within Normandy there are regular bus services and a special bus route along the D-Day beaches, see www.busverts.fr. If it is your first time in Normandy, you might consider an on-site battlefield tour first. There are many guides who offer this in the area, however, Paul Woodadge is highly recommended (www.ddayhistorian.com).

TOURIST OFFICES: The two principal tourist offices are in Bayeux and Caen. However, there are many smaller ones in the area, all of them offering a host of free brochures about the D-Day beaches. The contact details for the main ones are:

Office de Tourisme – Bayeux
Pont Saint Jean
14400 BAYEUX
Tel: 0033 231 512 828
Web: www.bessin-normandie.com

Office de Tourisme – Caen
Place St Pierre
14000 CAEN
Tel: 0033 231 271 414
Web: www.tourisme.caen.fr

ACCOMMODATION: As Normandy is a holiday area there is no shortage of accommodation. Many of the coastal villages have small hotels, and in cities like Bayeux and Caen there are larger establishments and many of the chain hotels, including budget ones. In addition, the area has a high concentration of bed and breakfast establishments. Another option is to rent a house and in this respect Gîtes de France Calvados is recommended (www.gites-de-france-calvados.fr). Details of all the accommodation in Normandy can be found at www.calvados-tourisme.com. The author's favourite place to stay in Normandy is the La Fière Battlefield B&B near Ste-Mère-Eglise. Run by Vivian and Rodolphe Roger, it has some high-quality but affordable rooms and a legendary breakfast! This was also a site that featured heavily in the D-Day story. For more details see their website at www.lafiere.com, or contact them at La Fière Battlefield B&B, 14 Moulin a La Fière, 50480 Ste-Mère-Eglise, France; tel: 0033 233 046 289.

WHAT TO TAKE: As always with a coastal area like Normandy, the weather can be mixed and changeable, and waterproofs, a spare jumper and strong shoes are never wasted on a trip to the

D-Day beaches. In the summer, extra water, sun lotion and a hat are equally useful. Good walking boots are recommended for all walkers. Although there are many inexpensive brands currently on the market, the more money you spend on a pair of boots, the longer they are likely to last. Ones that are already, or easily made, waterproof are essential. A small walker's rucksack is useful for carrying supplies, camera and other gear; again a waterproofed one would be a wise choice.

NORMANDY WEBSITES: There are a huge number of websites relating to Normandy and the Second World War. The author's site for this book is www.dday1944.co.uk and his main WW2 Battlefields site can be found at www.ww2battlefields.com. For the American side of the story www.americandday.org is recommended and the Canadians are well covered at www.junobeach.org. For the British side the D-Day Museum in Portsmouth has a good site at www.ddaymuseum.co.uk, and another useful site is www.normandie44lamemoire.com. The best Second World War discussion forum on the Internet is WW2 Talk at www.ww2talk.com. British and Commonwealth war graves can be traced at www.cwgc.org, American casualties at www.abmc.gov and Germans at www.volksbund.de.

NOTE: The author and publishers bear no responsibility for any events or injuries that arise through the walking of the routes described in this book, nor the interpretation or misinterpretation of any directions or maps, nor any changes that take place that affect the walking of the routes. All walks are conducted at the walker's own risk and responsibility, and vehicles and property are left at the owner's risk.

Sherman Flail   Petard   DUKW

Churchill AVRE

ABBREVIATIONS/GLOSSARY

AVRE	Armoured Vehicle Royal Engineers; this was a specialist piece tank used by 79th (Armoured) Division on D-Day. The majority were Churchill tanks
BAR	Browning Automatic Rifle
Bn	Battalion
Bren	Light machine gun found in every infantry section
C47	The Dakota aircraft used to drop British and American airborne troops on D-Day
CSM	Company Sergeant Major
DD	Duplex Drive, Sherman tanks adapted to be able to swim ashore
DUKW	An amphibious six-wheeled truck used to ship supplies and men to the beaches. Also known as the 'Duck'
DZ	Drop Zone
Flail	Sherman tank with a drum and chain device fitted to the front so it could clear paths in minefields
Funny	Generic name for the adapted tanks used by 79th (Armoured) Division on D-Day
H-Hour	The time an operation begins
HE	High Explosive
KSLI	King's Shropshire Light Infantry
LCA	Landing Craft Assault
LCI	Landing Craft Infantry
LCM	Landing Craft Mechanised
LCT	Landing Craft Tank.
LCT(R)	Landing Craft Tank (Rocket)
LCVP	Landing Craft, Vehicle, Personnel
LMG	Light Machine Gun
LST	Landing Ship Tank
LZ	Landing Zone
MG34	German machine gun

MG42	German machine gun capable of firing up to 1,500 rounds per minute
OP	Observation Post
PFC	Private First Class
PIAT	Projectile Infantry Anti-Tank; spring-fired anti-tank weapon used by British and Commonwealth troops
PIR	Parachute Infantry Regiment
PVT	Private (US Army)
RCT	Regimental Combat Team
RV	Rendez-Vous Point
SP	Self-Propelled
WN	*Widerstandsnest*, the German name for a defensive structure such as a pillbox or bunker

Browning Automatic Rifle

Bren Gun

Maschinengewehr MG34

Maschinengewehr MG42

PEGASUS BRIDGE WALK: 6TH AIRBORNE DIVISION AT BÉNOUVILLE

HISTORICAL SECTION

The 6th Airborne Division was one of two airborne formations created when the airborne forces came into existence from 1941 onwards. It was commanded by Major General R.N. 'Windy' Gale DSO OBE MC, an experienced regular soldier who had seen action in the First World War a generation before. Like all British airborne divisions, it was composed of three brigades: two parachute brigades and one airlanding brigade. The parachute brigades contained battalions of the Parachute Regiment, and would drop from either C47 Dakota transport aircraft or Stirling bombers. The airlanding brigade consisted of battalions of infantry regiments converted

Major General R.N. 'Windy' Gale DSO OBE MC.

6th Airborne Division Drop Zones on D-Day.

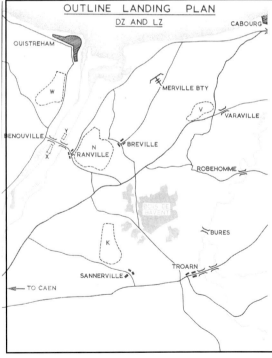

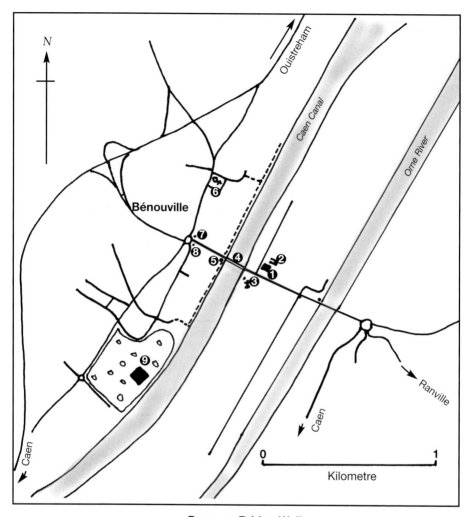

Pegasus Bridge Walk

1. Pegasus Museum
2. Pegasus Bridge
3. Landing Zone Memorials
4. New Pegasus Bridge
5. Gondrée Café
6. Bénouville churchyard
7. Para Memorial
8. Bénouville town hall
9. Bénouville chateau

to airlanding units which would be brought in by glider. Most of the support units in the division were gliderborne due to the nature of their heavy equipment and the need for vehicles. The only tank support was from the divisional reconnaissance regiment, and this was equipped with Tetrach light tanks, which could be brought in aboard the larger Hamilcar gliders.

The division's objective on D-Day was to drop in the area around and east of the Caen Canal and Orne River. There were two bridges over those waterways at Bénouville which had to be taken intact and held. In addition, the division was tasked with taking and neutralising the German gun battery at Merville (see pp.34–35). Further to the east specialist Engineers would land and destroy the bridges over the River Dives to stop German re-enforcements and armoured troops from entering the Normandy bridgehead. Once these tasks were complete the division would then link up with the Commandos and elements of 3rd Division landing on Sword Beach. From there they would establish an eastern flank to ensure the advance on Caen was secure and the bridges at Bénouville remained in Allied hands. Bénouville is a small village in Normandy, located just west of the Caen Canal and Orne River. There is a twelfth-century

Pegasus Bridge just before the war.

church, and on the southern edge of the village, set in parkland, an eighteenth-century chateau designed by the French neoclassical architect Ledoux, famous for his work in Paris. By the 1920s the chateau was a maternity hospital and latterly where the regional accounts department was based before it was requisitioned by the Germans. There were two bridges here. There was a lift bridge across the Caen Canal, and a swing bridge on the Orne. They were both moving bridges due to the passage of vessels along the waterways, although by the 1930s it was largely only the Caen Canal with its link to the deep-water facility in the city that remained in use. A pre-D-Day intelligence report stated that Bénouville, 'has a population of 589 spread over small farmsteads with a big chateau which commands views SW and NE along the Orne Valley. The mayor's name is M. Thomas.'[1] The same report said of the local people,

> there will be a considerable number of essential workers left in farms etc. They have been cruelly treated by the enemy but at the same time they will have been bombed by the Allies, so in the early stages there may be some anti-allied feeling . . . The Norman is a horse dealer and a notorious cider drinker and always he loves success in anyone and appreciates a sharp deal but is a stickler for justice and should be handled justly and firmly.[2]

The Germans had garrisoned Bénouville since 1940, but in 1944 defences had been expanded with a 50mm gun position on the eastern side of the bridge, trenches dug along the canal, a

The bridge across the Orne River.

Men from 6th Airborne board their gliders.

roadblock on the village side of the canal and barbed wire covering the position. Beyond the village, anti-glider obstacles (poles) had been placed in the fields. The troops guarding the position were believed to be from the 711th Infantry Division, a formation numbering 13,000 men backed up with artillery and anti-tank gun support, and tank support consisting of a unit equipped with captured French Renault 35 tanks. Intelligence reports rated this division as 'low category' and made up largely of men aged 35–40, or very young soldiers, with a large number of Russians or *Ost Truppen*. The 21st Panzer Division were the nearest armoured formation, and the gun battery at Merville could also provide support if needed.

The plan to take the bridges at Bénouville had been formulated in the spring of 1944. The unit detailed to make the assault on the bridges was the 2nd Bn Oxfordshire & Buckinghamshire Light Infantry. This was an airlanding unit, which came in by glider. It had been felt that a direct parachute drop on the targets would fail, and that a strike force should land almost on top of the objective and immediately engage the Germans before they had time to react. While landing a glider so close to a bridge over a waterway was a tricky call, the pilots of the Glider Pilot Regiment were confident it was possible. Within the battalion the commanding officer, Lieutenant

Colonel M.W. Roberts, selected 'D' Company for the task as it was led by his best company commander, Major John Howard. Reginald John Howard was a pre-war regular soldier who had served in the ranks as an ordinary soldier, and was a police officer in Oxford when the war broke out. He was commissioned in 1940, and was promoted to Major and commanded 'D' Company from 1942.

The task allocated to Howard and his men was to land two sets of three gliders close to the bridges to be taken; one party of three near the Orne Bridge and one near the Caen Canal. Each glider was packed with men from 'D' Company along with Airborne Engineers to clear any explosives and mines, and medics to assist with the expected casualties. Howard was set to be in the leading glider to land at the Caen Canal Bridge, but the assault would be lead by one of his platoons, with the others following in close support. A similar assault would take place on the Orne Bridge. Training for the mission had been intense, but as the group approached the Normandy coastline on the night of 5 June, Howard felt confident.

The order to release was given and the gliders began their descent. Unbeknown to Howard, one glider for the Orne Bridge group had been towed off course and landed miles away, the party rejoining later. In Howard's group the pilots began the tricky task of descent; the landing being the most difficult part with little space to stop the aircraft. Special arrester parachutes had been fitted to the gliders and these were used. Howard had joked about putting the gliders close on the enemy wire near the Caen Canal Bridge, but that was exactly where the lead glider, with Howard in it, came to rest. It was arguably the most impressive feat of flying in the whole war, something that Air Chief Marshall Leigh Mallory later commented on.

With the gliders down, and close to the objective, it was time to go into action. Private Clark later recalled,

Lt Danny Brotheridge, our platoon commander, quickly slid open the door and said 'get out!' I jumped out and stumbled on the grass because of the weight I was carrying and set the Bren up facing the bridge. The rest of the lads jumped out. Lt Brotheridge got in front of me. He looked around to make sure everyone was out and said 'Come on lads!' and up we got . . . we were about thirty yards from the bridge. We dashed towards it. I saw a German on the right hand side and let rip at him and down he went. Having shot the first

Aerial view of the Pegasus Bridge landings.

> German, I still keep firing going over the bridge. At the other side
> there was another German and he went down.[3]

But not every German had been accounted for. Return fire was
coming in the direction of the party crossing the bridge and the
first to get hit was Den Brotheridge. Caught by a bullet, he was
thrown onto his back where he died in the arms of one of his
men, Corporal Wally Parr. Lieutenant Herbert Denham
Brotheridge, from Smethwick in Staffordshire, was the first
British combat fatality and probably the first fatal Allied battle
casualty of D-Day.

Despite this loss the German defence had buckled, and the
firing died down as the men of Howard's company cleared the
trenches. Another one of the platoon commanders, Lieutenant
Wood, later recalled, 'by the time we got over to the other side
most of the enemy seemed to have run away; I found an MG34
intact with a complete belt of ammunition on it which nobody
had fired . . . On my '38 set I heard the magic words *Ham and Jam*
and knew that the operation had been successful.'[4]

John Howard himself later wrote an account of the unit's
activities on D-Day,

At 2354 hrs Monday 5th June 1944 an assault party consisting of 'D' Company and 2 platoons 'B' Company under command of Major R.J. Howard, took off in 6 gliders from Tarrant Rushton airfield. They were the first troops to leave England for the invasion of the continent and had a coup de main task of capturing two vital bridges intact, namely the bridges over the Caen Canal and River Orne at Benouville and Ranville respectively. These gliders were briefed to land within 50 yards of each bridge. Speed and dash on the part of the attacking troops was considered sufficient to overcome the garrison of 50.

At 0025 hrs the first glider crash-landed within 20 yards of Bénouville Bridge. It contained No 25 platoon commanded by Lt H.D. Brotheridge, and the company commander. According to plan they immediately attacked and crossed the bridge while they took on the defences, the Sappers who accompanied the party cut wires and removed charges. Lt Brotheridge was unfortunately shot while crossing the bridge and died two hours later, he gave a gallant display of brilliant leadership. The 2nd glider, 24 platoon, commanded by Lt D.J. Wood touched down a minute after 25, with 14 platoon commanded by Lt R.A.A. Smith half a minute later. While 24 took on the inner defences, 14 were ordered to reinforce 25 and start to form a small bridgehead to meet the first expected counter-attack. Both the platoon commander and platoon Sergeant of 24th were wounded in the initial assault, subsequently command falling on Cpl Godbold. On the Ranville Bridge only two platoons had arrived, 17 platoon under Lt D.B. Fox, and 23 under Lt H.J. Sweeney. Little opposition was met and 17 platoon soon had control of the bridge, reinforced by 23. Both bridges were captured and consolidation effected after mopping up, within 15 minutes of landing.[5]

With the bridges secure and Howard, as David Wood mentioned, having given the instructions to his signaller to send the code-words 'Ham' and 'Jam' to indicate the capture of both bridges to those off-shore (the information was also sent by pigeon), it was up to his small party to defend what they had captured. Some men were sent to guard the swing bridge across the Orne, but as airborne troops were dropping around Ranville beyond it, possibly tying up any small parties of Germans there, it was felt the main threat would come on the western bank. Moving up to the crossroads next to the *mairie* at Bénouville, Howard screened out his men here and into the neighbouring

Howard's gliders landed close to the bridge.

buildings around the church. Here they awaited the arrival of the expected German counter-attack.

Back at the bridge one building was increasingly in use, the first to be 'liberated' as such. This was the local café, owned and run by the Gondrée family. Georges and Therese Gondrée had purchased the café before the war, and had a young family. In the early hours of D-Day they had heard the gliders land on the opposite bank of the canal. They retreated to the safety of the cellar with their two children, Georgette and Arlette. Then the firing started and going upstairs to see what was going, Georges Gondrée came under fire when he opened a window to look down on what was happening. Thankfully, the burst missed him, and he went downstairs to speak with the soldiers. They advised him to go back down to the cellar, which is what he did until the battle for the bridges was over.

Howard's defences were about to be put to the test. He later wrote,

> the defence of the bridges until our relief arrived was expected to be a difficult task, within an hour two or three tanks approached the bridges from the West. The first tank was put out of action by a well aimed bomb from a PIAT [Projectile Infantry Anti-Tank] fired by 17 platoon. This platoon was brought over from the river bridge to form part of the bridgehead on the west bank.[6]

The man responsible for this feat was Sergeant Thornton. He later wrote that the PIAT had,

> fifty yards range only and you must never, never miss. You've had it because by the time you have reloaded and cocked it everything has

gone . . . Sure enough . . . this thing appears. You couldn't see very much, it was moving slowly towards the bridge. For a few second they hung around. Although shaking I took an aim and 'Bang!' off it went. The thing exploded. Two minutes later all hell let loose.[7]

The tank was immobilised and the crew bailed out. The tank was a Panzer IV, almost certainly from the 21st Panzer Division. The other tanks in the group that had approached the bridge withdrew, at least for now. The Germans had seemingly been surprised at the anti-tank capabilities of the airborne troops, thinking they would easily be overwhelmed by armour. For now it was a stand-off.

Finally, at 0300 on 6 June what Howard and his men had waited for finally materialised from the direction of Ranville.

Our relief, 7th Bn Parachute Regiment (Somerset Light Inf) reached us 3 hours after our landing, 2 hours later than expected. Being relieved by the Somersets made the bridge operation a light infantry show. Our first relief was intended to be 'C' Company 7th Para Bn commanded by Major R.H. Bartlett of the regiment, unfortunately his company were dropped dispersed and unable to reach us as soon as expected. Soon after first light a Gun Boat moved up the Canal from the sea and shot HQ 7 Para Bn. Another well aimed PIAT bomb put this out of action. The assault force was still defending the bridges when the regiment landed and crossed the bridge at 2300 hrs.[8]

Indeed, the arrival of the boats was a curious incident, also mentioned by 7th Bn Parachute Regiment in their account,

two boats, each about twenty foot long, chugged slowly past . . . keeping an interval of about a hundred yards between them. There was no sign of life to be seen on either but there was a closed wheelhouse aft where the crew were presumably watching events . . . Each had a pom-pom gun in the bows but these were apparently completely unmanned. It was obvious they did not know what the situation was and had come down to try and find out . . . A Bren gun of Thomas' platoon on the West end of the bridge and a PIAT of Howard's on the East end of it both opened up . . . almost simultaneously. The Bren splintered the wheelhouse and the PIAT stopped the engine completely. The second boat immediately turned round and made off towards the sea at full speed . . . The first boat drifted helplessly towards the East bank where a reception party of Howard's men were waiting . . . While it was drifting though the pom-pom gun, which was obviously remote controlled, swung round and started to fire tracer into the battalion position on the West . . . The crew of the crippled boat, who were all young soldiers and very nervous except for . . . an arrogant Nazi type, surrendered without trouble and the gun boat remained as a trophy.[9]

For John Howard, with the arrival of 7 Para and the establishment of a new perimeter, the day was over. It was the first of many he would spend in Normandy, but in August 1944 he was decorated with the Distinguished Service Order for bravery on 6 June.

The 7th Bn Parachute Regiment was commanded by Lieutenant Colonel Pine-Coffin. The unit had been formed from a nucleus of men from the 10th Bn Somerset Light Infantry in November 1942. The battalion had become part of the Parachute Regiment at this time, but retained its Light Infantry title and associations being known as the 7th (Light Infantry) Bn. Its men were also given permission to wear a small piece of green diamond-shaped cloth backing to the Parachute badge on their berets, a regiment colour showing a visible connection to the old regiment. After much parachute and invasion training, in February 1944 command of the battalion passed to Richard Geoffrey Pine-Coffin. He was a pre-war regular officer who had first been commissioned in 1928, served in India, fought at Dunkirk and had been awarded the Military Cross in North Africa with 3rd Bn Parachute Regiment. Pine-Coffin was highly respected by his men, and many described him as quiet and inspirational, and all recalled his fondness for smoking a pipe.

For D-Day his battalion had been selected to support the *coup de main* operation that John Howard and his men were detailed to make; the capture of the vital bridges over the Caen Canal and Orne River. They would be parachuted onto a Drop Zone (DZ) close to the bridges and then march to the objective to support Howard in the defence of the ground if his party had succeeded, and launch their own attack on the bridges if he had failed. The plan to land the gliders so close to the bridges made many think the latter situation was more likely. In case one or more of the bridges had been blown it would also mean a water crossing to secure the area, so Pine-Coffin's men would be detailed to carry boats into battle as well as their own gear.

With training over, the final briefing was made in the last hours leading up to D-Day when the exact locations could be revealed.

By 2230 on 5 June, the 7th Bn was airborne in thirty-three Stirling bombers adapted for parachute drops. They began the drop over the DZ at 0500 on the 6th and, as was common on D-Day, some men were scattered far and wide. There were two aircraft shot down by flak en route with the loss of all on board and one aircraft returned without dropping as the pilot had failed to find the DZ. Pine-Coffin had made it down and it was now up to him to bring the battalion together into a coherent fighting force.

> It was very difficult to pick up ones bearings and the CO and Lieut Rogers collected many other wanderers in their search for the RV. It was a most desperate feeling to know that one was close to it but not to know in which direction it lay. Time was slipping by and the Coup de Main party might well be in difficulties; everything could easily be lost if the battalion did not arrive in time. It was impossible to pick up a landmark though until a chance flare, dropped by one of the aircraft, illuminated the church at Ranville, with its most distinctive double tower and thus provided the necessary clue.[10]

Having got to the Rendez-Vous point (RV), Pine-Coffin summoned his bugler and gave the order to sound the battalion call, hopefully bringing in any personnel sheltering in the darkness. He also instructed that an Aldis lamp should be flashed, risking discovery by the Germans in the hope that if the scattered battalion didn't hear the call, they would see the flashes. The plan worked and, 'officers and men began to come in from all sides and it was good to see how many had joined up into groups to come in as formed bodies, with their own protective detachments and the senior of the group in command although there were several groups without officers or NCOs in them.'[11]

Although many figures had emerged from the dark, it was soon found all the companies were well under strength, with 'C' Company down to only 15 per cent of its original number. The men had seemingly been scattered far and wide, and it would take time for them all to reach the RV. Pine-Coffin therefore decided trying to stick to the timing of the operation was more important than numbers, so waited until the battalion was at 50 per cent strength and left his second in command at the RV, Major E. Steel-Baume, to await the arrival of others.

The battalion moved off, with the weak company leading

and the others following. Over the radio net the success signals broadcast by Major Howard at the bridges was picked up and so Pine-Coffin ordered the men to step up the pace. The swing bridge was reached first, and contact was made between the Paras and the Oxs & Bucks men. Pine-Coffin tracked down Major Howard and discovered that Brigadier Nigel Poett, commanding 5th Parachute Brigade, was also at the bridges. Discovering the bridges were intact and the position secure, Pine-Coffin brought the remainder of his force at the double as they crossed the 400yd between the two bridges.

> *The distances between the two bridges was only four hundred yards but it contained plenty of evidence of the thoroughness with which Howard's men had done their job. Many of the battalion got their first sight of a dead German on that bit of road and few will forget it in a hurry, particularly the one who had been hit with a tank bursting bomb while riding a bicycle. He was not a pretty sight.*[12]

Once across the Canal Bridge, Pine-Coffin sent his men out into defence positions at Bénouville. He had to use personnel from 'C' Company to bring the forward posts up to strength and kept what was left as a battle reserve. Radiomen were missing from the platoons and once the men were set up Pine-Coffin had no

The maternity hospital at Bénouville.

direct way to communicate with them. He realised the difficulty of his position.

> *The battalion was now pitifully weak in numbers and several of those that were present carried arms only adequate for close quarter fighting. The actual number available, including all ranks, did not quite touch two hundred, excluding Howard's party which could produce seventy more. There were no 3-inch mortars, no medium machine-guns and no wireless sets. There were, however, a few PIATs which were to give an excellent account of themselves.*[13]

The furthest post out from the Canal Bridge were the positions in front of and in the grounds of Bénouville chateau. Here one of the platoon commanders, Lieutenant Atkinson, set up his men so they could keep an eye on the towpath along the canal, watch the chateau and also control the main road from Caen, which offered the best route into the position for any major counter-attacks. Known for his love of the use of explosives, Atkinson's men were unusually equipped with more explosive charges than any other platoon in the battalion. They soon got a chance to use them, as several armoured vehicles approached and his men were able to knock out one tank and cripple another. His sections in the chateau grounds saw a figure walking around, and when ambushed discovered this person was a Madame Vian, who was in charge of the maternity hospital that had once been here. As Lieutenant Atkinson spoke fluent French he was able to ascertain a great amount of information as to the German positions and strength in the area.

The biggest threat to the positions held by the bridgehead party came when elements from 21st Panzer Division arrived for a counter-attack. A reconnaissance group of tank commanders came forward on foot, were seen by the forward outposts and came under heavy fire, and 'the noise of the seaborne effort became very apparent before the Germans had recovered from the shock of being shot up while on their feet; the survivors rushed back to their tanks and the whole lot swung off towards the beaches'.[14]

Back at the bridge, the problem was not with the enemy but the locals.

> *One of the chief daylight problems of the bridge platoon was how to deal with the very large numbers of extremely excited and voluble refugees who wanted to cross. They did not know which way they*

wanted to go but were very frightened and wanted someone to take them under control. Obviously they could not be allowed to stream across . . . as there was always the chance that they would later contact the Germans and report what they had seen.[15]

Lieutenant Thomas was given the task of dealing with them and when the civilians had all finished enthusiastically shaking hands with him and his men, he was forced to herd them all into hastily put up cages close to the bridge to stop them wandering off and appoint a handful of men to keep an eye on them. At this point Thomas also went into the Gondrée Café and roused Georges, his wife and children to reassure them about what was going on. Being made aware of the situation sometime before it was clear that their corner of Normandy had been liberated, it was only later that they were to discover they were the first building to be liberated in France on D-Day.

As it became light the seaborne landings and the battle for Ouistreham and SWORD Beach was audibly in full swing. It was just a matter of Pine-Coffin and his men sitting and waiting.

The attacks on the battalion bridgehead continued to be launched and to be beaten off, but now they were beaten off more as a matter of routine than as part of a life and death struggle on which everything depended. It seemed impossible that they [the Germans] could break through now and confidence was higher than at any period since the drop. The enemy was still very persistent though and although the attacks were driven off they were not so without casualties; each attack cost a few more and those that were still unwounded were beginning to feel the strain.[16]

Eventually the visible signs of success were evident and the men from the beachhead were on their way.

True to their word the Commandos were the first to arrive but it was not until 1pm that their pipes were heard in the distance . . . They came through in grand style and their mere numbers were sufficient to keep the snipers quiet for an hour or so . . . at 2pm the piper led the way across the bridge, skirling away on his pipes, followed by Lord Lovat. It was an impressive sight.[17]

With the initial link-up between the seaborne and airborne troops complete, a further wait ensued for Pine-Coffin and his men, as units of 3rd Division from SWORD Beach eventually made contact with the defence perimeter. However, instead of infantry arriving to relieve them, the first men from 3rd Division were Royal Army Service Corps lorry drivers and the driver of a Royal Engineers bulldozer from 79th (Armoured) Division. They had much to tell about the landings, but were of little use for the defence. Elsewhere, airborne headquarters had made contact with SWORD Beach and around 1930 Major General Tom Rennie, commanding 3rd Division, tore up at the bridge in a Bren Gun carrier to report personally to Pine-Coffin that the relieving battalion had been held up in hard fighting beyond the beach but the first elements would arrive shortly. Rennie was as good as his word as within 30 minutes men began to come into the battalion area, and shortly afterwards lorries arrived with the remainder of them. With their day's action over, Pine-Coffin and his men collected on the road in Bénouville with orders to move off to Ranville for the night. Their task successfully completed, they looked back to the field graves of their comrades who had died in the action and were led by their Colonel across the Canal Bridge – a bridge thereafter known as Pegasus Bridge in recognition of the incredible feats of the airborne troops who fought here on D-Day.

Walk 1: In the Airborne Area

STARTING POINT: Pegasus Museum, Bénouville

GPS: 49°14'32.4"N, 0°16'20.2"W

DURATION: 4.8km/2.9 miles

Park your vehicle in the car park of the 'Memorial Pegasus' Museum in Rue Major John Howard, taking care to keep an eye on opening times. There is further parking down the same street. Spend time visiting this excellent museum, which houses the original Pegasus Bridge and many other unique mementoes of the 6th Airborne Division operations on D-Day; a good 90 minutes is needed here before moving off.

From the museum return to the main road (D514) and **turn right** towards the new Pegasus Bridge. Before the bridge **cross the road** and walk over to the area near the gun pit where the memorials are located. This is where the three gliders landed; the marker stones indicate the position of the nose of each glider and details of who flew them and who was inside are included on plaques. It is only when standing here at the first marker that

The original Pegasus Bridge in the Memorial Museum.

you realise how close the glider pilots were able to put Major Howard and his men to the bridge. By the first marker is a bronze bust of Howard, who died in 1999. The nearby gun pit houses a 50mm anti-tank gun that was used on D-Day, and was re-used when *The Longest Day* was filmed here.

From the memorials **cross the bridge** to the far side of the canal. **Stop**. To your left is the famous Gondrée Café, the 'first house in France to be liberated' as the plaque above the front door proudly proclaims. Still run by the Gondrée family, it has always been a special place for returning veterans and inside it is a virtual time capsule of D-Day memories; no visit is complete without seeing it. From the café **cross the road** to the tank. This is a Centaur tank and has no connection to the

Memorial to Major John Howard DSO.

The Gondrée Café.

Pegasus Bridge story; it was used by Royal Marine units on D-Day and was presented to the original museum here (to the rear of the café) in the 1970s.

From the tank follow the canal path in the direction of the coast. Take the **first left**, a minor path across a small bridge and into the outskirts of Bénouville. Follow Rue du Bac du Port to the D35; this was Lieutenant Colonel Pine-Coffin's right flank in the defence of the village on D-Day and many of the buildings on your left were occupied by his men with, then, a clear field of fire. At the main road go **left** and enter the churchyard by the gate.

Bénouville churchyard is an unusual burial ground as it is an original D-Day cemetery; very few of them survive intact. The twenty-three burials here were made largely by units of 6th (Airborne) Division, along with a few from 3rd Division units that had landed on SWORD Beach. Most of the dead are from Pine-Coffin's 7 Para. Among them is the Revd George Edward Maule Parry (Grave 21), who was one of the 7 Para chaplains. He parachuted into Normandy on D-Day and died defending wounded soldiers when the battalion Regimental Aid Post was overrun in one of the German attacks. Private Michael John McGee DCM (Grave 12) was a 20-year-old who took on a German tank with a Bren Gun, distracting the crew and allowing others in his group to place

Bénouville churchyard.

Gammon bombs on the tank. He was awarded a Distinguished Conduct Medal for his bravery but was killed later in the day. By the main entrance are the graves of Georges and Therese Gondrée, who ran the café on D-Day; veterans often visit and place poppy crosses on the grave as a mark of respect for the kindness shown by the family.

From the churchyard go onto the D35 and go **left**; follow the road until you reach the roundabout. This was a crossroads in 1944 and was the heart of Pine-Coffin's defensive position in the village. The memorial to the 7th Bn Parachute Regiment is here, and battle damage to

The Gondrée family grave.

Bénouville crossroads, the town hall and battle-damaged war memorial.

the First World War memorial outside the town hall is clearly visible. This town hall, or *mairie*, was the first such building to be liberated on D-Day and a plaque records this.

From the town hall take Rue du Grand Clos to the left of the building, following it through the village. Further down take Chemin de Camilly on the **right** and at the end **turn left** onto Avenue du 5 Juin 1944. This area was part of the perimeter defended by 7 Para. **Continue** along the road to a crossroads with a large Normandy stone wall on the left. Here is the entrance to the Bénouville chateau, the maternity hospital, which was the left flank held by one platoon of 7 Para. The chateau is not open to the public. At this junction go **left** onto Rue du Grand Clos and follow it round then taking the **first right** into Chemin du Lavoir. This leads out onto the canal. There are good views of the chateau from here and also back towards the bridge and glider landing zone.

From here **walk back** along the canal to the bridge, cross over and follow the D514 past the museum, and straight across at the roundabout to the next bridge. **Stop**. This is Horsa Bridge, captured by the second part of Major Howard's men who landed by glider in the fields north of here. The bridge was taken without a fight and at no loss. A plaque on the western side of the bridge recalls events here in 1944.

At this point you can either return to the car park or take in a visit to Ranville War Cemetery where many of those who fell in the fighting for Pegasus Bridge and Bénouville are buried. From here go across the bridge and at the roundabout take the exit for Ranville. Immediately **turn right** onto Chemin du Bar de Ranville au Marais. Follow this and then take Rue de l'Eglise following this to the church to visit Ranville churchyard and the war cemetery (see pp.48–49). Return via the same route to the museum car park and your vehicle.

EASTERN FLANK WALK – THE MERVILLE BATTERY AND AMFREVILLE–BRÉVILLE

Historical Section

The Merville Battery was one of a number of German field gun battery sites constructed as part of their in-depth Atlantic Wall defences in Normandy. Looking north-west from high ground overlooking the Orne Estuary it was capable of firing on targets in Ouistreham, along the stretch of coast that would become SWORD Beach and any shipping in the Orne area. The battery site consisted of four concrete gun casemates containing the weaponry, and several headquarters and support bunkers; pre-D-Day intelligence reports put the garrison at between 150–200 officers and men. It was ringed with barbed wire and minefields, had two 20mm flak guns and a dozen machine-gun positions to protect it. At the time it was believed

Merville Battery from the air.

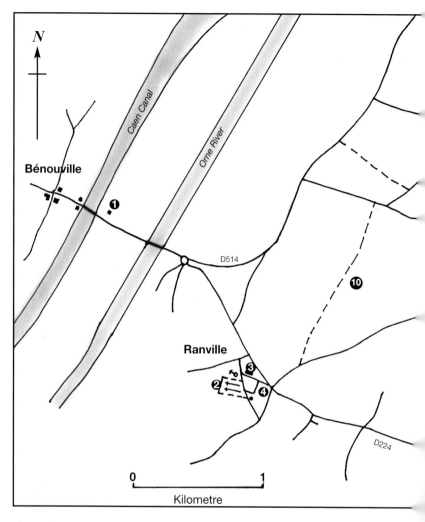

that the guns in the casemates were large-calibre 155mm howitzers or above. In fact they were 100mm Czech field guns dating from the First World War; but in either case they certainly did pose a threat for operations on D-Day.

The unit detailed to make the attack on Merville Battery was the 9th Bn Parachute Regiment, commanded by Lieutenant Colonel Terence Otway. It was part of Brigadier S.J.L. Hill's 3rd Parachute Brigade, and had been training for the operation for some time on a full-scale reconstruction of the battery site near Newbury in Berkshire. Issued with local French resistance

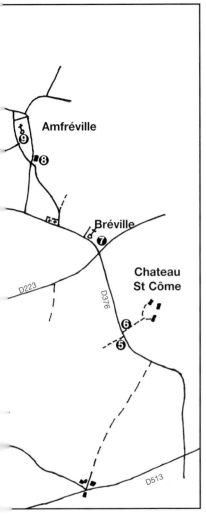

Eastern Flank Walk
1. Pegasus Museum
2. Ranville War Cemetery
3. Ranville Marie-Ecoles
4. 13 Para Memorial
5. 51 (Highland) Division Memorial
6. Chateau St Côme Memorials
7. Bréville churchyard
8. Farm complex
9. Amfréville church
10. Landing and Drop Zones

information, aerial photographs and maps, and following the construction of the model of the battery site, Otway had decided to attack the battery from the south. Surprise was the key, and as at the bridges at Bénouville, it was decided to put a glider party right on the objective to achieve this. This would consist of three Horsa gliders containing fifty-six men of the 9th Bn and eight Airborne Engineers from 591st (Antrim) Parachute Squadron Royal Engineers. The airborne troops selected for the gliders were specially chosen by Otway and he put Captain Robert Gordon-Brown in charge of them; the assault team soon became known as the 'G-B Force'. With them landing inside the perimeter, Otway would lead the remainder of the battalion in support from the south, from a 'firm base' position where the battalion's heavy weapons would be set up providing machine-gun and mortar fire.

With their intensive training over, and the operation postponed numerous times, finally Colonel Otway was able to go to his men on 5 June and give the final instructions; for the majority the final confirmation of where the target was. The battalion would be transported in thirty-two Dakota aircraft with the support weapons, heavy gear and additional Airborne Engineers coming in by glider. The parachute drop would be on DZ 'V', a few miles to the south of the battery. From here the men would assemble and Otway aimed to be on the Firmbase by around 0410/0420 on 6 June. He would then instruct the officers in respect of the final assault and send a diversionary team round to the main gate. This team, with two German speakers, consisted of a number of battalion snipers. Together they would take on the main gate and a bunker nearby and then the snipers would act in support of the main assault. Meanwhile, the battalion would be getting ready for the main assault by laying Bangalore torpedoes under the wire and the engineers assessing what could be done to clear the mines. The 'G-B Force' was due to arrive by glider at 0430 and as they came in the torpedoes would be blown, pathways in the minefields cleared and the bulk of the battalion go in at the point of the bayonet. The garrison would be dealt with by the main force, and the engineers would then use General Wade explosive charges to blow the barrels off the guns. Naval signallers would drop with the battalion and they were to signal to the fleet off-shore; if no sign of success was received by 0530 then they would open fire on the battery site. This meant Ottway had an hour to do the job. The plan was well thought out, Otway was positive there would be a successful outcome, but the events of D-Day were to push him and his men's training and bravery to the limits.

Crossing the Normandy coastline, the Dakotas carrying the battalion to the DZ came under immediate fire from German flak. As the aircraft approached the area where the airborne troops were due to land there was a great deal of confusion in receiving and understanding the signals being received from below. Because of this only a minority of the 9th Bn actually parachuted down onto the DZ. Among those on target were Otway and his group, although they had actually fallen right into a German headquarters. In some cases men had been dropped as much as 30 miles from the DZ, others had landed in the marshy ground around the Orne Estuary, losing their heavy equipment, and sadly some had been dropped into the sea where their chances of survival were slim. There were a number of reasons why this had been a less than successful drop. The aircraft bringing the battalion in was from the No. 46 Group

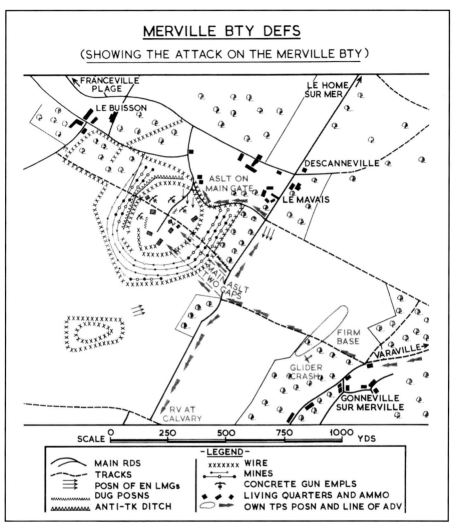

MERVILLE BTY DEFS

(SHOWING THE ATTACK ON THE MERVILLE BTY)

Plan of Merville Battery.

RAF which had only been formed in January 1944. The crews had little experience and there were fewer ex-Bomber Command men among them as in No. 38 Group, which did much of the rest of the 6th (Airborne) Division drop. The aircraft in this group also operated in 'loose' formation and dropped the paratroops following a signal from the leading aircraft. If that signal was wrong it would mean not only his stick would be dropped incorrectly but all those following him. It was made worse when aircraft were scattered following the flak as they flew over the coast, with aircraft going off formation and unable to ascertain where the DZ was. Finally, the Eureka Beacon systems used on this drop were partly faulty and some crews incorrectly or inadequately trained on their use, which again led men to be dropped far and wide. In the end men from the 9th Bn were dropped in an area of roughly 50 square miles, whereas the original DZ was only 1 mile by a $^1/_2$ mile.

Whatever the reasons, the men of the battalion were now faced with the awful truth of the situation. By 0235 Otway had collected some 110 officers and men at the RV. Among them were men with ten lengths of Bangalore torpedo, one machine gun and a few medical orderlies. There were no 3in mortars and none of the transport gliders had arrived so there was no additional heavy equipment or vehicles. There were also no navy signallers to liaise with the fleet off-shore. With so few men and so little equipment, what to do? Otway decided to go anyway and sent a reconnaissance team forward. They cut down the outer wire defences, created lanes through the minefield to the inner wire fence and pinpointed where the garrison was located by listening in to their conversations. The German defenders had no idea they were there. The lanes were taped out with little tape and largely by making marks in the soil, and the mines detected and removed without the normal equipment. It was a tough job made worse by the smashed up nature of the ground; the pre-D-Day aerial bombardment had turned the site into a crater zone. Otway gave his final orders,

> The Commanding Officer was calm and unperturbed. He gave his orders concisely and clearly, as though he were standing giving orders on a training demonstration . . . the CO's calm set a fine example which was followed by all ranks. His thoroughness in training paid a fine dividend, the troops were on their toes and ready for the job.[1]

The attack would go in following two lanes, instead of the three that had been intended. Both parties were only a fraction of the size originally planned. One of the men near the inner wire was finally detected and machine-gun fire opened up. Otway ordered the single Vickers machine gun to reply. A small diversion team then began to attack the area of the main gate and the assault parties then blew the Bangalore torpedoes under the wire. It was at this point Terence Otway shouted the now famous call, 'Get in! Get in!', and the assault started.

Above them were the gliders of the 'G-B Force'. One had crash-landed in the UK on the way over, and now the remaining two were under flak fire. Both crashed, and neither within the perimeter. The furthest was nearly 5 miles away, containing Captain Gordon-Brown himself, but the other one went down in an orchard nearby. The unwounded men among them then joined the fight.

A bitter struggle in the battery site then followed. Some men headed for the Germans firing from weapon pits. Others began to clear the casemates containing the guns. With a general lack of specialist equipment improvisation was the byword, and one man took out the breechblock of a gun with a Gammon bomb. The remainder were dealt with using plastic explosive. Within minutes the main battle was over and the garrison either prisoners, dead, fled or gone to ground. Officers confirmed all the guns were neutralised but how to signal the job had been done? Amazingly, a signals officer, Lieutenant Jimmy Loring, had a pigeon inside his Denison smock. It had survived the landing and the battle, and he now released it with the vital information hoping that it would be received. Without a single radio capable of contacting anyone outside the battalion, and no navy signallers, the only other means available was to light yellow signal flares indicating success and in the hope that they would be duly spotted by Allied aircraft. This was duly done.

At this point the battery site started to come under mortar and shell fire from the Germans. Someone had ordered a heavy 'stonk' knowing that the fire would likely hit friendly as well as enemy troops. The job done, Otway gave the order to withdraw and meet at a nearby Calvary, the selected RV point. But there was the question of the wounded; the walking could be evacuated but the pitiful facilities available meant that the majority had to be left behind. Wounded men were dragged into cover as the last of Otway's men pulled out. For many it was the start of a long period of captivity as prisoners of war.

At the Calvary the survivors gathered and Otway began to assess the casualties. The assault party had lost 1 officer killed along with 4 others wounded, and 65 men killed, wounded and missing. The party of wounded that had made it back were taken off to a farm building known as the 'Haras de Retz', south of the battery site, where a Regimental Aid Post was established. In addition, to them were three German prisoners from the battery, including a doctor and his two orderlies, who were there to assist. It had been a costly action for the men involved and for Otway there was now the issue of gathering what was left of his scattered battalion to pursue the rest of their D-Day objectives. He took his men to Amfreville chateau and dug in there to await the arrival of the Commandos who were meant to link up with them here.

While Terence Otway no doubt thought the battle for the Merville Battery was over, sadly no one aside from those who had taken part were aware of the success. There had been no 'Ham and Jam' moment here, no one had seen the yellow smoke success signal and no one in 6th (Airborne) Division was able to relay the success on 6 June. On that day during the landings on SWORD Beach shells had fallen among the landing troops, which some observers had calculated came from the Merville Battery. Orders were therefore passed down to Lord Lovat and 1st Special Service Brigade to ensure the battery was indeed silenced.

A second battle for the Merville Battery therefore began on 7 June. Men from No. 3 Commando, who had been in touch with elements of the 9th Bn Parachute Regiment, were selected and two troops were sent to take on the Battery under the command of Major J.B.V. Pooley MC. No. 5 troop would lead the assault and No. 4 would give covering fire. Upon arrival it was found the Germans had returned – in fact some of the garrison had hid in tunnels beneath the site and emerged when Otway's men had left. The Commandos came under machine-gun fire so a smoke barrage from 2in mortars was placed down as the assault troop went in. The Battery site was entered and guns found. Some of Otway's men left behind were also discovered, but they could not be evacuated. It was unclear to Pooley whether the guns were serviceable so a second attempt to incapacitate them was made. While supervising his men, Pooley was shot in the head and killed instantly. A German counter-attack then came in supported by armour, and so the Commandos were forced to withdraw. One party had to escape through an uncleared minefield and lost men as a consequence. The survivors withdrew to Sallenelles.

Commandos move up.

The Commandos recalled that the 'Germans in the Battery had fanatical courage and fought until they died'.[2] It had been a tough battle and in terms of what was known of the battery site, once more indecisive. Otway had got in and thought he had silenced the guns. Others thought they were still in action and had ordered the Commandos in, and they too thought they had silenced the battery. But within two days Merville Battery was once more in action and would remain so until the end of the Normandy campaign in August 1944.

Following the success of the initial D-Day objectives allocated to the 1st Special Service Brigade and elements of 6th (Airborne) Division in the Bénouville–Ranville and Merville Battery areas, the next phase of the battle involved the capture and securing of the high ground to the east of the Drop and Landing Zones (LZ). Here an eastern flank would be formed between the Orne and Dive rivers to protect the invasion forces and the advance on Caen. To support them units from the 51st (Highland) Division, an infantry formation, began to disembark on SWORD Beach late on D-Day. This unit had been in action constantly since the outbreak of war. It had been destroyed in France in June 1940 and reformed, and then fought in North Africa, Sicily and Italy before returning to the UK for invasion training.

The key to the success of securing this eastern flank was the capture of the northern and central areas of the high ground between Amfreville and Bréville, and high ground close to the Chateau St Côme. It had originally been planned to assault and take this ground on D-Day, but the fighting for the village of Ranville, in the heart of the airborne position, had proved somewhat more difficult. The 12th and 13th Bns Parachute Regiment had been detailed to take and hold Ranville. Like many others, they had been dropped widely on D-Day and in both battalions about 60 per cent of their strength made it to the RV and into action at Ranville. The village was taken and held against counter-attacks from Panzer Grenadiers and tanks from 21st Panzer Division, but by the afternoon of D-Day the situation was getting critical. The arrival of Commandos from 1st Special Service Brigade helped tip the balance, but it meant that further operations had to be postponed until the following day.

On 7 June the situation was more stable with the 3rd Division having taken over positions at Bénouville, troops from the Highland Division arriving, Ranville and the ground to the south being defended by glider troops of 6th (Airborne) Division and the Merville Battery silenced by the 9th Bn Parachute Regiment. The 1st Special Service Brigade cleared the coastal belt to the north with naval support from two cruisers off-shore, and the 12th Bn Devonshire Regiment, the final glider battalion, arrived on SWORD Beach as a seaborne trail and entered the battle area. With a more stable situation attention

Commandos at Bréville.

could now be turned to taking and holding the high ground.

The two key villages here were Amfreville to the north, with its small hamlet of Le Plein, and Bréville to its south-east. Both of these were small, with the usual collection of stone-built Normandy houses and farm buildings surrounded by *bocage* hedgerows and orchards, but sited on rising ground they dominated the positions around Ranville. Commandos from 1st Special Service Brigade made the first attempt to secure the villages. At 1400 on D-Day No. 3 Commando assaulted the village of Amfreville and the hamlet of Le Plein. Arriving on bikes, they formed up and were supported by men from Lieutenant Colonel Otway's 9th Bn Parachute Regiment, fresh from their action at Merville that morning. Lord Lovat himself arrived and sent the Commandos into action. They moved up the road into the village, with a section each side of the road, and soon ran into heavy small arms fire causing heavy loss. This route proved impossible, and the Commandos surveyed a new route in via the village school and post office. This was attacked, hand to hand fighting pushed the Germans back so that No. 3 Commando went through Le Plein and dug in among the hedgerows beyond.

With the Le Plein–Amfreville position now held, other Commando units moved up to strengthen it, among them No. 6 Commando. However, the Germans in Bréville made life difficult here and dominated the battlefield. The Commandos sent patrols in the direction of Bréville and found it well held with machine guns, mortars and 20mm cannon. Captain J.E. Thompson MC noted that on 7 June,

> *The OC sent for the troop commanders, the mortar Sergeant, and the Major commanding a Battery of SP [Self-Propelled] guns. He thought a successful raid would not only clear out the weapons that were troubling us, but would give us a high moral effect, giving everyone a chance to put into practice lessons they had learned from training during all those long periods back in England.*[3]

An attack therefore went in later that day.

> *The barrage opened up on time, three Verey lights were fired and the mortar smoke landed in the right places.*

> *Just before reaching the German battery positions, LMGs [Light Machine Guns] opened fire at point blank range from the left side of the wood. An SP gun was knocked out, and within 30 yards of the gun a German ran out trying to reach his cannon and was killed. The centre of the attacking troops came across a dugout with the body of a German sergeant laying across the entrance. Private Greenhill tossed a hand grenade into the dugout, and those who could walk came out with their hands above their heads. When the dugout was cleared, men of the Parachute Regiment who had been captured were now set free.*

> *The left of the assault had overrun the German gun position, and when we entered the village we found the Germans had evacuated the village in a hurry . . . 12 prisoners were captured along with 2 x 80mm mortars, 3 LMGs and many Schmeissers, Lugers and stores . . . The village was now quiet after the attack, except German ammunition exploding.*[4]

While in Bréville, one of the Commandos had found an

Fighting at Amfreville.

unposted letter from a German soldier to his wife which read 'The British have arrived, and are digging in but don't worry dear, they are too yellow to attack us.'

The position now remained static, and having silenced most of the German heavy weapons, was a little more pleasant for the Commandos in Le Plein, although they came under constant probing attacks.

Finally, the position at Bréville was taken on 12 June 1944. The units selected to assault were the 12th Bn Parachute Regiment and 12th Bn Devonshire Regiment (glider troops). They also had tank support from the 13th/18th Hussars equipped with Sherman tanks, along with 25-pounders from

Amfreville church.

four different Field Regiments and 5.5in howitzers from a Medium Regiment. Well supported, the attack would go in from the west, with the units forming up in Amfreville.

The 12th Bn Parachute moved up to take part in the attack the night before. Major Ellis 'Dixie' Dean later recounted the battalion's experience in the action,

At 8pm we were ordered to prepare for battle, and at 8.30 the Bn moved off, uphill, towards Amfréville. There, to our surprise we filed into the Church. The men sat in the pews, smoking, chattering or sucking sweets, or gazing at the gaily painted effigies of saints, of the Virgin and at the elaborate gilded cross on the altar. After some minutes there was a scurry and a bustle, quick orders were given and the Bn filed out of the Church. On the steps the Padre handed out bundles of the Div paper 'Pegasus'. We lined up on the road in the order 'C' 'A' 'B' & 'HQ' Coys, and were informed that an attack on Bréville was indeed to be executed. We were to be supported by a Squadron of Sherman tanks and a Company from the 12th Devons (Airlanding) Bn. We started off down the road towards Bréville at approximately 2150 hrs, the noise was colossal, shells whistling over our heads and exploded with a crash ahead. Trails of white smoke appeared overhead from smoke shells, then, suddenly, among and around us, everywhere, shells and mortars began with deafening noise to explode. We sought such cover as was available. It became evident that most of this fire around us came from our own guns (this being discovered true later), but it couldn't be stopped now – and was perhaps not misunderstandable with the attack mounted in such short notice. The firing ceased some ten minutes past 10, and the remnants of the Bn moved towards the start line. Men with limp arms, bloody faces, and men crawling on their hands and knees were passed. Of the Devons only 1 officer and some 6 men could be found. We approached the start line and assumed position along the hedgerow. Ahead was the burning, dust smoked village, and between it and us was a large open field. In the centre of the field four Shermans were blazing away with tracer into the houses. Steadily, and in line we advanced up to the tanks, and, as they were still firing, we halted and waited for them to stop. Behind and to the left,

*a pillar of black, oily smoke billowed up from one of the Shermans.
The fire from the tanks was switched to the left of the village into
some dark woods. Again the advance continued. 'B' Coy was joined
by Col. R.G. Parker DSO, our old Bn commander. Apparently he
was at a loose end and had come to see us in. He had just been
wounded in the hand.*

*With little fuss or bother 'B' Coy entered the village and deployed
into an orchard close to the blazing church. Dead Germans, with
their weapons – automatics, rifles, etc, lying around their empty
trenches, were to be seen everywhere. According to the drill the men
quickly found themselves trenches. In one was a live, shivering
German. On being made to come out he dived at one of our men who
immediately shot him. He turned and faced the Coy 2 i/c with horror
stamped on his face, saying 'God! Look what I've done.'*

*When the expected counter barrage came down the men were
safely in trenches. For ten minutes it was hell in that orchard with
mortar bombs and shells mercilessly pouring down – It ceased very
suddenly. The Company Commander was found lying half in and
half out of his trench, moaning. He died two minutes later.*

*In the other rifle Coys, much the same had been happening. But
the objective had been secured. And it was held.*

*General Gale visited Bréville, but few of the men saw him. We
were sorry to learn that the Commanding Officer had been killed
near the church at Amfréville, and that Lord Lovat had been
wounded by the same shell.*[5]

Lovat had come up to see how the fighting was going in Bréville
and as he stood with Lieutenant Colonel Johnson shells from
British artillery units fell short killing the Colonel and
wounding Lovat.

Meanwhile, the 12th Bn Devonshire Regiment had
committed 'D' Company, commanded by Major J.A.F.W.
Bampfylde. The unit formed up on the start line and also came
under 'friendly fire' when British shells fell short, killing
Bampfylde and several others. The survivors took part in the
assault, and what was left of the company consolidated in the
village.

Although it had been costly, the attack on Bréville had been
successful. The 12th Bn Parachute Regiment lost 8 officers and
133 men, nearly half its strength before the battle. The company
of the Devonshires involved had lost its company commander

killed and 35 killed or wounded. But, 'the Bréville gap had been closed, and the enemy never made any attempt to reopen it. The battle in that small battered village achieved results of the greatest importance to the whole Normandy campaign.'[6]

The eastern flank now settled down to one of stagnation. The men dug in around the villages, and to the south in the wood areas close to the Bois de Bavent experienced the type of warfare known to their fathers a generation before in the First World War: trenches, patrols and daily casualties from shell and mortar fire, even when no major activity was going on. Little would change until the German position here collapsed at the end of the Normandy campaign in August 1944. By that time the Airborne, Commando and Highland troops who had served here had suffered not inconsiderable casualties on what was 'all quiet on the eastern flank'.

Walk 2: On the Eastern Flank

STARTING POINT: Ranville War Cemetery

GPS: 49°13'51.7"N, 0°15'27.7"W

DURATION: 9.3km/5.8 miles

Park your vehicle in the car park close to the cemetery in Rue Comte Louis de Rohan-Chebou. There are also additional places to park in the area around the cemetery.

Start the walk in Ranville War Cemetery. There are a number of airborne graves here, and several of these soldiers fell in the ground covered by the walk. Among the Airborne graves is the first man credited to have landed in the 6th Airborne Division. Captain Robert Edward Vane De Lautour (IIA-E-2) was in the 22nd Independent Parachute Company tasked with marking the DZ and LZ, and was in the first stick to be dropped on the night of 5/6 June. He was killed two weeks later. Private Emile Corteil (IA-G-13) was in 9 Para and one of many dropped in the wrong place on D-Day. Emile was in charge of the troop dog, Glen, who had dropped with him. Both were killed by friendly fire because they were spotted in the wrong place by an RAF fighter and fired on. Emile and Glen were buried together; a rare example of an animal occupying a war grave. The youngest known airborne soldier to have died in Normandy is buried

6th Airborne pathfinders get ready for D-Day. Captain De Lautour is on the extreme left.

here: Private Robert Edward Johns (IVA-E-1), from Portsmouth, of 13 Para was only 16 years old when he died on the eastern flank on 23 July 1944. War Poet Major John Jarmain (IIIA-L-9) wrote poems based on his experiences in North Africa. He died in Normandy on 26 June 1944 while serving with an anti-tank regiment. His poem 'At a War Grave' seems strangely appropriate here.

> *No grave is rich, the dust that herein lies*
> *Beneath this white cross mixing with the sand*
> *Was vital once, with skill of eye and hand*
> *And speed of brain. These will not re-arise*
> *These riches, nor will they be replaced;*
> *They are lost and nothing now, and here is left*
> *Only a worthless corpse of sense bereft,*
> *Symbol of death, and sacrifice and waste.*

Top: Ranville Cemetery, 1946.
Inset: Captain De Lautour's grave at Ranville.
Above: Ranville Cemetery today.

From the main cemetery walk towards the wall that divides the military and civil cemetery and **go through the wooden gate**. This takes you through the civil graves to the rear of the church (if the church is open, go inside as there are several airborne memorials and a stained glass window to the rear). At the rear of the church is Ranville churchyard.

Ranville churchyard is a wartime burial site for forty-seven men from 6th Airborne and 1st Special Service Brigade who died on D-Day and the following weeks. Among the burials is Lieutenant Den Brotheridge who was killed in the assault on Pegasus Bridge. One intriguing grave is that of Bombardier Henry Hall of 53rd (Worcestershire Yeomanry) Airlanding Light Regiment Royal Artillery. This was an artillery support unit in 6th Airborne Division. Hall's date of death is recorded as 5 June, the day before D-Day. It appears he died in a glider en route to Normandy before midnight on the 5th, but the exact circumstances of his death remain something of a mystery.

From the churchyard exit near the First World War war memorial and **walk across the road** to Rue des Airbornes. On this street is the imposing *marie-ecole*, the old town hall and school in Ranville. It was used by General Gale as a headquarters in June 1944 and outside the right wing of the building is a bronze head and shoulders statue of Gale. To the right of it is a plaque commemorating the fact that Ranville was the first village liberated in France by the 13th Bn Parachute Regiment.

Ranville school, former 6th Airborne HQ.

Memorial to Major General 'Windy' Gale.

From the *marie-ecole*, follow Rue des Airbornes down to the main road and at the end **go to the right**. On a wall on the right is what is considered the 'original' airborne memorial in the village, unveiled when the first veterans returned in 1946. It actually commemorates the liberation of the village of Ranville at 0230 on 6 June by the 13th (Lancashire) Bn Parachute Regiment. Originally formed out of men from two battalions of the South Lancashire Regiment, it was commanded by Lieutenant Colonel P.J. Luard on D-Day and became known as 'Luard's Own'. On D-Day the unit had a fairly successful drop north of Ranville and was rallied on the DZ by a call from a hunting horn sounding 'L' for Lancashire. It cleared and secured Ranville by 0300, and its Support Company heavy weapons, including 6-pounder anti-tank guns, arrived shortly afterwards having come in by glider. During the rest of the day it came under heavy attack from units

The memorial to 13th Para when it was unveiled in 1946.

in the 21st Panzer Division, but the position held; its casualties by the close of D-Day were nearly a hundred all ranks.

Continue along Rue des Airbornes and follow it out of the town. On the eastern edge the road becomes Rue du General de Gaulle, stay left and continue, mindful of the traffic. Beyond the village this road meets a crossroads with a farm complex on the left. **Stop here**.

This was one of the positions held by the 13th Bn Parachute Regiment on D-Day, and subsequent days. With dug-in weapons, the infantry sections in foxholes and good fields of fire, clearly visible from here, it gradually beat off attack after attack from Panzer Grenadiers and self-propelled guns from the 21st Panzer Division. These included Marders and some of the hybrid vehicles converted from 1940-period French tanks; two were knocked out in an attack on 'A' Company on the morning of D-Day alone. On one occasion the Germans attempted to penetrate into the line held by the 13th Bn wearing airborne smocks and red berets. Here the battalion remained until the ground along the ridge from Amfreville was cleared and the line moved nearer to the Bois de Bavent. On 8 June they became one of the first British units to encounter the 12th SS Panzer Division, when four men from a Panzer Grenadier battalion were captured just outside Ranville.

Sunken lane leading to the eastern flank.

At the crossroads **go straight across**, the road now becomes the D224. Follow this until it meets the main D513, staying left for the last few hundred yards, and at the junction take a **minor road on the left** which has a 'no entry' sign for cars at the start called Chemin Guillaume. This takes you through some farm

buildings and is a recognised walking route; follow it uphill through typical Normandy terrain. It is worth stopping and looking back as you go.

At the top of the track you reach the Rue de l'Arbre Martin and here **turn left**. This area was essentially the front line from June to August 1944, defended by units of 6th (Airborne) Division and elements of the 51st (Highland) Division. Follow this road until it reaches an entrance to a chateau on the right. **Stop.**

There are a number of memorials here connected with the units who fought and served here. The impressive Scottish Piper is a large bronze statue that commemorates the fighting here in June 1944 involving the 51st (Highland) Division. The plaque on the memorial reads,

On 10th June 1944 the Highland Division made its first attack from this position in the Bois des Monts towards Bréville. In this and the action at Chateau St Côme 110 men were killed in two days. Vastly outnumbered and against ferocious counter-attacks the Highlanders helped to secure the Orne Bridgehead only by steadfast dedication, courage and sacrifice.

Memorial to the 51st (Highland) Division.

Opposite, at the entrance to Chateau St Côme, are two other memorials. The one on the right commemorates the 9th Bn Parachute Regiment and their involvement in the fighting here between 7 and 13 June when a much reduced in size battalion held this ground. The battalion's commander, Lieutenant Colonel Terence Otway, who had led them into the assault on Merville Battery, was wounded here in the sunken lane opposite the chateau entrance, close to the double water tower. In the lane on 12 June a shell landed between him and Lieutenant Christie and several other officers. Christie was killed and Otway and the other officers wounded. Otway was evacuated, command of the 9th Bn then passing to Major Napier Crookenden. The final memorial on the left is in memory of the Princess Irene Brigade, Dutch Commandos who fought here with No. 10 Inter-Allied Commando in August 1944.

Having seen the memorials look towards the chateau; the building is in private hands and cannot be entered. On 12 June 1944 while the fighting for nearby Bréville was going on the 5th Bn Black Watch, of 51st (Highland) Division, was dug in around the chateau and came under a concerted attack.

> *A terrific concentrated enemy barrage came down on our positions. When the barrage lifted our positions were attacked by a battalion of Germany infantry supported by tanks and SP guns. We had no armoured support and our MGs were knocked out in the early stages of the battle. Only one anti-tank gun was working. After a battle lasting all afternoon, during which the enemy fired . . . solid shot and oil bombs, we finally drove them off suffering heavy casualties in men and material. The enemy also suffered heavily and left his dead literally piled up on the battlefield. During the course of the afternoon many examples of personal bravery and sacrifice were carried out. Never did the battalion uphold better the traditions of the Black Watch.*[7]

This was typical of the sort of fighting that took place in this sector after D-Day and one reason why all the units that fought here were reduced to a mere shadow of their original strength.

Bréville church.

The farm at Amfreville.

Continue along this road into Bréville. The village was quite small in 1944 but sat on vital ground overlooking Ranville, the DZ and beyond towards Caen; this is clearly visible from here. Despite the ferocious fighting here there are many original buildings still remaining, including the *marie* visible on the right as you come into Bréville. On the walls outside are two original pre-Second World War cast-iron road signs, now rare in the region, and both survivors of the fighting. On the left of the crossroads is a memorial to the airborne forces and just beyond that a Battle of Normandy totem pole with text about the area. **Continue** on this road, Route de Sallenelles, and further on the right is the entrance to the civil cemetery. **Go in here.**

This part of the village was heavily shelled in June 1944 and

Commando Memorial at Amfreville.

many of the graves and memorials show signs of battle damage. The ruins of the original church were kept as a memorial to destruction and the old Normandy stonework now lies in the shadow of the post-war church. There are two war graves in the cemetery, both of men from 6th (Airborne) Division. Private Charles John Bertram Masters was killed in the attack on Bréville on 12 June 1944, aged 21. Originally he had served with

The Landing Zones near Ranville.

the Duke of Wellington's Regiment, but had volunteered for the Parachute Regiment and did his parachute training in November and December 1943 and was afterwards posted to the 12th Bn. On D-Day he dropped into DZ 'N' and fought in Ranville before the action here. Among the civilian graves to the right of Masters is the grave of Captain Hugh William Ward, 53rd (Worcestershire Yeomanry) Airlanding Light Regiment Royal Artillery. He also died in Bréville on 12 June while commanding C Troop of the 211th Battery. From Bedfordshire, he was a married man aged 34 when he died.

Leave Bréville on the Route de Sallenelles and then take the **first right** into Rue des Champs Saint Martin. **Stop here.**

The short strip of land separating the villages of Amfreville and Bréville was the scene of the assault on 12 June 1944, and shows how close both sides had been to each other in the days before that. This open ground, which could easily be swept by machine-gun fire, was only possible to cross that day because of the huge amount of artillery support that was available, artillery support that often fell short causing casualties. Among those wounded close to here was Brigadier Lord Lovat of 1st Special Service Brigade and Brigadier Honourable Hugh Kindersley of 6th Airlanding Brigade; the loss of two brigade commanders on one day was a serious blow to the units in this area.

Stay on this road into Amfreville. At the far end it brings you into the main square of the village, with a large farm complex on the right and a memorial ahead. **Stop at the memorial.**

The memorial commemorates the men of No. 6 Commando. This unit had taken part in the fighting for Ouistreham on D-Day and moved into Amfreville on the 7th. They had silenced the troublesome German gun firing on the unit's positions in a raid, and then held the front line here until the attack on the 12th. They then remained here until the summer of 1944. Opposite the memorial is a large Normandy farm complex known as Ferme des Commandos 6 Juin 1944. This was often used as headquarters for the platoons dug in beyond Amfreville and for wounded coming back from the attack on the 12th.

From here **go across the village green** to the church. **Stop.** The church is rarely open, but this is where the 12th Bn Parachute Regiment formed up before the assault on Bréville. This is the original building which the men had a brief respite in, and as they emerged from the door in front of you their

Digging in on the Landing Zone.

padre handed out copies of the divisional magazine to the men; a somewhat surreal event on the eve of a big attack.

Go across the green to the right to a white fenced memorial. This commemorates the 1st Special Service Brigade and their role in the fighting here in 1944. Close by on the far end of the green are memorials to No. 3 Commando, No. 4 Commando and the French Commandos under Commandant Philippe Kieffer. By the time the French Commandos dug in at Amfreville they were down to less than 50 per cent of their original D-Day strength.

From the 1st Special Service Brigade Memorial take the **first turning on the right**, Rue du Gable Harel. Follow this out of the village until it meets another minor road. Here **turn right** and a short while afterwards take the first cart track on the **left**. At the start of the track, **stop**.

This is DZ 'N'. The 5th Parachute Brigade landed here by parachute and the 6th Airlanding came in with their Horsa and Hamilcar gliders in the early hours of D-Day. This vast flat field was a perfect landing area, as can be clearly seen and was covered with gliders on D-Day.

Follow the track towards Ranville. The track emerges onto Rue de Petworth in Ranville. Here **turn right** and continue to the junction with Rue des Airbornes. Follow this street back to the Ranville War Cemetery and your vehicle.

Area Three

COMMANDO WALK: THE 1ST SPECIAL SERVICE BRIGADE ON D-DAY

HISTORICAL SECTION

The 1st Special Service Brigade was a mixed Army Commando and Royal Marine Commando unit commanded by Brigadier Lord Lovat. The story of the Commandos goes back to the period after Dunkirk when the Prime Minister, Winston Churchill, called for the formation of a special force to continue to carry the fight to the Germans in mainland Europe, but in small teams. Army Commandos were then formed, each consisting of ten troops, comprising three officers and forty-seven men. The Army Commando units in this brigade – No. 3, No. 4 and No. 6 – had taken part in a number of such sorties into Europe, including Norway and the Dieppe Raid. By 1944 the Army Commandos were also joined

The men of 1st Special Service Brigade approach SWORD Beach. Piper Bill Millin is the third man in on the right, pipes just visible.

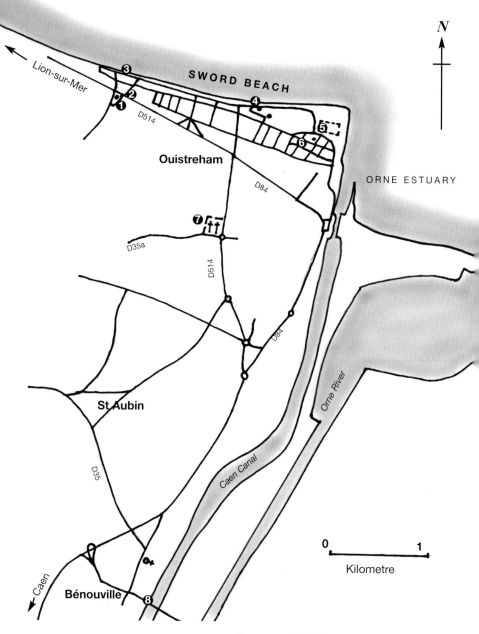

Commando Walk
1. Montgomery Memorial
2. Commando Memorial
3. WN-18 and Commando Memorial
4. Kieffer Memorial
5. Ouistreham Gun Battery (site of)
6. Ouistreham Bunker Museum
7. Communal cemetery
8. Pegasus Bridge Area

by Royal Marine Commandos of 45 Commando and men from the No. 10 (Inter-Allied) Commando, which included Belgian, Dutch, French, Norwegian, Polish and Yugoslav troops. The bulk of the French Commandos were attached to No. 4 Commando for D-Day.

The brigade's task on D-Day was to land on the left flank of 3rd Division's assault at La Brèche at Queen Beach Red, and then fight their way along the lateral roads by the coast into the port of Ouistreham. Here they were to neutralise the German defences around the casino and a coastal battery and positions close to the port so they did not threaten the follow-up waves on SWORD Beach. Having secured Ouistreham, they were then tasked with moving inland along the Caen road to Bénouville and linking up with troops of 6th (Airborne) Division. This link-up would secure not only the vital bridges that the airborne troops had been tasked to capture but also the eastern flank, allowing the main assault on Caen to continue.

The first to land was No. 4 Commando, which touched down at La Brèche at 0830, thirty minutes after the first landings by 3rd Division. As the men beached it was clear the initial landings were opposed as the air was thick with gunfire. Lieutenant Murdoch McDougall of No. 4 Commando recalled,

> I splashed forward into the shallower water and up onto the smoke-laden beach. Through the wreaths of smoke I could see the hazy outline of the ridge of dunes. The air was full of peculiar whines and whizzing, while the clumping of the mortars and the tearing, searing rattle of machine-guns seemed to dominate everything.[1]

The unit suffered more than forty casualties as they exited the landing craft, among them their commander, Lieutenant Colonel R.W.P. Dawson, who was lightly wounded. His men, seeing the assault infantry pinned down, assaulted the German positions and fought their way through the maze of bunkers and slit trenches. This short, sharp fight enabled the 2nd East Yorks to get off the beach but in the link-up between the Commandos and the infantry Colonel Dawson was wounded again, this time in the head.

Meanwhile, No. 6 Commando had landed 10 minutes after No. 4. As they landed two of their assault craft received direct hits, causing heavy casualties. The site that greeted them as they followed No. 4 off the beach was later described by the Adjutant

Commandos landing at SWORD Beach on D-Day.

as a 'Martian landscape' – gaunt and gutted buildings, a maze of tangled wire and craters everywhere. Landing with No. 6 was the Brigade Commander, Brigadier Lord Lovat DSO MC and his piper, Bill Millin. Wearing his father's borrowed Cameron kilt, he was to accompany the Brigade commander for the whole of D-Day.

My job as Piper, I was personal Piper to Lord Lovat. My job was to play the bagpipes for the invasion . . . to play the pipes going ashore. I was completely unarmed, all the weapons I had was a skinundoo in my stocking. Coming ashore the landing craft touched down, the ramps went down, Lovat jumped off, I jumped off behind him. Of course Lovat being a tall man unlike me; the water came up to his knees but it came up to my waist when I jumped in. I struggled through the surf until I got level with him and then struck up the bagpipes. I played 'Highland Ladee' through the surf until I got onto the beach and then I stopped.

For some Commandos it was a tricky landing in the rough sea.

Commandos push off the beach.

When I went onto the beach other people were furiously digging in. Other Commando had managed to get off the beach but my group . . . had been pinned down. I was standing at the water's edge with Lovat when the Brigade Major came up and said the Paras had captured the bridge at Bénouville. Lovat turned to me and said 'Now Piper do you mind very much playing the Road to the Isles. You can march up and down a bit if you wish.' I thought it was rather an odd thing when the beach was under fire . . . the noise was terrific. Anyway I struck up the bagpipes and marched up and down; the comments I received, some were complimentary, others were not so complimentary.

At the time it didn't cross my mind about being killed but on reflection . . . I wondered why they didn't kill me coming ashore when many others were killed and wounded. I think I was lucky but being a young man I didn't think I was the one going to be killed. Later prisoners said they didn't shoot me because they thought I was mad!²

Soaked with coming through the surf in his heavy kilt, Millin changed into his denim trousers once the beach was clear, but continued to pipe the brigade into action.

Thus with the arrival of these men from Brigade Headquarters and then the Inter-Allied Commandos, No. 3 Commando and 45th Royal Marine Commando, the brigade was now complete and moved to the lateral roads for the next phase of operations. Lieutenant McDougall remembered,

> *Once clear of the wire and first line of emplacements, we looked for and quickly found the assembly area of partially demolished buildings. Here, a little off the beach, things were unnaturally quiet. After the chaotic din of the beach itself, which had been almost numbing in its intensity, it seemed extraordinary that we should be able to speak in a normal tone of voice here . . . The next part of the operation was to be the approach through the little town on our left, culminating in the assault on the battery at the far end.*[3]

The move on Ouistreham was lead by the French Commandos, commanded by Colonel Philippe Kieffer. Kieffer was 'tall, burly and determined, whose family was still in France, and whose son was at that moment fighting with the Maquis in the Haute-

The old railway line that ran along the coast was used as a line of advance on D-Day.

Commandos moving closer to Ouistreham.

Savoie'.[4] His men encountered harassing fire from snipers and the occasional machine gun in the fortified houses, but they cleared these with some relish. On the outskirts of the town they came across a French *gendarme*, who was also a member of the French Resistance. He was able to lead the assaulting troops down a better route avoiding the main strongpoints. Another elderly Frenchman, Monsieur Lefevre, also approached Kieffer and his men and explained that during the bombardment of the German defences he had slipped out and cut the cables to

Monsieur Lefevre, a French Resistance leader who cut the power to the flamethrowers at Ouistreham.

One of the electrically fired flamethrowers with the bunker visible in the background.

the dug-in flamethrowers covering the defences around the casino and gun battery. These were electronically controlled from distant bunkers, but now they were out of action.

At this point the Commando force broke off, with the French Commandos heading to take on the casino area, and No. 4 Commando making the assault on the gun battery. No. 4 Commando was now well into the town. Here they began to encounter French civilians, once residents of a quiet seaside port and now in the midst of battle. Lieutenant McDougall turned one corner and found,

> *a cafe in front of which a beaming figure in pyjamas was rushing from group to group, cheering and waving . . . My attention was caught, however, by what was happening at the other side of the street, where a young woman, sobbing distractedly, was being hurried indoors by another, older woman. I wondered what was the cause of their grief; was it simply a result of reaction at having had to contain and conceal their feelings for so long? Or had the girl perhaps formed some sort of attachment to one of the German garrison?*[5]

The troops of No. 4 Commando pushed on. As they neared the objective the fighting became a matter of taking possession street by street, and in some cases house by house. Using cover, fire and movement to cross open ground and grenades to clear defenders in confined spaces, the men gradually reached the buildings overlooking the gun battery. The assault went in, again covered by the fire of Bren Guns. The air was full of tracer rounds, most gunners having loaded their magazines with one in five tracer bullets. One troop brought up a PIAT and silenced a machine-gun position and mortar pit that was impeding the assault, and then the men went in at the point of bayonet. It was soon found that the concrete emplacements protecting the guns had survived the pre-D-Day bombardment from both the air and sea, so it was a tough fight from casemate to casemate. Gradually, each casemate was reached, and as was to be a familiar story on 6 June 1944, the casemates were found to be empty. There were no guns of any calibre, and no signs of recent occupation. The cost of this discovery, as welcome as it was for the overall plan for the landings on SWORD Beach, was high. Casualties had been heavy – at one stage medics from both sides worked together to attend to the considerable wounded from both sides. Lieutenant McDougall caught the tail end of the gun-battery fight and got an immediate report from his comrades,

E Troop reported that [the] gun emplacements were . . . empty of big guns. D Troop in their first rush upon the various defences of the battery had taken over a hundred prisoners, while the crews of various machine-gun posts had been killed. At least it had been ascertained that the battery contained nothing that could in any way hinder the landings of the follow-up troops.[6]

Part of the Ouistreham gun battery.

With this threat neutralised and the casino dealt with by the attached French Commandos in an equally tough battle, No. 4 Commando withdrew and marched south to link up with 6th Airborne.

As the fight for Ouistreham was going on, No. 6 Commando had been working on the vital link-up between the Special Service Brigade and the airborne troops. This unit was led by Lieutenant Colonel Derek Mills-Roberts DSO MC, an ex-Irish Guards officer who was an old friend of Lord Lovat; the two had attended Oxford together. No. 6 Commando was charged with advancing on Pegasus Bridge, ensuring it was secure and then to push on to secure the vital eastern flank beyond the bridges. The ground beyond the beaches towards Bénouville was marshy and intersected with deep ditches, some of them up to 6ft deep, often with thick mud at the bottom of them. This made the Commando's advance somewhat difficult and scaling ladders had to be used to cross some of the larger obstacles. They also encountered some opposition, but they were latterly supported by tanks from the 13/18th Hussars, who had come ashore at La Brèche. One of the troop officers left a detailed report of the unit's action that day:

On reaching the Commando forming-up position, the Commanding Officer only gave the troop enough time to get into proper formation before continuing the advance inland. The country was by this time

heavily wooded, and the troop stuck to fairly well defined paths, which were luckily going in the same direction as the line of advance. The enemy had stuck 'Minen' signs all over the place which must have been bluff as no mines were encountered despite the fact the troop walked over many of the signed areas. Continuing in a southerly direction the troop soon came to the two pill boxes which had been allotted to 3 Troop to either attack or neutralize until the remainder of the Brigade had passed through. Although no firing was coming from these pill boxes at the time they could be seen quite easily through the trees – another strong point also being discovered in the corner of a field which was not shown on the photograph.

The troop commander decided to attack all three positions and despatched No. 2 Section to the more westerly and went himself with No. 1 Section to the other two. No. 2 Section attacked and found the position had been vacated at very short notice, and signs of bombing were evident everywhere. The section then returned to support No. 1 Section in the event of their needing it. No. 1 Section were formed into two parties and a third gave covering fire onto a hedge ahead whilst the attack went in from the flank. The first pill box was cleared by grenades after putting up minor resistance. The second pill box was attacked in a like manner and two prisoners were taken. Returning from this attack fire was turned on the section from a hedge in the rear. In the attack one man was severely wounded.

No. 2 Section then proceeded off to destroy the six-barrelled mortar which had been firing fairly close all this time, in co-operation with two Sherman tanks which had by this time come up with some other infantry. On reaching the road in the area . . . the section came under small arms fire from a distance. After penetrating a little further the mortar was nowhere to be seen and having gone somewhat over our boundary the section returned, and on the orders of the Brigadier continued the advance to Breville.

The route that was taken was Colleville [to] Bénouville bridges [via] Breville. During the advance several snipers were contacted but they always fired and retired through the undergrowth. On reaching the Bénouville area small arms fire was heard in the village so the Troop Commander decided to by-pass the village and make for the bridges which had been reported captured by the Airborne. On nearing the bridges a group of men were seen through a hedge 200 yards away and these were first thought to be Germans; on looking at them through the glasses, however, they were recognised as paratroops. The Troop Commander waved the Union Jack carried for this purpose and shouted to us. On seeing us the paratroops cheered frantically and moved towards us. The party consisted of a paratroop Brigadier, Colonel Pine-Coffin and their HQ. The Brigadier said to our Troop Commander: 'We are very pleased to see you'. The Troop Commander characteristically answered, looking at his watch: 'I am afraid we are a few minutes late, Sir!'[7]

In the final advance on Bénouville Lovat caught up with No. 6 Commando, and still had his Piper, Bill Millin, with him. Bill recalled, 'after leaving the beach I played the Commandos from Ouistreham to Bénouville, about 4½–5 miles, and there were pastures and built up areas where we were being sniped at and mortared. We reached the bridge at Bénouville and I doubled over there as it was under fire. Lovat and I led them over.'[8] Indeed, Lovat was given the honour of making the final link-up with Pine-Coffin, commanding 7th Bn Parachute Regiment, which was defending the area. The link-up had been made, the bridges were secure, the Commandos had taken out their initial D-Day objectives at Ouistreham and now the next phase of their D-Day task was put into operation. They would move across Pegasus and Horsa Bridges, as Lovat and Millin had done by leading them, and move onto the ridge, into the woods and villages beyond, and secure the vital eastern flank.

Walk 3: In the Commando Area

STARTING POINT: Seafront Colleville-Montgomery

GPS: 49°17′36.5″N, 0°17′02.2″W

DURATION: 18.1km/11.2 miles

Park your vehicle in the car park just off the Avenue des Bruxelles on the seafront at Colleville-Montgomery. There is plenty of parking available here and along the seafront.

This site overlooks where the 3rd Division landed on 6 June 1944 on what was SWORD Beach. Infantry battalions from the division ran into a lot of opposition on these beaches and suffered numerous casualties in pushing off them. The men from 1st Special Service Brigade came in later, only to find the beach still under fire and very much a battlefield. No. 4 Commando was the first to beach, and as the battle for the beach moved into the battle for the buildings in this area, the Commando plan was put into action and the men moved from

The Commando Memorial at Colleville-Montgomery.

the beachhead along the lateral roads towards Ouistreham.

From the car park **follow the shoreline** along Boulevard Maritime. The beach to your left is where most of the Commandos landed. The huge bunker at strongpoint Widerstandsnest 18 (WN-18) comes up on the right. **Stop here**. Strongpoint WN-18 was a huge German pillbox complex more than 300m across. It was equipped with an anti-tank gun and machine guns and had caused many of the casualties to the landings on SWORD Beach. Opposite, on the shore side, is a memorial to the landings and the Commando units.

Continue along Boulevard Maritime. Further along take Avenue du 4eme Commando on the **right**, and the **first left** Boulevard du Marchal Joffre. Follow this road; this is a route used by the Commandos to approach Ouistreham and the wall on the right is typical of the Normandy walls in this area, which appear in many of the wartime photos. The area was much more open along this road in 1944, and few of the original buildings from that period still exist.

Further along the road reaches Boulevard Winston Churchill. Here **turn left** and return to the shore into Boulevard Aristide Briand, **turning right**. Further up on the left is the memorial to Commandant Kieffer and the French Commandos. **Stop here**.

Capitaine de Corvette Philippe Kieffer was a French naval

officer who commanded 1er Bataillon de Fusiliers Marins Commandos, which became part of No. 10 Inter-Allied Commando. Born in Haiti in 1899, he first worked in a bank in New York. He volunteered for service in the French Navy in 1939 and served at Dunkirk. Having escaped the fall of France, he joined the Free French Forces in the UK and joined the Commandos in 1941. Kieffer led his men ashore on SWORD Beach and they spearheaded the attack on the casino area of Ouistreham on D- Day and then moved up to Pegasus Bridge and beyond to the high ground on the eastern flank. The memorial is located on top of an observation cupola, part of the Ouistreham gun-battery site.

Follow a sandy path along the beach from the memorial behind the casino and then **turn right** and walk across a car park to Place Alfred Thomas to visit the Musée du Commando No. 4. **Stop here**. The museum is run by the French and dedicated to the Commandos who attacked Ouistreham on D-Day and in particular focuses on the role of the 177 French Commandos under Kieffer. It contains many unique photographs and artefacts, often donated by the families of Commandos who served here. The museum is open every day from mid-March to late October from 10.30am to 6pm.

From the museum **continue** along Place Alfred Thomas to the next roundabout and then **go left** along Boulevard Maritime. Go through the trees towards the beach. **Stop**. This is the site of the Ouistreham gun battery. Little of it remains today as most of the concrete gun pits and bunkers disappeared with the post-war redevelopment of the site. However, you can walk out onto the edge of the beach and see the potential field of fire of the battery up SWORD Beach and looking back the tall concrete observation bunker can be seen rising above the rooftops.

From the Boulevard Maritime take Avenue de la Plage to where it meets Avenue du 6 Juin. The huge observation tower of the bunker is visible on the right. It has since been converted to an excellent museum. The Ouistreham bunker was part of the gun-battery site and acted as its eyes. The 52ft-tall structure gave commanding views out to sea and up the coast and was linked by radio to a number of artillery positions well away from the beachhead. The defenders of the bunker sealed themselves in on D-Day and would not surrender. The bunker did not fall until 9 June when Lieutenant Bob Orrell of 91st Field Company Royal Engineers mustered enough explosives to blow the doors off the entrance, a feat that took some 4 hours. Once the position was breached, the garrison of two officers and fifty men surrendered. Today, the museum has numerous vehicles outside, including a Higgins Boat used in the film *Saving Private Ryan*. Inside you can climb to the top and see the original range finder and enjoy spectacular views over SWORD Beach.

The Bunker Museum, Ouistreham.

From the bunker **continue** up Avenue de la Plage until it meets Rue Leon Gambetta. Here **turn left** and take the **first right**, Rue du Hamel. Follow this to the end, take the **first left**, Rue du Fonteny, and then **first right**, Rue Cite Jardin. Follow this to the end and **cross** Avenue de la Liberte to the civil cemetery. Go in via the main gate.

Located in Rue Gustave Flaubert in Ouistreham, this large communal cemetery has five British and Commonwealth graves from the Second World War, and

The tower of the bunker is impressive and even today dominates the area.

gets very few visitors compared to other D-Day sites, as few realise it is here. Among the pre-D-Day casualties are Sergeant Pilot Edward Appleton-Bach who flew with 131st (County of Kent) Squadron RAF. He was shot down on 18 November 1942 when his Spitfire VB took part in Operation 'Rhubarb' – an ongoing plan with aircraft working in pairs to take on key targets in fighter range in German-occupied France. Of the D-Day casualties Private Frederick Burkett, Corporal Frederick Maskell and Private Orlando Farnese died with No. 4

Commando, the latter serving as one of their medical orderlies. Flight Sergeant John Francis McCullum was a Canadian who died on 24 October 1942 flying with 207th Squadron RAF. He was part of a Lancaster bomber crew that had been on an operation against Milan. The aircraft was shot down and crashed in the sea, the crew all being killed but being washed up along the French coast in different places and McCullum's body found on the beach at Ouistreham.

At this point the walk can be cut short. You can take the route back to the car park on SWORD Beach via Avenue de la Liberte and back to the seafront, and then follow the shore back to La Brèche. Otherwise, the walk can be continued in the footsteps of the Commandos to where they joined up with the airborne troops, and the Pegasus Walk in Chapter 1 could be linked up to this walk to make a full day's walking on the battlefield.

To continue with the walk, **follow** the Avenue de la Liberte (D514) to where it meets the second roundabout from the cemetery. Here **turn right** onto the Route de Saint Aubin d'Arquenay. Follow this up the rising ground to the village of Saint Aubin d'Arquenay, taking a route used by Lord Lovat and men from 1st Special Service Brigade. Just before the village take the **first left** onto Chemin de la Maladrerie. At the end **turn left** onto the D35 and follow it downhill to Bénouville. On reaching the church in Bénouville the Pegasus Walk can be followed, or simply stay on this road until you reach the next roundabout and **turn left**.

Follow this road down to Pegasus Bridge where the Gondrée Café and Pegasus Museum will be seen. This is the point that having met up with Lieutenant Colonel Pine-Coffin, Lord Lovat assembled his men and had Piper Bill Millin lead them across the bridge to the eastern flank.

After a visit here you can walk back to the seafront at Ouistreham by taking the towpath along the canal, and then following the shoreline back to the parking at La Brèche. At a steady pace this would take around 90 minutes. An alternative is to get a local bus back to Ouistreham and then walk the last section to the car park.

Area Four

SWORD BEACH WALK:
3RD DIVISION ON D-DAY

HISTORICAL SECTION

The 3rd Division was an infantry formation that had fought in France in 1940. Then commanded by Bernard Montgomery, it had acquired the name 'Monty's Ironsides' and while it had been heavily mauled in the retreat to Dunkirk, on arrival in the UK it was reformed. By 1943 it was in the Scottish Lowlands engaged in invasion training and by 1944 it was arguably the most highly trained Combined Operations formation outside of the Commandos. It was commanded in 1944 by Major General Thomas Gordon 'Tom' Rennie, a tough and experienced solider. An officer in the Black Watch, he was taken prisoner in 1940 but escaped and fought in North Africa, where he was wounded. After Sicily he went

Major General Tom Rennie, commander of 3rd Division.

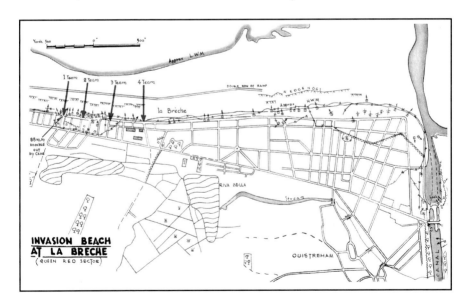

The defences on SWORD Beach close to Ouistreham.

77

back to the UK where he was given command of the division, and proved a popular and respected commander.

The sector allocated to the landings of 3rd Division on D-Day ran from Luc-sur-Mer in the west to an area just short of Ouistreham. Overall part of SWORD Beach, like all other D-Day

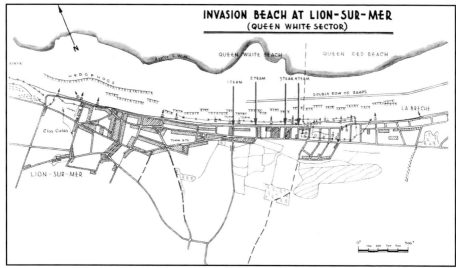

The defences on SWORD Beach close to Lion-sur-Mer.

Approaching SWORD Beach on D-Day.

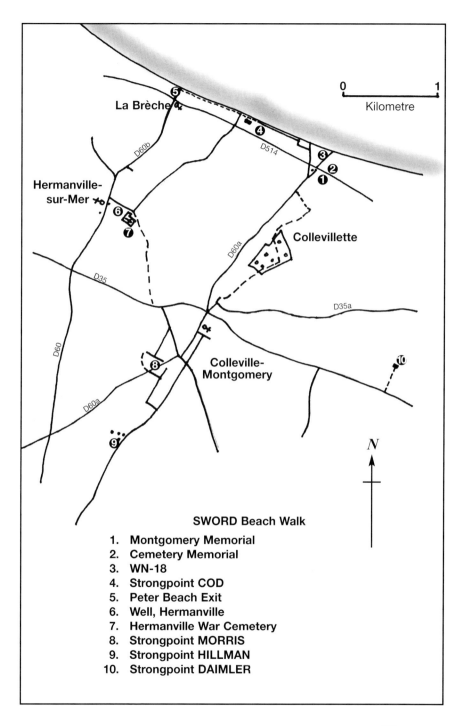

SWORD Beach Walk

1. Montgomery Memorial
2. Cemetery Memorial
3. WN-18
4. Strongpoint COD
5. Peter Beach Exit
6. Well, Hermanville
7. Hermanville War Cemetery
8. Strongpoint MORRIS
9. Strongpoint HILLMAN
10. Strongpoint DAIMLER

beaches it was broken down into small sectors named Oboe, Peter and Queen. The division would employ an assault brigade – 8th Infantry Brigade – in the first wave with the 185th Brigade in support and 9th Brigade in reserve. Armoured support would be from tank units in the attached 27th Armoured Brigade and tasks on the beach would be assisted by the 5th Assault Regiment Royal Engineers, from 79th (Armoured) Division. The task of Rennie's division was to effect a secure landing, push inland to 'Poland' (the code-name for Caen) and link up with the 6th (Airborne) Division at the vital bridges over the Orne. On the right Commandos from 41st Royal Marine Commando would land at Luc-sur-Mer and link up with the Canadians at JUNO, but there would be an empty 'corridor' between SWORD and JUNO and Rennie's men would have to keep an eye on that flank as the advance moved inland.

In the early hours of 6 June more than 250 ships of all sizes were assembled taking the 3rd Division and its supporting units towards the Normandy coast. It has been a rough crossing.

> *In mid-Channel the waves were between five and six feet high, and a force 5 wind (16 to 20 knots) was blowing from the west. Still there was no resistance from the enemy, and it was gradually becoming clear that we had achieved the tactical and strategic surprise that had seemed too much to hope for.*[1]

While there was no sign of any immediate resistance, the area was defended by elements of the German 716th Division, a formation pre-D-Day intelligence had stated consisted of upwards of 40 per cent of non-Germans: Poles, Russians and other nationalities swept up in the Nazi domination of Europe. Compared to the well-trained, well-motivated and well-led 3rd Division they may have appeared second-rate troops but their defences were formidable,

> *The assaulting troops would first meet two groups of ramp type obstacles starting 300 yards down from the back of the beach. Then they would come to a double row of stakes running continuously across the beaches, 30 to 60 yards between stakes, 230 yards down from the back of the beach. The last of the underwater obstacles began 180 yards from the back of the beach and consisted of overlapping rows of 'hedgehogs' twenty feet apart and fourteen to seventeen in a row. Hedgehogs were constructed of angle-iron after the pattern of*

caltrop used in the Hundred Years War . . . and the possibility of mines below high water was anticipated.[2]

In addition, the bunkers of the Atlantic Wall protected the defenders with a series of concreted machine-gun nests, Tobruk pits and larger bunker complexes such as at a position on the beach at La Brèche, called WN-18; a huge bunker housing an anti-tank gun. Firm believers in defence in depth, the Germans also had major defence complexes just inland at locations known to the British as DAIMLER, HILLMAN and SOLE. All of these defences were scheduled to be neutralised or destroyed by the pre-D-Day bombardment and aerial strikes, and if not, taken by direct assault once the beach was cleared.

The initial landings took place at 0725 – H Hour here – on 6 June. The first troops to reach the beach were those to secure it allowing the main infantry assault to begin – the men of 13/18th Hussars. This unit was equipped with Sherman Duplex Drive (DD) tanks which could swim ashore with a canopy to protect the tank and a motor to drive it in the sea. Launched at 5,000yd from the beach by driving out into the water from Landing Craft Tank (LCT), only a handful of tanks were lost in the water from the two squadrons leading the assault, but the weather conditions slowed them down and not all landed on time. The German defenders were already replying with anti-tank fire, and as the DD tank canopies dropped, the first shots were fired along this stretch of SWORD Beach. Close behind were the men

Men from 3rd Division pinned down on SWORD Beach.

from the Assault Squadrons of the Royal Engineers. To clear the minefields, Sherman Flail tanks from 22nd Dragoons were used and the 77th Assault Squadron equipped with Churchill Armoured Vehicle Royal Engineers (AVRE) tanks were to provide the other engineer support. The Petard mortars on the AVREs would be used to deal with strongpoints and blow holes in concrete obstacles, and a variety of kit from brushwood fascines, dropped bridges and 'carpet' from Bobin tanks would allow vehicles to exit the beach area. The landing for these men was far from easy and as in most places on SWORD Beach, it was clear the pre-D-Day bombardments had done little to the defences; the majority were intact and in use by the defenders. One gun opened up on a LCT bringing in equipment from the Assault Regiment headquarters causing an explosion onboard and killing the unit's commander, Lieutenant Colonel A.D.B. Cocks.[3]

Close on the heels of the first wave were the infantry. Touching down on the two beach sectors were the leading platoons from the 2nd East Yorks on Red Beach to the left and the 1st South Lancashires on White Beach to the right. The battle was only minutes old and here at La Brèche defenders from *10. Kompanie Grenadier-Regiment 736* commanded by *Hauptmann* Heinrich Kuhtz were putting up some stubborn resistance. As

Tanks and men caught on the beach.

The price of victory.

the infantry landed, as per the drills practised time and again in the preceding years, they came under withering fire. Well-sited machine guns and mortars had not yet been silenced and casualties in both battalions quickly mounted. The leading company commander on White Beach, Major John Frederick Harward, an Oxford graduate,[1] was mortally wounded taking his men to the barbed wire on the beach. Hit by a burst of Spandau fire, he crawled in agony to the Bangalore torpedoes his men had placed under the wire to cut a land through it and lit them, collapsing in pain as the explosion ripped through the wire. Sadly, Harward died of his wounds the following day at Hermanville. In the confusion near Strongpoint COD, which was still firing on the beach, the commander of 1st South Lancs, Lieutenant Colonel Richard Burbury, was trying to organise his men when he was killed instantly by a sniper's bullet. The only officer then present was Lieutenant Robert Bell-Walker who assumed command until he, too, was killed while assaulting a pillbox.

On Red Beach it was equally chaotic. One officer, Major 'Banger' King, had inspired his men by reciting Shakespeare to

83

them through a loud hailer but as the ramps went down the men came under terrific fire; survivors recall seeing many bodies floating in the water as their ramps went down. The commanding officer of 2nd East Yorks, Lieutenant Colonel Charles Hutchinson, was in the thick of it, 'The beaches were under very heavy fire and the assault companies suffered many casualties, but he rapidly collected his battalion and organised the mopping up of the remaining beach localities. During this period he was continuously under enemy artillery and mortar fire.[5] Close by one of his officers, Lieutenant Arthur Oates, organised the breach of the wire defences.

> This officer himself was wounded in the arm, but carried on with the assault. On reaching the wire obstacles at the top of the beaches it was found that the assault pioneer section were casualties and the Bangalore torpedo for clearing the wire was not available. This officer returned to the water edge and recovered the torpedo which he carried forward and exploded against the wire, enabling his platoon to cross over the beach. The platoon next attacked a defended locality which contained several pillboxes all of which this officer captured in every case personally leading the assault parties himself.[6]

Close by Private Arthur Wilson found that the Bangalore torpedo issued to him to cut the wire would not explode, so he, 'forced his way through the wire obstacles and attacked a pillbox which he reached in spite of enemy fire. On reaching it he managed to throw in a grenade which silenced the enemy and his platoon were able to move away. This gallant action . . . undoubtedly saved many lives.'[7]

All three men were decorated for bravery in this part of the battle: Lieutenant Colonel Hutchinson the Distinguished Service Order, Oates the Military Cross and Wilson with the Military Medal.

The tank support was proving crucial to the outcome of the battle on the beach. Major Derrick Wormald of 13/18th Hussars was a tank commander on D-Day who,

> showed tremendous courage and leadership when commanding a squadron of swimming tanks . . . The full weight of the enemy fire was directed at these tanks who were leading the assault on the beaches in broad daylight. Many rocket projectiles were falling in the water in front of the tanks. Major Wormald led his squadron through the curtain of enemy fire and on through the mined beach

Strongpoint COD from an assault craft.

obstacles when heavy seas were breaking on the beaches. He personally directed the fire fight and successfully silenced the enemy beach defences thus enabling the assault to proceed.[8]

For his gallantry he was awarded a Distinguished Service Order. Close support from these tanks had certainly helped tip the balance in the favour of the infantry when it was clear more of the defenders had survived than originally expected.

With the tide of battle going in favour of the men from the 3rd Division, the work that had been going on while all the shot and shell fell around the beach by the men of the Royal Engineers was coming to an end. Sappers from the demolition parties in 246th Field Company, who had landed 40 minutes into operations, had crawled their way to the edge of White Beach and became the first unit to complete an exit off the

Strongpoint COD photographed by an officer of 79th (Armoured) Division.

Prisoners taken at strongpoint COD.

beach, finally finished with a bulldozer loaned by the 79th Armoured Division. Through this exit poured elements of both infantry assault battalions supported by the surviving tanks of 13/18th Hussars and Forward Observation Officers from two of the Field Regiment Royal Artillery units attached.

The hinterland was not hard to defend . . . Behind Red and White Beaches and the houses scattered

With the beach secure, follow-up waves now arrive.

Troops from 3rd Division begin the move inland.

The same building today.

all along the front lay a strip of marshland impassable to vehicles. This extended back some 500 yards and then gave way to an area covered with orchards, where the green cornfields were hedged and the hedges were buttressed by poplars and elms. These and the apple trees almost hid Hermanville, a straggling little village about a mile from the sea.[9]

This was the next objective for the assaulting battalions. The 2nd East Yorks on the left began to moved inland beyond the urbanised area close to the beach and across the fields beyond towards Colleville. Here were a number of bunker complexes on the high ground between Colleville and Ouistreham. Of these, two were the objectives of the East Yorks: SOLE and DAIMLER. By this stage the reserve companies of the battalion had arrived and brought the battalion up in strength, and more units were arriving on the beachhead all the time. As the battalion moved off, they now had M7 Priests, self-propelled 105mm howitzers, from 76th Field Regiment and M18 Wolverines, self-propelled 17-pounder anti-tank guns, from 20th Anti-Tank Regiment to support their advance. The German complex WN-14, SOLE, was the first objective.

After emerging from the houses and beach defences and into the lane behind, there was a fair amount of stuff coming down. Two very large and very frightened cart horses came galloping down the lane. A Lance Corporal with a small party of men told them to get out of the way and take cover behind a low wall, as they might otherwise get hurt. To take cover to avoid getting hurt by shells and mortar bombs had never occurred to him!

Under enemy observation, mortared and shelled, the move across country to 'Sole', the first objective, was slow. The naval artillery Observation Officer could not be found when naval artillery fire against 'Sole' was wanted, but 76 Field Regiment shelled the place, and 'C' Company finally took it. 'A' Company had meanwhile been clearing the beach area, but arrived at 'Sole' in time to help in consolidating.[10]

SOLE had contained the headquarters unit of *1. Batallion Grenadier-Regiment 736,* and as a command and control complex it did not have considerable defences and had proved straightforward to overrun, even without the naval gunfire support. Colonel Hutchinson, the battalion's commander, had again been instrumental in the fighting.

After clearing the beach defences he led his battalion against two strongly defended localities which commanded the beaches from the high ground inland. The country was very enclosed and considerable opposition was experienced from these commanding positions. It was very difficult to get observations from which to make a recce of the positions and heavy mortar fire caused numerous casualties. Col Hutchinson, with complete disregard for his own safety, moved forward to where he could control the attack and was successful in capturing the first locality.[11]

The next objective, only a short distance away, was the gun battery at WN-12, otherwise known as DAIMLER. Intelligence reports showed this to be a 155mm gun battery that if not silenced would fire into the follow-up waves landing on SWORD Beach. Colonel Hutchinson now had a Bren Gun Carrier at his disposal as the battalion's transport was gradually arriving, and with several other officers took it up to a sunken lane to recce the next position when they were seen and got hit by mortar fire. Hutchinson was wounded and evacuated, bringing his eventful day to a conclusion. By now it was well past midday, and the attack went in, well supported by the battalion's 3in mortars, tanks from the Hussars, guns from 76th Field Regiment and a well-thought-out infantry assault.

Moving through the buildings on the coast road towards Hermanville.

With the aid of some tanks of the 13/18 Hussars and under cover of artillery fire from the 76 Field Regiment, 'A' and 'C' Companies put in an attack on 'DAIMLER', which was quickly taken with little loss. Seventy of the enemy surrendered. Many German weapons were captured. In their dugouts, the Germans had been liberally supplied with wines and champagne. These the troops gladly 'liberated'.[12]

While the fighting for these two complexes was taking place, the 1st South Lancs had moved inland towards Hermanville. Setting up their battalion headquarters near the church, radio communications was established and contact with all the battalion's companies made. At this point, late morning on 6 June, the men were fighting their way through the streets of the village and dealing with small pockets of resistance and snipers. With the beach behind them clear the follow-up battalion of their brigade, 1st Suffolk Regiment, had landed at 0825. There was a handful of casualties on the beach, but as per the D-Day plans, the battalion moved inland to a wooded area close to Hermanville. Contact was made with the South Lancs, who confirmed that flank was secure, and Lieutenant Colonel J.G.M.B. Gough set about organising his men for the assault on the two bunker systems beyond. The first of these was WN-16, MORRIS, and beyond that was the more substantial WN-17, HILLMAN. MORRIS was bombarded by 6in guns from HMS *Dragon* before air support from 2nd Tactical Air Force went in. An infantry assault was planned but just as the Forward Observation Officer for 76th Field Regiment was ranging in his guns on the site, the defenders put up a white flag and surrendered. That was the easy part; HILLMAN was much more formidable.

HILLMAN covered an area of 600 yards by 400 yards and consisted of deep concrete shelters and pillboxes and 3 cupolas and a complete system of connecting trenches about 7 feet deep. The armament consisted of two infantry guns, several machine guns with A.A. and ground roles. There was also normal riflemen of approx strength of one platoon and the Bn HQ of the unit guarding the beach defences. The position was surrounded by two belts of wire between which were anti-tank and anti-personnel mines. The whole position was very well equipped with modern instruments, telephones and every comfort possible in the circumstances. It was in fact very much stronger and better guarded and equipped than had been supposed prior to the operation. It was not known that there were any of the deep concrete shelters.

Captain Ryley went forward to make his recce at about 11.30 . . . while the company moved up through the village to its FUP [Forming Up Position] and in doing so it sustained a number of casualties . . . one section of No 9 Platoon was almost wiped out. After a short recce the plan was put into action.[13]

Protected by wire and covered by mines, once more the men of the Royal Engineers were called in to deal with the problem. An officer of 'D' Company crawled forward with Lieutenant Arthur Heal of the 246th Field Company Royal Engineers and four Sappers. Carrying a mine detector, white tape and wire cutters, they cleared and marked a path through the minefield and cut the wire, all the while supported by fire from the infantry. Heal later wrote,

I was ordered, in the nicest possible way . . . to clear a path through the perimeter minefield so that tanks could enter the locality. During training in Scotland I made sure that we could all recognise and disarm any mine we were likely to find. I was therefore disconcerted that I could not identify the first mine that I uncovered. It turned out to be an obsolete British Mk 11 anti-tank mine left behind at Dunkirk in 1940. However, lying flat on the ground, and with the help of covering fire and smoke from the tanks of the Staffordshire Yeomanry and the assault company this was achieved by the early evening. It was only much later that it was appreciated what a formidable obstacle HILLMAN had been.[14]

Finally, Heal's party dragged some Bangalore torpedoes through the high grass, which had been covering the small party throughout the operation, and blew the final approach allowing the infantry to go in.

No 9 Platoon under command of Lieut J. Powell was the first platoon through the gap which was effected under cover of a squadron of 13/18th Hussars Sherman tanks, two batteries of RA and 2-inch mortar smoke from 'A' and 'D' Companies. No 8 Section went through the gap and immediately came under heavy MG fire and Cpl Jones was killed while trying to get his section forward. The platoon commander now came forward and got the PIAT team forward and into action so as to be able to fire three shots at a cupola which was the cause of most of the trouble.

A message was sent back to the company commander that the

platoon was pinned down. The platoon runner was killed in trying to get this message back and a second runner then had to be sent.

A further concentration of fire (HE and smoke) was put down and the rest of the company were then led in by the company commander. Once again MG fire held up the advance and only 4 men (Capt Ryley, Lieut Tooley, Lieut Powell and Cpl Stares) managed to get through and went forward for about 200 yards and took a few prisoners. As it was obviously impossible to continue this without further assistance Lieut Powell went back while the others remained until his return. He was only able to get one Sergeant (Sgt Lankester) and two men, and they again went forward and found that Lieut Tooley and Cpl Stares had both been badly wounded. Captain Ryley was killed very shortly afterwards when returning for assistance. The position was now a stalemate and a new plan on a battalion level had to be made.[15]

Another reason for making a new plan was that the Divisional Commander, Tom Rennie, was now ashore and had come up for a personal reconnaissance of what was taking place. Typical of Rennie, he arrived wearing a cap and no steel helmet, and informed the local commander that HILLMAN had to be captured before dark so the units of 8 Brigade could dig in on their D-Day objectives and be ready for any counter-attack; it was already being reported that German armour was coming down the gap between his division and the Canadians from the direction of Caen. Fresh tank support from A Squadron of the Staffordshire Yeomanry, equipped with Shermans, came up and mine-clearing tanks were requested.

It was decided to call up two Flails and about 8 or 9 extra tanks. The Flails were too long arriving and the attack went in immediately the artillery had fired again onto the position. The tanks moved into the perimeter followed by Nos 8 and 9 Platoons who moved out and mopped up the area by using No 75 and No 36 Grenades. One Platoon of D Company also moved in to assist while one Platoon of C Company acted as a left flank protection. A number of the Boche surrendered, others died in the emplacements and the success signal was given.[16]

This was around 2000 on 6 June, so the battle for HILLMAN had lasted for nearly 9 hours. However, events there weren't quite over as the site came under sporadic shell and sniper fire, and on the morning of the 7th a group of more than seventy officers and men emerged from a hidden bunker that had been missed and finally surrendered. For 8 Brigade, with the East Yorks, Suffolks and South Lancs dug in along the slopes of the Périers Ridge, D-Day was over.

With the ground around the beachhead now secure, the next phase of the battle plan envisaged 185 Brigade moving further inland and taking the division's main objective 'Poland' – Caen. The battalions from this brigade – 2nd Royal Warwicks, 1st Norfolks and 2nd King's Shropshire Light Infantry (KSLI) – had all landed between 1000 and 1100 as the fight for the bunker systems between MORRIS, HILLMAN, SOLE and DAIMLER were going on. The beaches were all under fire, and each of the battalions had lost men upon landing and as they moved inland to their forming up points. The Warwicks, in particular, suffered from machine-gun fire coming from the direction of Lion sur Mer. But by midday the next phase of the plan began and Brigadier K.P. Smith ordered the men to begin the advance on Caen supported by tanks from the Staffordshire Yeomanry, and AVREs from 79th (Armoured). Other supporting units, such as the artillery, were not available at that point as they either

The HILLMAN complex under new owners.

hadn't cleared the beach or were engaged in the fighting for the bunker sites, although Forward Observers did accompany the brigade.

Beyond the beachhead the ground rose to Périers Ridge, a long stretch of high ground that went from Plumetot in the west – where the gap between the divisions were – through Périers-le-Dan which gave a route towards Bénouville. Beyond that was a clear approach over open fields, and a clear view towards Caen itself. As they approached the ridge all three battalions had come under fire, often from different directions; the Norfolks, for example, had taken substantial casualties as they passed the on-going battle at HILLMAN. On the ridge itself mortar and shell fire came in. The latter was from a battery of Russian 122mm howitzers in a known gun position near Périers village, which should have been silenced in the pre-D-Day bombardment, but which like much of the defences had survived intact. At 1425 Lieutenant Colonel Maurice, commanding 2nd KSLI, sent his 'Z' Company, commanded by Major Wheelock, to deal with this battery. He was to discover it wasn't just a few guns in a field, but a proper position protected by wire and mines.

Major Wheelock's company managed to drive the German gunners from their emplacements but they went to ground and covered the wire with dense machine-gun fire. The Yeomanry Colonel directed a Regimental Shoot of 7th *Field Regiment on to them, but several times the Germans got back to their guns and continued to shell the road until stopped again by the small-arms fire of Z Company. Eventually a Pole was captured who knew the way through the wire at the back of the battery. The gunners fled into the woods, harried for some hundreds of yards by the Company. The guns were then blown up.*[17]

Wheelock was later awarded a Military Cross for his bravery here and Sergeant Rawling of the 2nd Middlesex machine-gunners, supporting the infantry, was awarded a Distinguished Conduct Medal for taking over when his officer, Lieutenant Dixon, fell mortally wounded.

The advance continued towards Caen and the villages of Beuville and Biéville were taken. At Biéville the advance halted as a large tank force was seen advancing on the right flank towards the gap between 3rd Division and the Canadians. A

Squadron of the Staffordshire Yeomanry had moved up, fresh from the battle at HILLMAN, and their B Squadron was in position at Périers-le-Dan. The 2nd KSLI support company had moved up their 6-pounder guns, now equipped with the new Armour Piercing Discarding Sabot ammunition, and close to Biéville a troop from the 41st Anti-Tank Regiment, equipped with M10 Wolverines, was also ready. Some accounts claim as many as forty German tanks were in the Battle Group, which comprised largely Mk IV tanks from *Major* Vierzig's *II. Bataillion Panzer-Regiment 100*, part of *21. Panzer-Division*. Leading tanks were hit by 2nd KSLI's 6-pounders and the Shermans from the Staffordshire Yeomanry. The column moved further to the right, and then were hit by fire from the Anti-Tank Regiment, and other squadrons of Shermans. With a bloody nose, *Major* Vierzig called off the counter-attack and withdrew.

The 2nd Royal Warwicks continued to move on Caen. They had reached the road that ran along the Orne Canal towards the city and advanced on Blainville. Here they came under fire from 88mm guns and encountered substantial defenders. The Forward Observers' tank was knocked out, which meant no artillery support and by midnight the battalion was on the outskirts of the village, only a few miles from Caen. Over to their right, just north of the woods at Lebisey, were 2nd KSLI. Both close to Caen, but for now it remained an objective for another day, and another battle.

The memorial to Field Marshal Montgomery at Colleville-Montgomery.

Walk 4: 3rd Division's Sector

STARTING POINT: Montgomery Statue, Colleville-Montgomery

GPS: 49°17'25.9"N, 0°16'56.8"W

DURATION: 17km/10.6 miles

Park your vehicle in a side street next to the Field Marshall Montgomery Memorial just off the Rue de la Mer where it meets the D514. Start at the Montgomery Memorial.

This memorial commemorates Field Marshall Bernard Montgomery who as commander of 21st Army Group landed on the beach at Colleville on 8 June 1944. Collville-

95

Memorial to the first burial ground. The graves are now in Hermanville War Cemetery.

sur-Orne, as it was originally known in 1944, was renamed Colleville-Montgomery in honour of the Field Marshall after the war.

From the memorial take the road to the **right** of it, now a dead end, and follow to the D514. **Cross** the road and **stop** at the entrance to Rue du 4eme Commando. There are two memorials here. The one on the left commemorates men of Commandant Kieffer's French Commandos who formed up here before moving off along the lateral roads towards Ouistrehem (see the Commando Walk, page 62). The one on the right commemorates the first British cemetery made on European soil in 1944. The graves here were part of the first formal cemetery on French soil and were all of men from the 3rd Division, and some of the 1st Special Service Brigade, who died in the landings on SWORD Beach on 6 June. The graves were moved to Hermanville War Cemetery after the war and this memorial was on the site for the first anniversary of D-Day in 1945.

Continue along Rue du 4eme Commando to the Boulevard Maritime. Here **turn left** and cross the road onto the marked footpath (do not walk on the cycle lane). Here you are standing on the left flank of Queen Beach looking straight down the beachhead where the 2nd Bn East Yorkshire Regiment landed. **Continue** on the Boulevard Maritime and on the left is a large German bunker, now part of a house.

This is WN-18, a German strongpoint which housed a 75mm gun. It was protected by a huge concrete wall, still clearly visible, which substantially reduced the effect of direct fire from the sea and on D-Day it was only neutralised by tank fire at short range from the 13/18th Hussars. Its potential field of fire is clear. Opposite the bunker is a modern memorial to the landings which includes plaques commemorating the 1st Special Service Brigade and the men of the Royal Norfolk

Regiment who landed here in the follow-up waves.

Continue along the footpath and along SWORD Beach to where there is a grassed area in front of the seaside housing. This was open ground in June 1944 and the defences of Strongpoint COD were here. COD consisted of a system of trenches, machine-gun positions, mortar pits, bunkers and 50mm guns that defended this stretch of the beach. Churchill AVREs and armoured bulldozers from the 79th Assault Squadron landed here, supported by tanks of the 13/18th Hussars and men from 2nd East Yorks landing on their right flank. The two period houses – the so-called 'Twin Villas' – which appeared on many wartime images are the only indication of where COD was located and can be seen set back from the beach on Rue de Rouen.

Again **continue** along the footpath, and the road soon becomes Promenade Henri Spriet. Where this meets Place du Cuirasse Courbet, **stop**. Look back in the direction you have just walked and you are now overlooking Peter Beach where the 1st South Lancashire Regiment landed at H Hour, and while assembling his men at this point their commanding officer, Lieutenant Colonel Richard Burbury, was killed by a sniper. The small square just off the beach is home to a large number of memorials, including a plaque to the South Lancs, and a large representation of the 3rd Division battle insignia on the pavement. Other plaques and memorials commemorate the 13/18th Hussars, East Yorkshire Regiment, 5th King's Liverpool Regiment, who manned SWORD Beach from 6 June until the end of the campaign, Norwegian sailors who took part in

Operation 'Neptune' and an older memorial to the Royal Artillery units of 3rd Division. Many of the buildings off this square date from the pre-Second World War period and appear on a number of the photographs taken on D-Day. There is also a lively café here, which makes a good stop before continuing with the walk. On certain days a small hut next to the beach is open and displays a panoramic photograph of SWORD Beach and a number of other relics of 1944.

From the Place, **walk south** towards the D514. Go **straight across** onto Rue du 6 Juin following signs for Hermanville. This is the route 1st South Lancs followed after the beach was secure, as the second phase of their D-Day objective was to move forward, take Hermanville and guard this flank while other units of 3rd Division continued with the advance. The streets of Hermanville in 1944, as they are today, were narrow and walking the route into the centre of the village gives a sense of what it was like clearing the area, and how the nature of Normandy buildings and the close terrain favoured the defender.

Continue past the church, and **stop** at the village war memorial in Grande Rue. This appears on wartime images showing men from 3rd Division marching past to continue with the battle towards Caen. Just beyond the memorial is the entrance to a chateau, now a building owned by the local council. This chateau was used by General Tom Rennie and the headquarters of 3rd Division from D-Day, once Hermanville had been cleared. Medical units of the division also established a Dressing Station here and the grounds of the chateau had graves of men who died of their wounds here, now re-buried at the nearby war cemetery.

Retrace your steps to the church, and opposite is a memorial to the Hermanville water well. This well, when tested, showed no signs of any water pollution and for the first few weeks of the campaign in Normandy was the principal source of water for the troops as they pushed inland. A staggering 1.5 million gallons of water were drawn from here. Over the years of visiting Normandy with veterans, many of them had read about the well and wanted to visit it, having once indirectly drank

The important well in Hermanville.

Hermanville War Memorial.

from it, and often owed their lives to it, all those years before.

Just past the well **turn right** onto Rue du Cimetiere Anglais and follow to the entrance of Hermanville War Cemetery. **Stop.** The entrance has paved design similar to the 3rd Division badge. Enter the cemetery. It was once called 'SWORD Beach Cemetery' but the name was changed in the 1950s when the site was made permanent. The cemetery contains 903 burials, most of them men from 3rd Division who died in the fighting here on 6 June, and also some from the 1st Special Service Brigade who fell on SWORD Beach in the initial landings. Among the burials are Lieutenant Colonel Richard Percival Hawksley Burbury

(I-A-18). Originally, he served with the Duke of Cornwall's Light Infantry, but he died commanding 1st South Lancashires on D-Day, although his headstone wrongly states that his date of death was on 7 June. Aged 38, he was an experienced soldier who had been twice mentioned in despatches. Close by is Lieutenant Charles Bell-Walker (I-M-14), from Bickley in Kent. He took over command of 1st South Lancs when Burbury and all the other officers were dead or wounded, and led them until he fell mortally wounded attacking a strongpoint.

Return to the entrance of the cemetery. **Turn right** onto a track and follow this until it reaches the D35, close to a water tower. It was close to here men from the 1st Suffolks assembled for the assault on Strongpoint MORRIS, located where the housing estate is ahead of you. MORRIS fell without a fight, but beyond it on the rising ground was the HILLMAN complex, a far more formidable defence work.

Turn left onto the D35 and then take the **first right** onto Rue du Stade. Then take the **second right** into Rue du Crespley. Follow this to the end and then **turn right** into an area where new houses have been built and in early 2011 were still being constructed. This was the area where Strongpoint MORRIS was located. MORRIS was a gun battery made up of four 105mm howitzers. Originally, these were on turntable gun mounts but in early 1944 efforts were made to place them in bunkers that had not been finished by D-Day. It was surrounded by two belts of barbed wire, along with anti-personnel and anti-tank mines. Little of the battery is visible now, but the remaining turntable position and one of the 105mm bunkers have been incorporated into the housing estate, with the nearby road being named Impasse Morris in recognition of the importance of the site. The road layout is changing as the housing estate develops, but return to Rue du Crespley and then take Rue du Clos du Moulin

A gun turntable from Strongpoint MORRIS.

onto the Rue du Caen (D60a). Go **straight across** to Rue Porte-Morin and then **turn right** onto Rue du Tour de Ville. Stay on this, and follow it **left**, where it joins Rue du Regiment du Suffolk. Here **turn right** and take the road uphill to the HILLMAN Bunker complex.

Artillery bunker from Strongpoint MORRIS.

The HILLMAN site is now locally owned and managed by the Friends of the Suffolk Regiment, a joint Anglo-French group. The site has gradually been improved, trench systems restored and bunkers cleaned and opened up. The site is always open but on certain days there are guided tours. Care should be taken when walking round the site as the trenches, gun pits and bunkers are not always easily visible. A good place to start is the observation cupola, which has excellent views back across the ground already walked and also onto SWORD Beach.

The observation cupola at HILLMAN.

The HILLMAN Bunker complex.

From HILLMAN **go back** downhill on Rue du Suffolk Regiment and take a minor track on the **right** called Rue des Petites Rues. Follow this until it meets the D35 and then go **straight across**, following the road to the church. Just past the church **turn right** onto Sentier de l'Eglise. Follow this out of Colleville-Montgomery onto Chemin des Pelerins. Follow this for just over a mile and take the **second track on the left**. The remains of WN-12 Strongpoint DAIMLER is here, captured on D-Day by the 2nd East Yorks. Manned by Artillery Regiment 1716, it was equipped with four 155mm howitzers in bunkers, and had Tobruks and 20mm flak positions. Like many of the howitzers used in other gun sites, the weapons were of First World War vintage and captured French Schnieders. The bunkers are still visible but parts of the strongpoint have been redeveloped and the site is largely on private ground and this needs to be respected.

From DAIMLER retrace your steps back to the outskirts of Colleville-Montgomery and **turn right** onto Rue du Bocage. At the end **turn left** onto the D35a and take the **first right** down a small cul-de-sac called Rue de la Fontaine. Follow this left then right, and on the right follow signs for a marked walking trail (part of a route called 'sur les traces du 4eme commando'). Follow this through the countryside, past a wooded area and in the woods **turn left** and follow it to Collevillette, and then back to the Montgomery Memorial and your car.

Memorial to the 1st Suffolks.

JUNO BEACH WALK: NAN BEACH – INLAND TO TAILLEVILLE

HISTORICAL SECTION

The troops allocated to the landings on JUNO Beach were men of the 3rd Canadian Division commanded by Major General R.F.L. Keller. Keller had joined the Canadian Army in the latter stages of the First World War, although he saw no active service, and became a regular officer after the war. On the outbreak of war in 1939 he was a Brigade Major and within three years was commanding the 3rd Division; quite a leap in rank and his promotion was largely due to his patronage by Harry Crerar, commander of the 1st Canadian Army. Keller's division had been based along the south coast in Sussex, and like the 3rd British Division which landed on its left flank on SWORD Beach, it had undertaken extensive assault and battle training; in fact, it had been working on such training for a full year in the lead up to D-Day. Keller was a popular commander with his men, although he

Harry Crerar, commander of 1st Canadian Army.

The defences on Nan Sector, JUNO Beach.

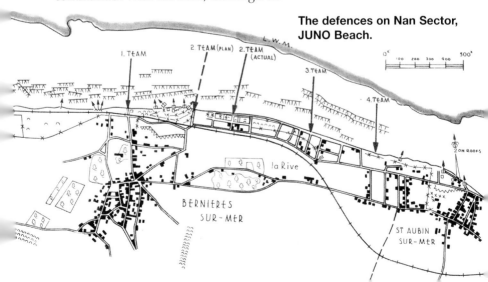

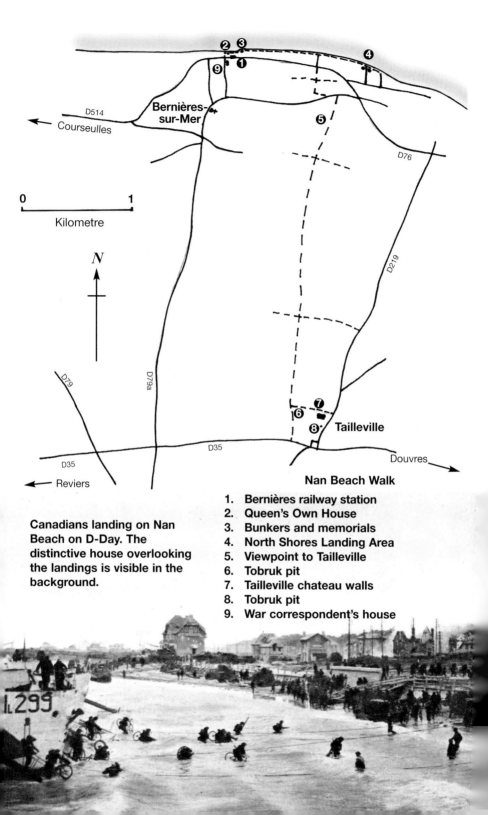

D514

Courseulles

Bernières-sur-Mer

D76

D219

D79

D79a

D35

D35

D79

Reviers

Douvres

Tailleville

Nan Beach Walk

2 ③ ②
④
⑨ ①
⑤
⑦
⑥
⑧

0   1
Kilometre

N

1. **Bernières railway station**
2. **Queen's Own House**
3. **Bunkers and memorials**
4. **North Shores Landing Area**
5. **Viewpoint to Tailleville**
6. **Tobruk pit**
7. **Tailleville chateau walls**
8. **Tobruk pit**
9. **War correspondent's house**

Canadians landing on Nan Beach on D-Day. The distinctive house overlooking the landings is visible in the background.

L.299

drove them hard, and the training they received in the numerous live-fire exercises and in the battle schools would pay dividends in Normandy.

The men of the 3rd Canadian Division were different to some of the Allied troops who landed on D-Day in that they were entirely volunteers. There was no conscription or National Service in Canada as there was in the UK and the men in the divisions' infantry battalions and support units had all willingly volunteered to fight for Canada and the mother country – the United Kingdom. Unlike a generation before in the First World War, a much higher percentage of them were Canadian born; in 1914 some 70 per cent of Canada's army had been born outside of Canada, but in 1939 the majority of men who enlisted were Canadian born.

On D-Day Keller's division was charged with landing on two flanks of the seaside town of Courseulles-sur-Mer. Nan Beach, the left flank of the Canadian landings, was itself sub-divided into three beaches: Nan Red on the left, Nan White in the centre and Nan Green on the right. These three beaches skirted the villages of St Aubin-sur-Mer, Bernières-sur-Mer and Courseulles-sur-Mer. The assault units landing here were the North Shore Regiment on Red Beach, Queen's Own Rifles of Canada on White and Regina Rifle Regiment on Green. They would be supported by swimming DD Sherman tanks from the 6th Armoured Regiment (1st Hussars) and 10th Armoured Regiment (Fort Garry Horse). The sea wall along Nan Beach was quite high compared to other areas, and there were a number of strongpoints and bunker complexes. Compared to other beaches there were also many more buildings here that directly bordered the beach area, several of which were concreted and contained defences. To assist the Canadians in their ability to overcome these defences if the pre-D-Day bombardment had not knocked them out, and to help get off the beach, British troops from the 79th Armoured Division were allocated to Keller. These included a large variety of so-called 'Funnies' ranging from Sherman mine-clearance tanks to Churchill AVRE tanks capable of dropping bridges onto the sea wall to allow access off the beach, and using their specialist Petard mortars could take on concrete emplacements.

The overall divisional plan on D-Day was to land at JUNO and then push inland towards the Bayeux–Caen road, capture the Authie Heights and reach the Carpiquet airfield west of Caen itself. There was a gap between the Canadians and the British 3rd Division, but both formations were to meet near Caen as the British took the city. The landings at Nan Beach were tasked with securing the bridgehead from Courseulles to St Aubin, then moving inland to capture a German strongpoint in the hamlet of Tailleville. Other troops were then to pass through and continue with the advance southwards to the Bayeux road.

The German troops facing the Canadians on Nan Red were from the *736. Grenadier-Regiment*, part of the *Infantrie-Division 716*. A substantial proportion of men in this unit were in *Ost Battalion* – former Soviet Army troops taken prisoner on the Eastern Front and offered the chance to escape the awful conditions of a prisoner-of-war camp and fight for Hitler. As such they were hardly willing combatants, and the pre-D-Day Canadian briefings had them down as low-quality troops with poor morale. Having said that, they had formidable defences to fall back on. Aside from the usual bunker, trench and minefield complexes, there was a substantial command centre inland at Tailleville, and close to that a *Wutzburg* radar station. There were 88mm gun positions inland on the high ground west of Tailleville and well-sited artillery batteries. The only available armour, however, was the *21. Panzer Division* beyond Caen.

The North Shore Regiment landing further up the beach on D-Day.

As D-Day dawned the armada of taking the 3rd Division into Nan Red assembled off the coast. The weather had already delayed operations, and in this area there was a high wind and heavy swell. An immediate decision was made not to launch the DD tanks at sea due to the conditions; they would have to land direct from the LCTs onto the beach. This meant that the initial infantry landing would be made with no tank support. At 0705, just 25 minutes before H Hour at Nan Red, a signal was received that the landing craft bringing in the AVREs from 79th Armoured Division were late, which meant the whole operation was now put back 30 minutes. The plan was already beginning to go wrong. One factor that was in accordance with the plan was the final bombardment. Cannon fire from the Landing Ship Guns was opening up on Nan Beach, along with fire from the rocket ships and also, as was common on all the British beaches on D-Day, there was a 'run-in shoot' from the 105mm M7 Priest self-propelled guns of Lieutenant Colonel F.P.T. Clifford's 13th Canadian Field Regiment. Despite poor visibility, they did well in dropping shells onto some key targets in the immediate beach area.

Finally, at around 0800 the assault troops began to land. On the left Lieutenant Colonel Donald Bowie Buell's[1] North Shore Regiment's leading companies touched down at 0810. Once again, despite the fire from several cruisers and destroyers, along with aerial bombardments, it was found that the German defences were pretty much intact. On Nan Red this left a 50mm emplacement on the right and a twin 50mm/75mm emplacement on the left still able to fire, and this was already beginning to cause problems. And without the initial tank support there was no easy way to solve it. One officer recalled the landings, 'Things weren't going as planned and unless we captured those heavy guns Jerry was potting landing craft with, things were going to get worse. And worse they got, for there we were with nothing heavier than Brens with which to attack heavily fortified enemy posts.'[2] Lieutenant C.F. Richardson was facing the same problems,

Tracer bullets from German anti-aircraft seemed to fill the air as we came in . . . Once we were out of the boat everyone acted mechanically, heading for the beach and the cover of the beach wall . . . we used our Bangalore torpedoes with good effect and were at close quarters with the enemy after traversing through what we later discovered was a minefield. The Germans were [behind] concrete and we were without armoured support. Soon the sniping became the most demoralising aspect of the day as we began to lose one man after another.[3]

Buell's company commanders began to prove their worth. Major Robert Borden Forbes, commanding 'B' Company, personally led his men against the strongpoints and using what weapons they had, they gradually began to neutralise the German defences; for this he was later awarded a Military Cross. Then, finally, tank support began to arrive. The Sherman DD tanks from C Squadron 10th Armoured Regiment (Fort Garry Horse) had left the LCTs and got ashore to support the North Shores. They soon found the infantry pinned down, so the Shermans began to direct fire onto the defences. But it was a tricky task; several tank commanders were sniped and the gun positions soon accounted for four Shermans knocked out. Supporting armour from the 'Funnies' were also present. No. 4 Team of the 80th Assault Squadron Royal Engineers landed here and lost their Churchill Bridgelayer when it collided with a landing craft. The crew immediately dismounted and came under sniper and grenade attack, which killed or wounded most of them. Sherman Flail tanks from the 22nd Dragoons began to sweep a lane through the minefields, but for most tanks in the Fort Garry Horse this was taking too long. Major William Roy Bray had had enough; stuck on the beach under sniper and direct anti-tank fire was no place for a tank commander, so he made the decision to brave the uncleared minefields and push on. In doing so, three tanks were lost, but the area was soon bypassed and now the tanks were beyond the beach. The fighting for St Aubin itself was now on.

On Nan White Beach the Queen's Own Rifles of Canada were detailed to assault the beach at Bernières-sur-Mer. There was a 50mm anti-tank gun in a bunker here on the battalion's frontage, and a very distinct gabled house to the left defined their flank there. As at Nan Red, the landings were delayed by 30 minutes, and one company found itself bobbing up and down off the beach in a heavy swell; as they had approached on time they had not encountered any opposition. They floated there like sitting ducks for half an hour. Finally, the assault went in just after 0800 and two companies touched down. The unit's

Coming ashore at Nan Beach.

commander, Lieutenant Colonel W.T. Barnard, later reported,

> 'A' Company on the right and 'B' Company on the left touched down at 0812 hours. The line between the companies was the railway station. Several LCA [Landing Craft Assault] hit mines on the run in but casualties were light . . . The rising tide had now left about two hundred yards or so of the beach between the water's edge and the sea-wall. The strip was swept by enemy enfilade fire but, with a rush 'A' Company, under Major H.E. Dalton, was over, clambered up the sea-wall, and reached the railway line.[4]

Charlie Martin DCM MM.

Company Sergeant Major Charles Martin was in a LCA on the left flank of the battalion's landing area, close to the gabled house.

Everyone seemed calm and ready. The boat commander was in charge of this part. He would give our landing order. We waited for it. In just a few inches of water the prow grated onto the beach. The order rang out: 'Down ramp.' The moment the ramp came down, heavy machine-gun fire broke out from somewhere back of the seawall. Mortars were dropping all over the beach . . . The men rose, starboard line turning right, port turning left. I said . . . 'Go!Go!Go!' we raced down the ramp . . . the men closely following. We fanned out as fast as we could, heading for that sea wall.[5]

Martin and his men got to the sea wall, got over it and across the railway line close to Bernières station and pushed into the town where the real fighting began, although it had cost his company dear in just getting there. Martin noted that the leaders, platoon and section commanders, were often the first to get hit, targeted by the Germans,

To both sides of us we had minefields. The machine-gun fire and mortars never let up, a barrage of shelling that seemed to come from everywhere. Once over the railway we had some grass cover, but we ran into heavy barbed wire . . . We decided to cut the wire and . . . go straight ahead.[6]

The next obstacle was the minefield beyond, and while seeing his men across Martin stood on an S Mine, which jumped out the ground and exploded ball bearings at chest or head height. He stood firmly on the men until everyone was across, and was just about to flop when a bullet hit his helmet and he dived badly. Luckily, he had ducked enough to avoid the mine exploding; only minutes into D-Day Martin was leading a charmed life that would take him into Germany the following year.

Elsewhere on Nan White beach the 80th Assault Squadron of the Royal Engineers were coming into to assist.

Door dropped . . . 4–5 feet of water at door and all AVRE with one exception got out and on to beach. The main items to ensure the reduction of most of the opposition did not take place . . . The AVREs were the first in this sector . . . The tide was rising fast and it was obvious from the outset that beach obstacles could not be cleared . . . Shelling was not bad but mortars did get some vehicles. Sniping was increasing.[7]

Mine clearance, as on Nan Red, was by the Sherman Flails of 22nd Dragoons. The AVREs were in action here, too. One tank

The battle-damaged railway station at Bernières-sur-Mer.

Prisoners taken when the German defences were overrun by the Queen's Own Rifles of Canada. One of the bunkers is visible on the sea wall.

from No. 2 Team took out the 50mm gun position with a 'flying dustbin' charge from the tank's Petard mortar. The same weapons were used to clear a beach ramp blocked only by 'Element C' obstacles, like big iron gates. A few shots from the Petards and the ramp was clear. Mines along the beach were swept by the Dragoons and an AVRE carrying a fascine dropped it into the ditch beyond creating the first main exit off Nan White Beach.

By 0900, an hour into the landings, the infantry battle had the Queen's Own well into Bernières. Battalion Headquarters caught up with them, coming in one of the final wave of LCAs, and as they entered the town discovered a café still open and selling wine! An hour later Bernières was secure, beach exits had been made and the next battalion – the Regiment de la Chaudière, French Canadians – had landed and would now take up the advance inland.

On the right at Nan Green on the edge of Courseulles-sur-Mer, the Regina Rifle Regiment hit the beach at 0805. 'A' Company landed first on the extreme right, close to the jetty where the mouth of the Seulles River was located, followed by the other companies in 20-minute gaps. The assault was supported by Sherman DD tanks from the 1st Hussars. This unit had successfully launched its floating tanks at 2,000yd with fourteen out of nineteen of them making it to the beach. Royal Engineer support was given by the 26th Assault Regiment and another squadron of the 22nd Dragoons with their Sherman Flail tanks to clear the mines.

Ted Hindmarch was in 'A' Company and one of the first to land.

We were going into the beaches in landing craft and the Germans didn't fire on us till we were close in. As number 2 section was in the centre of the landing craft they had to jump out first. Their last man of that section was their Bren Gunner. I followed him out. We had to jump into waist deep water. He was hit and started to sink so I grabbed him by his webbing and pulled him to shore, but he was dead when I got them there. He still hung on to his Bren Gun. His name was Cutler, from Moosemin, Sask.

I took off across the beach, bullets flying all around, men being shot down. I could see where the Germans had been driving over the barbed wire so that's the place I ran for. I thought of mines being laid there, so I took the longest steps I could to get across the wire. I got

Prisoners being guarded against the very distinctive sea wall here which was a major obstacle for vehicles

to the bank and went down on my belly, two of my men dropped down beside me . . . It was hard to see where all the firing was coming from. We were still a long way from the first building up ahead.[8]

The fire grew with intensity as the other companies came in, and tragedy struck when one of the landing craft hit a mine, killing Major J.V. Love, commanding 'D' Company. However, the infantry were now getting off the beach and into Courseulles. The 'Funnies' from the Royal Engineers were busy on the beach itself, however. No. 3 and No. 4 Teams from the 26th Assault Regiment had a long section of 'Element C' to clear on the right flank near the mouth of the Seulles River. From here the Flails cleared the minefield and the exit ramp near where Ted Hindmarch had crossed the wire was opened up by an armoured bulldozer. By 0900 the first exit ramp was open and the Sherman DD tanks that had landed in support of the infantry were now joining them in the battle for Courseulles town; within the space of another hour the beachhead battle was almost over and the Regina Rifles were pushing inland to the village of Reviers.

With the beachhead secure, the next stage of the advance was to move inland and take the villages and objectives towards the Bayeux road. One of these, south of St Aubin, was the small hamlet of Tailleville. Here the *736. Grenadier Regiment* had made their headquarters in the chateau, re-enforcing parts of the location with concrete shelters, tunnels and bunkers. The walls of the chateau park had been loop-holed for machine guns and parts of it dropped so that self-propelled guns could fire over it from a hull-down position. One part of the wall had been concreted with a firing aperture for a field gun, and Tobruk pits had been built into the wall giving further potential covering fire. It was certainly a formidable defensive position.

The approach to Tailleville in 1944, as it is today, is marked by wide open fields with little cover, save the occasional depression of ground. From the edge of the buildings that marked St Aubin to the chateau walls was potentially a death trap for any unit advancing in daylight. But this was only part

Canadian troops moving inland from JUNO Beach.

of the next phase of the North Shore Regiment's D-Day objectives. Having taken Tailleville, they were to push onto the woods around the radar station at Douvres and end the day at the village of Anguerny, some 6 miles inland. An ambitious plan.

Lieutenant Colonel Buell, commanding the North Shore, had fought his way off the beach with his men to St Aubin, where they waited for support. No attack on Tailleville would be able to succeed without tanks, and machine guns and mortars from the divisional support battalion. These were still landing, but by midday all were in place and Buell was able to send C Company forward in a probing attack towards the chateau. Their company commander, Major Daughney, had reconnoitred the area on a bicycle before his men moved off, a brave stunt in broad daylight. His recce had not noted anything like the sort of indications he would have expected to see if a German battlegroup had been in position, so he led his men in with some degree of optimism. With tanks from the Fort Garry Horse and a Forward Observer from the self-propelled guns of 19th Field Regiment, his plan was to send two platoons forward and use the carrier platoon to swing round the west of the chateau in their Bren carriers and cut off any retreating enemy.

The first sign of Germans came when mortar rounds began to drop on C Company. The advance sped on and reached a position a few hundred yards from the chateau. Here intense machine-gun fire brought the men to a halt, but then the Shermans fired High Explosive (HE), and the field guns and heavy mortars dropped rounds into the chateau grounds. With the German defenders suppressed by the fire, the platoons rushed the chateau and began the task of clearing Tailleville. Colonel Buell was hot on their heels and after a short while Daughney optimistically reported that the village was clear. Buell ordered a more comprehensive sweep and sent another company round the flank of Tailleville. The commander of that company, Major McNaughton, walked straight into an ambush just beyond the main chateau buildings and was killed along with his radioman and several others. The fight continued and it soon became clear that the Germans were using a system of tunnels beneath the village to go to ground and come up behind the Canadians just when they thought the area was clear. It finally took six attempts before Tailleville was completely clear and it wasn't until 2100 on 6 June that the message to say the objective was secure was given. It had cost the North Shores a score of men, and the German garrison had been reduced to just fifty men.

While it was late in the day, Buell considered pushing on to his other objectives. Getting to Anguerny was unlikely, but he might be able to clear the woods near the radar station. However, orders came down from Brigade Headquarters to stop and hold Tailleville. Unbeknown to Buell, the British on their flanks had run into opposition and were held up before Caen, and some of the Canadian units that had penetrated further south had run into units thought to be in reserve or away from Normandy. Indeed, one of them had even captured men from the Reconnaissance Battalion of 12th SS Panzer Division. For Buell his long D-Day was drawing to a close and while it had been tough and cost him casualties, his men would soon be encountering more than recce units from the 12th in some of the toughest battles of the Normandy campaign.

Walk 5: From Nan Red to Tailleville

STARTING POINT: Car park close to Bernières railway station, just off D514

GPS: 49°20′05.7″N, 0°25′22.4″W

DURATION: 10.4km/6.5 miles

Park your vehicle in the car park just west of the old Bernières railway station off the D514, here part of Rue Victor Tesniere. Start with a visit to the station.

Bernières railway station is now de-commissioned and is the local tourist office. Tourist information, postcards and some useful local guides can be obtained inside. It is the original building that was here in 1944 and appears in many period photographs. There is a series of

The railway station at Bernières.

images around the town at places where key events took place on D-Day, and outside the station is a colour image.

From the station return to the car park and **continue** to the seafront. The wall of the building to your right displays further images from D-Day and the house itself is also a survivor from

117

The Queen's Own Rifles of Canada House on JUNO Beach.

1944. Known as the 'Maison de Queen's Own Rifles of Canada', the building was part of the German defences at this point – WN-28 – and came under fire when the Germans inside refused to surrender. It overlooks the landing point that was on the left flank of the Queen's Own Rifles of Canada. The D-Day defences were intact here, and immediately came to life as the Queen's Own hit the beach, but with the assistance of Churchill AVREs and tanks from the Fort Garry Horse the positions were overwhelmed and the battalion pushed inland. The house owners are proud of their association with D-Day but visitors should remember it is private property. In front is a memorial that reads,

> *This house was liberated at first light on D Day 6th June 1944, by the men of The Queen's Own Rifles of Canada who were the first Canadians to land on this beach. It may very well have been the first house on French soil liberated by seaborne Allied Forces. Within sight of this house over 100 men of The Queen's Own Rifles were killed or wounded, in the first few minutes of the landings.*

From the house walk along the promenade going east. Further up on the left is a Tobruk pit. Walk down onto the beach to the

The distinctive sea wall at Nan Beach is still visible.

The field of fire from a German bunker looking down Nan Beach.

far side of it; there is a plaque here to the Queen's Own. Returning to the promenade **continue** to the next bunker, a strongpoint that contained a 50mm gun that could fire right down the beach. A further memorial to the Queen's Own was placed on the bunker, but earlier plaques commemorate other units including the 22nd Dragoons, the unit that operated Flail tanks here on D-Day, and the 5th Bn Royal Berkshire Regiment.

Today this former German bunker is covered with memorials to the units who fought here on D-Day.

This unit, a Territorial battalion from Hackney in London, defended the beach from D-Day until the end of the campaign. A Canadian Battlefield Foundation map can be seen further along the sea wall and just beyond that another Tobruk pit.

Staying on the promenade **continue** for about ⅔ mile until you reach Rue des Hirondelles on the right. **Stop**. This is the

119

sector where the North Shore Regiment landed on D-Day. The regiment had a cinematographer from the Army Film and Photographic Unit attached to them who filmed men from either 'A' or 'B' Companies of the North Shore approaching this stretch of beach on an LCI (Landing Craft Infantry). This section of film has become an iconic image of D-Day, and two of the buildings visible on it are either side of Rue des Hirondelles. This area also marks the extreme left flank of JUNO Beach.

Return along the promenade in the direction you just came from until you reach Rue de la Caline on the left. **Turn left** into this street and continue to the D514. Here go **straight across** onto Chemin Huet and **continue** into Passage de la Rive. At the end **turn left** onto Rue Moisant de Brieux and follow it onto the D7. Stay left and then take the first track on the **right**.

This track takes you across the fields towards Tailleville. It is as open as the ground was in June 1944, and the advance of the North Shore Regiment was to your left running parallel to the track. The first section of the track has a battle-damaged wall on the right, and at the second junction of tracks stop for a good view of the approach to the battlefield around the Tailleville chateau. Then continue to the north-west corner of the chateau wall. There is a Tobruk pit built into the corner of the wall here. Go along the wall to another

Tobruk pit in the corner of the wall at Tailleville.
Inset: A similar position in use.

Artillery position built into the wall at Tailleville.

Tobruk. The machine-gun position is open here and an appreciation of its potential field of fire is gained by looking back towards the beach. Further examples of how the chateau was fortified can be seen along the wall, included slits for machine guns, lower walls to place self-propelled guns behind and a concreted gun position.

At the end of the chateau wall **turn right** and go into the chateau grounds. The chateau is owned by a charity that helps the homeless by selling reclamation goods, and normally they welcome visitors who want to look at the outside of the chateau, but the grounds are private. The chateau shows signs of battle damage, but modern buildings now cover some of the positions that were in the grounds.

Machine-gun position at Tailleville.

Return to the road and **turn right**. Round the next bend on the right is a Tobruk pit. It was here Major J.A. MacNaughton and his party was ambushed. This part of the village has now been named in memory of one of the North Shore men who was wounded here that day. **Continue** through the village until you reach the D35. Here **turn right** and on the next bend walk across to the memorial on the left. This is the village war memorial but it also has another memorial to the North Shore

Tailleville chateau.

Regiment on it. The Canadian flag is flown here for most of the year.

On the D35 **stay left** and continue west, taking the second track on the **right**. Follow this track back into Bernières. On the outskirts of the village go **straight across** at a junction of tracks and roads onto Route de Tailleville. Take the first **right** onto the Rue de la Corderie. At the end **turn left** and then take **first right** onto Rue du Regiment de la Chaudière. At the end of this street on the right is the building used by Allied war correspondents, photographers and cinematographers from the late morning of D-Day onwards. From here go **straight across** on the D514 and return to the car park and your vehicle.

Area Six

JUNO BEACH WALK: MIKE BEACH – THE FIGHT FOR COURSEULLES

HISTORICAL SECTION

The 3rd Canadian Division, commanded by Major General R.F.L. Keller, had been allocated to land on JUNO Beach on D-Day (for more information on this formation see the previous chapter). Their beachhead had been divided into two sectors: Nan Beach from Courseulles-sur-Mer to St Aubin-sur-Mer, and Mike Beach west of Courseulles. Mike Beach was the responsibility of units from the 7th Canadian Infantry Brigade, and itself divided into Mike Red on the left and Mike Green on the right. To the right of Mike Beach was Love Beach, but no landings were due to take place here on D-Day.

The assault at Mike Beach was led by the Royal Winnipeg Rifles of 7th Canadian Brigade. It would transpire that the pre-D-Day bombardment here had been the most ineffectual on a British beach on D-Day,

Major General R.F.L. Keller.

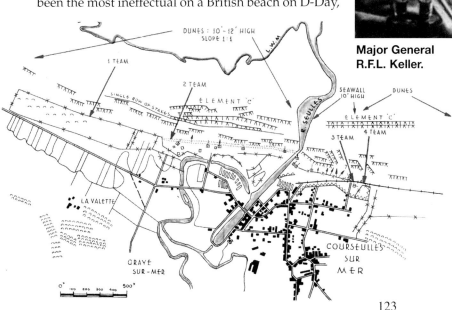

The defences on Mike Sector, Juno Beach.

123

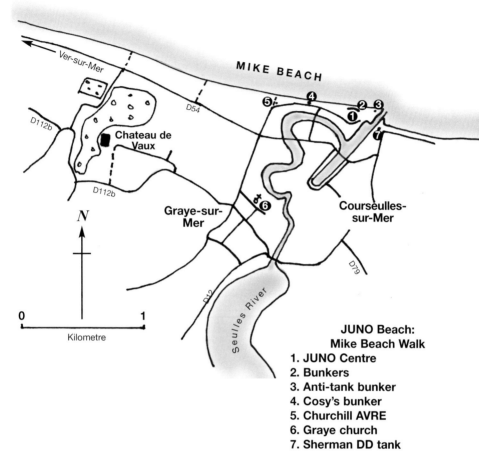

**JUNO Beach:
Mike Beach Walk**
1. JUNO Centre
2. Bunkers
3. Anti-tank bunker
4. Cosy's bunker
5. Churchill AVRE
6. Graye church
7. Sherman DD tank

and the defences were pretty much intact as the landing craft approached the coast at H Hour. As such, it would prove one of the toughest fights on D Day, but a combination of the level of training the Canadians had received prior to Normandy and the full range of armoured and engineer support meant that, despite the difficulties, the troops here were able to overcome the problems, albeit at some cost. The Winnipegs, or 'Little Black Devils', a name given to them because of the design of their cap badge, landed on the join of Mike Beach and Love Beach. The official history of the Canadians on D-Day records,

> *The infantry's experience on the right battalion front of the Canadian division was a mixture of good and bad. The Royal*

Winnipeg Rifles state that they touched down at 7:49 a.m., all three assault companies landing 'within seven minutes of one another'. On the far right, 'C' Company of the Canadian Scottish, which was prolonging the Rifles' front here, reported that it landed with slight opposition, and the platoon which had the job of knocking out the 75-mm. casemate north of Vaux approached it 'only to find – thanks to the Royal Navy – the pill-box was no more'.

Quite different was the experience of 'B' and 'D' Companies of The Royal Winnipeg Rifles, a short distance to the left, whose task it was to deal with the western portion of the Courseulles strongpoint. The battalion diary remarked grimly, 'The bombardment having failed to kill a single German or silence one weapon, these companies had to storm their positions "cold" – and did so without hesitation.'

'B' Company met heavy machine-gun, shell and mortar fire beginning when the LCAs were 700 yards from the beach. This continued until touchdown, and as the men leaped from the craft many were hit 'while still chest high in water'. But the Little Black Devils were not to be denied. 'B' Company, with the aid of the tanks, captured the pillboxes commanding the beach; it then forced its way across the Seulles bridge and cleared the enemy positions on the

Aerial view of Mike Beach on D-Day.

'island' between the river and the little harbour. The fierceness of the fight on the beach is attested by the report of the Special Observer Party which later examined the German positions: 'Big guns in this area were probably all put out of action by close range tank fire, and the machine gun and mortar positions gave up when surrounded by infantry.' When the strongpoint was clear 'B' Company had been reduced to the company commander (Capt. P. Gower) and 26 men. Gower, who had set a powerful example of leadership and courage as he directed the clearing of the successive positions, received the Military Cross. An assault party of the 6th Field Company Royal Canadian Engineers, which landed with the infantry, had similar losses; the company had 26 casualties during the day.

'D' Company met less fierce opposition when landing, since it was clear of the actual strongpoint area. It had relatively little difficulty in 'gapping' a minefield at La Valette and clearing the village of Graye-sur-Mer beyond it. When the reserve companies landed the beach and dunes were still under heavy mortar and machine-gun fire.[1]

Tank support on Mike Beach came from the 6th Canadian Armoured Regiment (1st Hussars), equipped with Sherman DD tanks. They were launched at 2,000 yards from the beach direct from the LCTs into the sea. They later reported,

Canadian troops landing on Mike Beach.

all were being subjected to mortar and other enemy fire. Ten tanks succeeded in launching . . . seven succeeded in reaching the beach, the other three going down, one to rough seas, one having the screen damaged by mortar fire and one being run down by rocket craft . . . Of the seven which touched down and the six which landed dry, three were put out of action either on the beach or among the underwater obstacles . . . While on the beach or in the water the ten tanks definitely destroyed two 75mm guns and 6 LMGs. . . . A very noticeable event was that very shortly after the tanks deflated back of the [amphibious screen] and commenced firing on the beach fortifications, the enemy manning these casements surrendered. It has since been learned from some of these prisoners that the presence of tanks at this stage of the attack came as a complete surprise and were the main factor in their decision to surrender instead of fighting.[2]

Lieutenant C.M. McLeod of 1st Hussars recalled a typical experience of a tank troop commander on Mike Beach as the landings began,

My tank touched down at the right position on the beach with the other two tanks of my troop, one on either side of mine. A few of the infantry were engaging the pill boxes to our immediate front. About fifteen minutes later the AVREs landed to clear the beach and make exits. They did this job in half an hour then I led my troop through the gap to find the infantry company I was supposed to working with.[3]

Once again on the British sector, the use and implementation of the Sherman DD tanks proved successful, despite the weather and enemy fire. With these tanks now on the beach, and as the infantry fight was proving difficult, they were able to provide the vital armoured support the Winnipegs needed. In 'A' Squadron,

seven DDs succeeded in passing through the hail of shell, mortar and small arms fire that the Germans threw out over the water whatever [sic] they could see the odd-looking two feet of canvas screen protruding ... The sudden appearance of tanks on the beaches in front of their positions had a [sic] momentarily disorganised the German gunners ... Landing on the right of 3rd Troop, Captain Powell's tank was fired upon from a concrete fort. An armour piercing shot hit the 75mm, went about half-way through the barrel and glanced off taking a gouge out of the turret ... As soon as the anti-tank guns on the beach had been liquidated, the seven DD tanks began to cruise up and down the beach engaging the machine-gun nests.[4]

Captain John Wilson Powell was awarded the Military Cross for bravery on Mike Beach on D-Day. His citation reads,

> *he was immediately engaged by an anti-tank gun in a concrete casemate. Before being able to neutralise the gun, his tank was hit three times, the third shot putting his master gun out of action. Captain Powell moved his tank forward and neutralised the enemy gun with his Browning machine-gun whilst directing the fire of the other tanks onto enemy gun positions.*
>
> *During this action he received an injury in his left hand and while still on the beach he changed tanks and continued to engage enemy coast defences, as well as organise part of the squadron which had succeeded in landing on his section of the beach.*[5]

The Royal Engineer support came from two teams of the 26th Assault Squadron and Sherman Crab Flail tanks from the 22nd Dragoons, both from 79th (Armoured) Division. Both teams landed near No. 2 Team's exit, a small lane running from just beyond the beach towards the Arromanches–Courseulles

Canadian LCI bringing in the follow-up waves.

road. The Sherman Crabs cleared a lane through the minefields over the dunes, and one tank commanded by Lieutenant P.D. Barraclough pushed on in line with the exit lane. The field here and part of the lane were cut by water-filled bomb craters from the pre-D-Day bombardment. Much of the field was flooded and the tank soon foundered and sank in the mud, immobile. Barraclough did not abandon the vehicle, and used it to support the advance of the infantry, at one point shattering the church tower of Graye-sur-Mer, which was being used by the Germans as an observation tower.

A Churchill AVRE with a fascine fixed to the hull came up to fill in the hole and possibly rescue the bogged Sherman Crab, but it was also bogged in the lane after ditching the fascine. The crew then bailed out and was hit by mortar fire, several of them being killed. Another fascine was bulldozed into the craters and a Churchill Bridgelayer tank, commanded by Captain R.J. Hewitt, pushed the AVRE in the hole and placed a bridge across it, opening the exit lane. After the war the bridge was removed but the tank covered over; it remained here until 1976 when a Royal Engineer team excavated it.

Major Anthony Younger commanded the assault teams on Mike Beach.

His AVRE carried a mine clearing plough which necessitated him steering it through the mined beach obstacles with his head exposed. A mortar shell landing on the turret destroyed his wireless communications and burst his ear drums. His communications gone Major Younger dismounted from his AVRE and proceeded to direct the operations of his squadron on foot in advance of the dunes behind which groups of assaulting companies were still held by mortar and sporadic MG and rifle fire. He arranged covering fire from the dunes with CO 6th Armoured Regiment and then organised and supervised his own men and elements of Beach Group RE . . . He then went forward on foot into Courseulles to the bridges which were mined and prepared for demolition. He organised the removal of mines from the arc bridges and then personally with the assistance of a Canadian cleared the demolition charges from the others and swung it across the lock, thus completing a lateral [opening] between the two assaulting battalions of his Brigade.[6]

With Mike Beach secure, the tanks moving inland along the exit roads and engineer tasks in hand, the fight now moved beyond the beachhead and inland to the villages towards the Bayeux road. In the immediate vicinity were two small villages, Graye-sur-Mer close to Courseulles and a hamlet dominated by a chateau, La Valette. The Royal Winnipeg Rifles, in the vanguard of the assault on Mike Beach, now went forward and with Royal Canadian Engineers began to clear the minefields between La Valette and Graye. With this clear they moved on to the villages of Ste-Croix and Banville, which were taken by 'A' Company. From here the remnants of 'C' and 'D' Companies pushed on to Tierceville and Creully.

Creully was a large settlement sitting on high ground, the approaches to it cut by the Seulles River which meant taking several bridges to get into the village. Lieutenant John Mitchell was in the leading platoon of 'D' Company and south of Tierceville reached one such bridge.

> *Approaching Creully from the left Lt Mitchell was crossing the river Seulles when he came under terrific cross-fire from two enemy machine-guns on the opposite bank in the woods. The officer managed to cross the river but two men of the leading section were hit, causing the remainder to go to ground. Lieutenant Mitchell was, at this time, wounded in the hand. Returning to the north bank of the river through a hail of fire, Lieutenant Mitchell managed to summon a troop from 6th Canadian Armoured Regiment to his aid, gathered his platoon and charged across the bridge against the MG positions. Lieutenant Mitchell's gallantry, prompt action and cool disregard for his personal safety in neutralising the enemy position contributed immeasurably toward maintaining the vital impetus of the advance and in gaining the company's portion of the battalion objective.[7]*

For his bravery Mitchell was awarded a Military Cross and this action brought the Royal Winnipeg Rifles' D-Day engagement to an end.

Back at the beach earlier that day, behind the Royal Winnipegs had been the 1st Bn Canadian Scottish. Landing in 3ft of water, they had helped clear some of the positions towards Love Beach,

> *We left our landing craft when we found we had to wade ashore . . . close to the obstacles. At first there was no enemy fire, but as we moved forward, enemy mortars began to drop amongst us, and machine gun fire was coming from the left flank . . . 13 Platoon moved west along the beach to their objective to find, thanks to the*

Royal Navy, the pillbox had been knocked out. They now moved inland towards the chateau clearing snipers who were giving trouble.[8]

The chateau was in the hamlet of La Valette and dominated it. A huge main building was flanked by numerous outhouses and stables, and all were defended. Sections began the task of clearing it. One squad took ten Germans prisoner; another found a frightened French family looking on in fear and amazement at the battle that raged around them. Lieutenant Schelderup's platoon captured a German MG42 position at the chateau and some parked trucks were fired upon; the trucks caught fire and as the men passed them to move on it was found one was full of ammunition and exploded, killing Privates Fahnri and Evans.[9]

From here the Canadian Scottish pushed further inland.

The Canadian Scottish, on the right flank of the beachhead, reached their intermediate objective about 16.30 hours. Here they paused only briefly before pushing on deeper, suffering more casualties from enemy mortar and machine-gun positions that had not been touched by the shore bombardment. By dusk they were six miles inland from the sea . . . of all the infantry battalions of the 2nd British Army landing [on D-Day] the Canadian Scottish in its present positions had gone farthest through the enemy's defences . . . During this march, Captain W.H.V. Matthews organised a party of men to search barns and buildings en route, flushing out a large number of German stragglers and others, and making the route safer for those coming behind.[10]

Later Captain William Matthews would be decorated for bravery with the Military Cross for his actions on D-Day and the first few days in Normandy. The battalion had meanwhile advanced from the chateau at Vaux into the village of Ste-Croix-sur-Mer, and then crossed the next river valley at Colombiers-sur-Seulles. In this phase they met little resistance but they encountered many dead and wounded, indicating the Germans were present somewhere. A German headquarters was overrun in the village and an enterprising sergeant liberated a fine-looking typewriter which was used by the battalion for the remainder of their work. Here the commanding officer, Lieutenant Colonel P.N. Cabeldu, requested to push on to his final objective, but he was so far ahead of the rest of the

Canadian units that his brigadier told him to dig in around the hamlet of Pierrepoint, south of the Seulles River. By midnight the battalion was dug in, patrols were out and the advance of the units from Mike Beach had for now come to an end.

Walk 6: The Mike Beach Sector

The Juno Centre.

STARTING POINT: Juno Centre, Courseulles-sur-Mer

GPS: 49°20'11.2"N, 0°27'39.0"W

DURATION: 7.29km/4.5 miles

Park your vehicle in the car park of the Juno Centre. Start with a visit to the centre, which tells the story of the Canadian involvement in the Second World War, focusing on their role in Normandy and North-West Europe. A good hour is needed here. On leaving the centre take time to look at the personal memorials to Canadian soldiers before walking towards the sand dunes. Immediately visible is a large German command bunker. This was the observation and

In the summer of 2011 a dig was carried out on some of the German tunnels at Mike Beach, exposing them for the first time in more than fifty years. It is hoped that eventually they will be open to the public.

German bunker on the extreme left flank of Mike Beach overlooking the Seulles River.

command centre for the German defences on Mike Beach. In 1944 this bunker was right on the seafront but the layout of the beach has changed slightly in seventy years and the dunes now obscure the view this observation bunker once had. It was linked by radio and telephone to artillery batteries beyond the beach and connected to the other bunkers by a system of tunnels. Part of the bunker can now be explored and there are plans to open up some of the tunnels.

From here walk to the **right** to the extreme left flank of Mike Beach overlooking the mouth of the Seulles River. There is another large bunker here, and this housed an anti-tank gun that could fire right down the beach in 1944. Unusually, it was neutralised in the pre-D-Day bombardment. From the bunker walk down onto the beach and walk **west** along the foot of the dunes. After about 500 metres there is a gap in the dunes on the

Cosy's Bunker.

Churchill AVRE '1 Charlie' now overlooking the spot where it fought on D-Day.

left, follow this to another bunker, now on its side. This is Cosy's Bunker, named after Lieutenant W.F. 'Cosy' Aitken, who commanded number 10 platoon of B Company Royal Winnipeg Rifles. His men stormed and took the bunker but suffered heavy losses – 78 per cent casualties – in doing so.

Go back to the beach and walk along to the next exit in the dunes. There is a Normandy memorial here. Walk past this down to the tank visible ahead. This is an example of a Churchill AVRE used by all the Royal Engineer Assault Regiments on D-Day. With a crew of four, it was equipped with a Petard mortar capable of destroying hard targets like sea walls and bunkers. The tank could also carry a variety of bridging equipment from drop bridges to fascines. This particular example was used here on D-Day by the 26th Assault Regiment when it was knocked out and pushed into a bomb crater. Another AVRE placed a bridge across it so traffic could pass, and after the war the hole it was in was just filled in, entombing the tank. It remained here until 1976 when a British Army team excavated the tank. It was later restored and then put on display here.

Return to the beach and then walk along the remaining stretch of Mike Beach. In doing so you have walked the area where the Royal Winnipeg Rifles came ashore supported by the 1st Hussars (Sherman DDs), and at this far end, where the Canadian Scottish landed. Continue past the first exit where a caravan camp is located to a second exit. Before leaving you can walk to a bunker visible ahead. This contained an anti-tank gun and was neutralised by naval gunfire on D-Day. **Leave the beach** by the exit, and follow the minor road to the D514. Here **go straight across** and follow the road into the wooded area of the hamlet of Vaux. At the next junction **turn left** on the D112B and continue to the high ground above Vaux chateau, which is now to your left. This was ground fought over by the Canadian Scottish as they pushed inland on D-Day and was where they ran into a German convoy parked up which when fired upon exploded, killing several men.

At a water tower on the left, **turn left** down a track and follow it along the edge of the chateau wall until the modern entrance to the chateau is reached. This is now a building owned by the local municipality and is not open to the public, but can be seen at this point. From the entrance go east on Rue du Chatcau de Vaux to where it rejoins the D112B and **turn left** following the road into Graye-sur-Mer. In the village follow the Rue Grande and take the **third left** into Rue du Carrefour. This will lead you to the church. **Stop.** This eleventh-century church was used as a German observation post (OP) on D-Day as the beach defences were overrun by the Canadians. At one point snipers operated from here until the church tower was fired on from Shermans coming over the dunes, destroying the main tower, which today is a later replacement. The church normally open and inside is a plaque from the village in memory of the Canadians who liberated the village on 6 June.

From the church follow a minor road leading to the D112C (Avenue du General de Gaulle) and **turn right** onto it following it back towards the beach. Where it reaches the D514 go **straight across** onto Voie des Francais Libres taking you back to the Churchill AVRE. **Continue** past the tank. In the dunes on the left is a large Cross of Lorraine which can be visited; here General de Gaulle landed on 14 June and went inland to Bayeux to make his first radio broadcast on French soil. Continue back to the Juno Centre and your vehicle.

The church in Graye-sur-Mer, a sniper's nest on D-Day, until the church tower was fired on from Shermans coming over the dunes and destroyed.

Sunset at La Fière.

Left: Iron Mike.

Below: US Airborne memorial window in the church at Ste-Mère-Eglise.

Above: The start of the 'Liberty Way' at Utah Beach.

Right: Pointe du Hoc.

Below: At Trévières a Sherman tank shell passed through the head of the local war memorial and remains a macabre reminder to this day.

Above: Omaha Beach after the winter tide showing Rommel's Asparagus.

Right: Nature has reclaimed the killing fields.

Below: Tracks across Omaha Beach.

Above: Sunset at Arromanches.

Left: Memorial at Pointe du Hoc.

Below: Normandy's missing.

Above: The Green Howards memorial at Crépon.

Left: Veteran Ken Cooke returns to Crépon, where he fought with the Green Howards.

Below: 1 Charlie at Juno Beach.

Above: Juno Beach.

Right: Battle damage is visible on many buildings in Normandy.

Below: Veterans remember.

Above: Battle of Britain Memorial Flight flypast on the 65th Anniversary.

Centre: Veterans from York gather at the Gondrée Café during the annual D-Day commemorations.

Right: The original Pegasus Bridge, scene of the first battle casualty of D-Day.

Above: Commando veterans remember.

Left: Not forgotten.

Below: Remembering.

Area Seven

GOLD BEACH WALK:
50TH DIVISION ON D-DAY

HISTORICAL SECTION

T he 50th (Northumbrian) Division that was destined to land on GOLD Beach on 6 June 1944 was unlike the other British and Canadian formations involved in the landings that day. A pre-war Territorial formation, it had fought in France in 1940 like the 3rd Division, but instead of remaining in the UK the division had gone to North Africa and taken part in the campaign there, and later in Tunisia. In 1943 it fought in Sicily, and by this time it was considered a 'veteran' division. As winter approached in Italy, the 8th Army Commander, Bernard Montgomery,was appointed to command the newly formed 21st Army Group and given orders to prepare for the invasion of France. He was given a free hand to select units in Italy to take back to the UK with him, and one of those was the 50th

The landings at Gold Beach on D-Day.

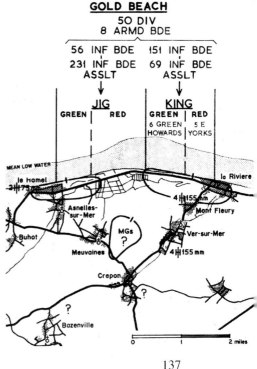

Major General Douglas Alexander Graham, 50th (Northumbrian) Division.

137

Division. They began arriving back home in November 1943, as the majority of men had been away fighting for two or more years. Widespread leave was granted and then the division knuckled down to invasion training for the next six months in preparation for D-Day.

The division at this time was commanded by Major General Douglas Alexander Graham. Graham was a regular officer whose service went back to before the First World War. He had been wounded in October 1914 while serving with the 1st Scottish Rifles and was rescued by one of his men, Private Henry May, who was later awarded a Victoria Cross for his bravery. He ended the war a decorated brigade major, and by the outbreak of the next war was commanding a battalion of his old regiment. By 1943 he was a divisional commander, and led

the 56th (London) Division in the landings at Salerno, before returning to the United Kingdom to take command of 50th Division for Normandy. He was the only British divisional commander on D-Day who had previously taken part in an amphibious operation, and no doubt this was one of the reasons his formation was chosen to lead the assault on GOLD Beach. On the eve of the operation he sent a message to all his men, part of which read,

much has been asked of you in the past and great have been your achievements, but this will be the greatest adventure of all. It will add yet another fine chapter to your already long and distinguished record – the grandest chapter of all.[1]

Major General D.A. Graham, commanding 50th Division on D-Day, talking to Montgomery.

The area the division was to assault was the widest British and Commonwealth beachhead on D-Day, and second only to

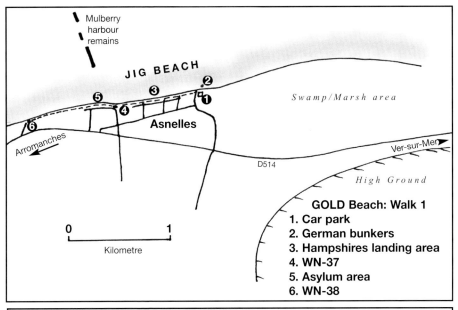

GOLD Beach: Walk 1
1. Car park
2. German bunkers
3. Hampshires landing area
4. WN-37
5. Asylum area
6. WN-38

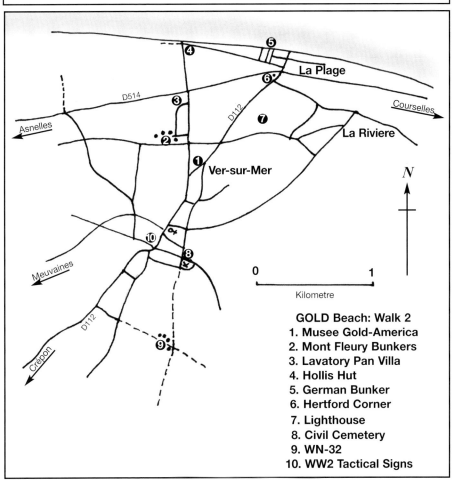

GOLD Beach: Walk 2
1. Musee Gold-America
2. Mont Fleury Bunkers
3. Lavatory Pan Villa
4. Hollis Hut
5. German Bunker
6. Hertford Corner
7. Lighthouse
8. Civil Cemetery
9. WN-32
10. WW2 Tactical Signs

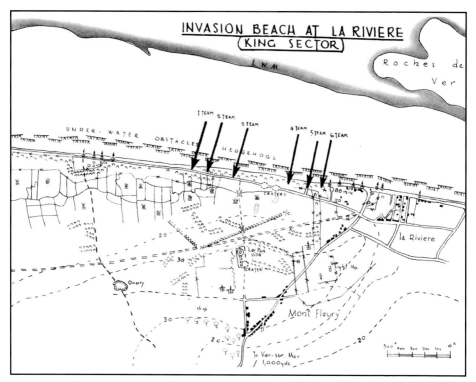

The defences on King Sector, GOLD Beach.

OMAHA Beach in terms of the distance between the flanks of the landing. It was subdivided into two smaller beaches: Jig Beach at Asnelles and King Beach at Ver-sur-Mer. Each of these was divided in two with sectors known as Green and Red. The division's overall objective was to land in the GOLD Beach area, secure a bridgehead then push inland to Bayeux and cut the Bayeux–Caen road at the village of St Léger. On its left flank it would link up with the 3rd Canadian Division landing on JUNO Beach, and on the right, some of its units would push on and take the coastal town of Arromanches, where it was planned to built an artificial harbour.

The western sector at Asnelles, was known as Jig Beach. The initial landing was planned here for 0725 on 6 June with the 1st Bn Hampshire Regiment coming in on Jig Green and 1st Bn Dorsetshire Regiment on Jig Red; both units being from Brigadier Sir Alexander Stanier's 231 Brigade of 50th Division. The final unit in the Brigade – 2nd Bn Devonshire Regiment – was in reserve. Supporting them, aside from the overall pre-D-

Day bombardment, were the 90th (City of London) and 147th (Essex Yeomanry) Field Regiments Royal Artillery. These units was equipped with Sextons, self-propelled 25-pounder field guns. As with many D-Day sectors, this unit was detailed to fire a 'run-in shoot' firing their guns from the Landing Craft as they made the final approach to the beach. In the first wave was engineer support from AVREs of 82nd Assault Regiment Royal Engineers and mine clearance would be done by B Squadron Westminster Dragoons, equipped with Sherman Flail tanks. Tank support was from the Sherman DD tanks of the Sherwood Rangers with B Squadron accompanying the 1st Hampshires and C the 1st Dorsets.

The Churchill AVREs in the first wave on Jig Green were from 82nd Assault Regiment Royal Engineers. They had three teams, numbered one to three, each of them comprising varying types of Churchill AVREs from the Assault Squadron and Flails from the Westminster Dragoons. No. 1 Team landed close to a large and untouched German bunker, inside of which was an

The defences on Jig Green Sector, GOLD Beach.

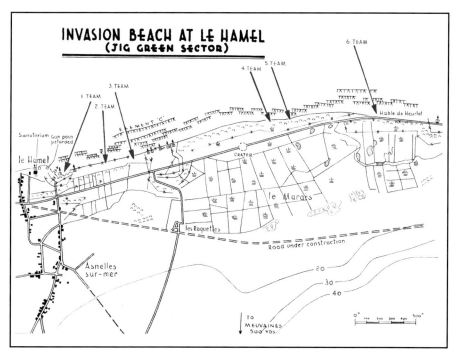

88mm firing down the beach. It immediately opened up on the Churchills on the beach, and among the casualties was Major Harold Elphinstone, a 34-year-old Cambridge graduate whose father was Canon Emeritus of Wakefield Cathedral. Commanding the Assault Squadron he was leading by example, and was fully exposed in the turret of his tank. He died in one of the early bursts of fire from the beach defences. Elsewhere, tanks fell to shell fire and also mines on the beaches but as the infantry landed, as the minefields were cleared, gradually the surviving vehicles of each team got off the beach.

'B' Squadron of the Westminster Dragoons approached Jig Green in six LCTs containing the teams of Sherman Flail tanks. The sea, being rough off the beach, caused one LCT to falter and then it came under fire putting it out of action and unable to discharge the tanks. The other five beached and the Sherman's touched down at half-tide, and, again because of the rough seas, not always in exactly the place planned. Dropping into nearly

Officers of the 1st Hampshires.

5ft of water, they found that despite the pre-D-Day bombardment they were confronted with intact belts of wire, minefields and beach obstacles, and more importantly all the defence bunkers seemed to be in operation and already opening fire. The beach was, however, flat here and they began their task of flailing through the minefields and into Le Hamel itself. With the battle for the beach still going on, much of the German support had yet to be neutralised and one Sherman Flail was knocked out by an anti-tank gun as soon as it got into the village. At this point it was just a matter of waiting until the defences had been overrun and then continuing with the next phase of the advance.

Behind the 82nd Assault Squadron the 1st Hampshires came in on their LCAs. As the AVREs had found, the beach defences were very much active and the battalion was about to pay the price for the failure of the pre-D-Day bombardment.

During the last half-mile enemy mortar and artillery fire, as well as small-arms fire, came down on the sea, but fortunately without

much effect. Some of the landing craft were lost through striking the underwater obstacles which had been dug deep into the beach. These were stout wooden posts and pieces of steel rail about four feet high, with mines or explosive charges fixed to the top. The beach was thickly sown with these . . . The landing craft beached some thirty yards from the edge of the sea and the men leapt into the water; some were up to their armpits in the sea, others up to their thighs, and at once they came under concentrated small-arms fire, so that many were killed. There were casualties, too, as the craft, lightened as the men jumped out, became water borne again and were swept inshore by the sea, overrunning some of the wading soldiers. It was apparent that the assault of the beach was going to be more difficult than had been expected.[2]

The battalion landed with two companies in the first wave, and two in the second. The initial companies were landed slightly off target and had come under the heavy fire described in the regimental history. The first men ashore were from A Company,

landing in the thick of very heavy fire slighty east of their intended position, so that they could not get forward to deal with the enemy at Le Hamel East, nor could they get up the beach to make their own gaps through the mines and wire, which were very thoroughly covered by enemy fire. The left platoon got inland and dealt effectively with two pillboxes at the edge of Les Roquettes, while the

The Asylum at Asnelles.

High tide at Asnelles showing the beach defences and why there was no direct landing here.

other two tried to work their way towards Le Hamel, but they ran into such violent machine-gun and mortar fire from the village that they were pinned down.[3]

C Company was on the right, closest to the large German 88mm bunker with its field of fire right down the beach. They lost all their officers in the first few minutes, along with many of the men, 'C Company . . . were caught on the beach . . . and tried in vain to get up the beach to get into Le Hamel'.[4] By this time the battalion's commander, Lieutenant Colonel Nelson Smith, had been wounded for the third time. This final wound was so serious that he had to be evacuated. Normally, the Second in Command would have taken over, but as Major A.C.W. Martin DSO was still at sea, the commander of C Company, Major Warren, took over. It was a role he would resume for the rest of D-Day as Martin was killed by a sniper as soon as he disembarked from a landing craft later that morning. Major Warren reorganised the survivors and by lunchtime they were fighting their way along the lateral road just off the beach into Le Hamel. One of the key defence points was the so-called 'Asylum' on the front at Le Hamel, a hospital building which was proving a tough position to crack.

A knocked out Churchill AVRE on GOLD Beach.

'B' Company then advanced grimly on Le Hamel, but they were held up about fifty yards from the hospital by a torrent of fire. By good fortune an AVRE came down the road from Asnelles at this critical moment. This drove close to the hospital and fired a petard bomb which exploded with its typical violence. The enemy machine-gun fire was only checked for a second or so, however, and it was not until five rounds had been fired by the AVRE's petard that 'B' Company was able to close with the hospital and silence this very obstinate and costly enemy position.[5]

As the fight for the Asylum was reaching its climax, the 88mm pillbox was silenced when 86th Field Regiment fired shells through the front aperture and another AVRE fired a Petard charge into the rear of the bunker, causing much damage and forcing the crew to surrender. By this time tank support had arrived from the Sherwood Rangers. The sea had been too rough to launch the DD tanks and the Shermans arrived late, but with the combination of small parties of infantry infiltrating inland, AVREs finally taking out the defences and the DDs giving tank support, the position at Jig Green was won and the advance inland could begin. But it had been costly. The battalion had lost its commander along with five other officers dead, and including the Colonel, eleven wound. Casualties in the ranks amounted to six sergeants, twelve corporals and 148 privates. These were the greatest casualties suffered to any single unit on any British and Commonwealth beach on D-Day.

On Jig Red the 1st Dorsets were destined to land in very different terrain to Jig Green. Here, at a location known as Les Roquettes, instead of a close lateral road and seaside villas, there were open fields and boggy ground beyond the beach, there was a track close to the coast but the main road was nearly a thousand yards away and aerial photographs showed it to be still under construction. Beyond the road was rising ground, with known gun positions that could potentially fire down onto the beach. On the beach itself were the usual Atlantic Wall defences and a variety of bunkers. On the right flank the defences relied heavily on minefields and barbed wire and due to the 'wild' nature of the ground the Germans had never built anything here, probably never expecting a landing at this point. In the first wave Nos 4, 5 and 6 Teams of 82nd Assault Squadron were the first to beach with Churchill AVREs and Flail tanks from the Westminster Dragoons. The initial response was not as intense as on Jig Green and the Flails quickly cleared the lanes to the road. Here bomb craters were filled by AVREs dropping fascines into them, but one tank was knocked out in the process. Close to No. 4, No. 5 Team lost two tanks on the beach due to the conditions and one Churchill equipped with a Bobin road-mat-laying fixture created a good route off the beach and

German bunker that protected the beach where 1st Dorsets landed.

through the boggy ground. A similar mat was laid on the left by No. 6 Team, and with the mine clearance done, the Sherman Flails engaged German machine guns beyond the beach.

Between 0725 and 0730 the first troops from 'A' and 'B' Companies of the 1st Dorsets touched down on Jig Red. For this battalion it was the third time in eleven months they had made an amphibious landing under the eyes of the enemy.

> By virtue of consideration of the tide, the Hampshires and ourselves claimed to be the first British troops to land on Normandy . . . The Battalion was actually put ashore slightly to the east of the appointed place . . . On the left 'B' Company had to swing right for some distance before reaching Les Roquettes, and on their way they suffered considerably from shell and mortar fire, machine-gun fire, and from mines. But the Company was ably led by Major Chilton across the minefields – he saw the need for advancing rapidly inland and away from the beaches . . . The enemy opposition so far had been mainly from shelling and mortaring, with some machine-gun fire and mines. Unfortunately the bombardment, naval and air, had done less damage than had been hoped for.[6]

Casualties getting off the beach and into the marshland had been heavy. In both assault companies the Company Sergeant Majors had been wounded and one of the most highly decorated men in the battalion, Sergeant W.J. Evans MM and

A view across the beach where 1st Dorsets landed on D-Day.

Bar, had been killed. But despite this, things were going better for the Dorsets than their neighbours on Jig Green, where the battle was still audibly in full swing.

On the left flank landings were taking place on King Beach. Here units from 69 Brigade were detailed to land with the 5th Bn East Yorkshire Regiment on the left at La Rivière and 6th Bn Green Howards on the right in front of Ver-sur-Mer, with 7th Green Howards in the follow-up wave. The latter's task was to push through Ver-sur-Mer and neutralise a German gun battery, WN-32, beyond. All units were then to continue to Crépon and push on beyond towards the Bayeux–Caen road. On this sector the final pre-H Hour bombardment consisted of not just aerial bombing but a huge amount of naval gunfire from the flotillas offshore, perhaps more intensive on one strip of defences than almost any other British beach on D-Day. Fire from nineteen Royal Navy ships, including 6in guns from HMS *Belfast*, dropped shells onto the bunkers and trenches and Brigadier F.Y.C. Knox, commanding 69 Brigade, watched from HMS *Kingsmill* as,

> the landmarks on the coast soon became obliterated by vast clouds of dust and smoke rising from the coastal belt. The terrific pounding from cruisers, destroyers and small supporting craft as well as from aircraft rose to a crescendo immediately before H Hour, and very little enemy battery fire was directed at the larger ships now lying off shore.[7]

The 5th East Yorks, commanded by Lieutenant Colonel G.W. White, landed at 0725 and the LCAs put them down in the correct sector of the beach. On their left they immediately came under heavy fire and 'D' Company got pinned down by machine-gun fire and 88mm guns in the bunkers. Here the pre-H Hour bombardment had missed a small strip of defences which were now punishing the East Yorks closing up on the sea wall at La Rivière. The 88s also accounted for the AVREs from the Assault Regiment and several exploded on the beach, causing more casualties to the East Yorks infantry moving past them, among them the company commander of D Company, his second in command along with three of his platoon commanders. This meant that the men on the beach were now virtually leaderless and sought cover against the sea wall they were assaulting. Coming behind them was C Company which was then picked off in the water by the same German defences. One platoon sped forward, supported by a Sherman DD tank and a surviving AVRE, and overran the defences, forcing the remaining garrison to surrender; forty-five Germans were taken prisoner here, but the battle on this part of the beach had cost six officers and eighty-five men.

On the right A Company had hit the beach, meeting only spasmodic opposition. Pushing through the defences cleared by the Assault Engineers, they pressed on to their objective, the German gun battery on the high ground above King Beach, the Mont Fleury Battery. This was a system of concrete bunkers protecting German field guns. The position was taken at the point of the bayonet, as the 6th Green Howards passed through it, and 5th East Yorks took thirty prisoners here, at the loss of only eight men. As the battery was finally overrun the German commander took his own life in front of his captors. They then sent one platoon to assault La Rivière from the rear, which helped the units pinned down on the beach trying to get through the defences.

Meanwhile, Lieutenant Colonel Robin Hastings's 6th Green Howards had landed several hundred yards west of where they should have touched down on the beach.

We swung about broadside on to the shore, missing by a few feet the shells on poles on either side of us . . . mortar shells kept landing quite near us on either side. We came to rest . . . quite a long way from the beach . . . I ordered the ramp to do be lowered. Nothing happened at all; the mechanism was broken. This was the worst place to delay . . . A huge-ex Guardsman . . . put his shoulder to it. It opened. . . . The beach looked a long way off; the water looked deep. I walked reluctantly to the edge of the ramp, sat down and dangled my feet like a Brighton paddler over the edge – not a very dashing or inspiring performance. The water was only

Lieutenant Colonel Robin Hastings.

up to my knees. Without the slightest difficulty we waded forward and scrambled up the beach.[8]

A strongpoint on the beach was overcome by Hasting's men, and the battalion had suffered a few casualties as they moved up from the shore; one of Hasting's company commanders had walked straight into the first shell he had encountered in action and been killed outright. Ahead of them was an access road which the battalion moved up, with the familiar site of Lavatory Pan Villa ahead of them on the slopes. Sherman Flail tanks moved up and cleared the minefields, and elements of the unit then moved through the Mont Fleury Battery. One of those who assisted in the fight here was Company Sergeant Major Stan Hollis. Robin Hastings recalled what happened,

> *As they were going uphill, Major Lofthouse, the company commander, and CSM* [Company Sergeant Major] *Hollis noticed a pillbox which had been bypassed and walked over to it. At twenty yards range fire was opened on the CSM who immediately charged the pillbox and killed the inmates – one of the outstanding actions on D Day which earned him the VC.*[9]

Indeed, Stan Hollis became the only man to be awarded a Victoria Cross on D-Day. Born in Loftus, Yorkshire, he had worked in a fish and chip shop, had gone to sea as a young man until Blackwater fever ended his naval career and on the outbreak of war was a lorry driver in Middlesborough. He was a pre-war Territorial in the Green Howards and had fought with them at Dunkirk, in North Africa and Sicily before Normandy, having been wounded at Primosole Bridge in July 1943. His Victoria Cross was in fact awarded for a series of brave acts on 6 June 1944.

> *In Normandy on 6th June, 1944, during the assault on the beaches and the Mont Fleury Battery, CSM Hollis's Company Commander noticed that two of the pillboxes had been by-passed, and went with CSM Hollis to see that they were clear. When they were twenty yards from the pillbox, a machine gun opened fire from the slit and CSM Hollis instantly rushed straight at the pillbox, firing his Sten gun. He jumped on top of the pillbox, re-charged his magazine, threw a grenade in through the door and fired his Sten gun into it, killing two Germans and making the remainder prisoner. He then cleared several Germans from a neighbouring trench. By his action, he undoubtedly saved his Company from being fired on heavily from*

the rear and enabled them to open the main beach exit. Later the same day, in the village of Crépon, the Company encountered a field gun and crew armed with Spandaus at 100 yards range. CSM Hollis was put in command of a party to cover an attack-on the gun, but the movement was held up. Seeing this, CSM Hollis pushed right forward to engage the gun with a PIAT from a house at fifty yards range. He was observed by a sniper who fired and grazed his right cheek, and at the same moment the gun swung round and fired at point-blank range into the house. To avoid the fallen masonry CSM Hollis moved his party to an alternative position. Two of the enemy gun crew had by this time been killed, and the gun was destroyed shortly afterwards. He later found that two of his men had stayed behind in the house and immediately volunteered to get them out. In full view of the enemy who were continually firing at him, he went forward alone using a Bren gun to distract their attention from the other men. Under cover of his diversion, the two men were able to get back. Wherever fighting was heaviest, CSM Hollis appeared and in the course of a magnificent day's work, he displayed the utmost gallantry and on two separate occasions his courage and initiative prevented the enemy from holding up the advance at critical stages. It was largely through his heroism and resource that the Company's objectives were gained and casualties were not heavier, and by his own bravery he saved the lives of many of his men.[10]

Mont Fleury bunker, 1944.

Aerial view of the Mont Fleury defences.

Follow-up waves coming ashore from Jig Beach.

Hollis fought throughout the Normandy campaign, was later wounded in Holland in September 1944 and commissioned as an officer before the end of the war. Back in Yorkshire he ran a pub and died in 1972.

From Mont Fleury the advance continued, but it did not quite go as planned and the hope of advancing on the Bayeux–Caen road was soon dashed. Hastings noted,

> from now on it became a battle like any other. C Company and one squadron of tanks took our next objective, which turned out to be a German HQ containing a Colonel. . . . The first village, Crépon, contained some determined Germans with a 75mm gun, who took a good deal of removing. It was clear that each farm and village would have to be fought for.[11]

While Hastings and his men were pushing through Crépon, across to their left their sister battalion, 7th Green Howards, was moving into Ver-sur-Mer en route to the gun battery WN-32. Commanded by Lieutenant Colonel P.H. Richardson, they had landed ¾ of an hour after H Hour and after some problems had made their way through the narrow streets of the village, encountering only limited opposition. Beyond the houses they had formed up north of WN-32 and waited until tank support from 141st Royal Armoured Corps arrived. This unit was part of 79th Armoured Division and was equipped with Churchill Crocodile tanks. A troop of them arrived and before an infantry assault, Richardson directed them to open fire on the casements of the bunkers with their 75mms. The Germans responded with machine-gun fire, so the troop let rip with some jets of flame, way off mark and out of range. This resulted in the raising of a white flag and the capture of the position with no casualties. Conflicting reports exit, but it appears the pre-H Hour bombardment had put the gun battery out of action. Some fifty prisoners were taken here, and 5th East Yorks arrived shortly afterwards. The advance then continued into Crépon, just as the 6th Green Howards were clearing it.

With Crépon cleared, the 5th East Yorks took the lead and made an assault on the high ground near Villers-le-Sec. Here,

there was some opposition, including self-propelled guns, and two of the tanks supporting the leading battalion were knocked out and 'brewed up' in the valley before these guns were dealt with. The enemy was found to be dug in in the cornfields on the reverse slope of the ground south of Villers, and the battalion moved in extended order through the cornfields, beating out the Germans. Enemy mortar fire was heavy, and Lieutenant Colonel White was seriously wounded by a mortar bomb early in the action. The 5th East Yorkshire Regiment smashed this enemy position and went on

Knocked out Sherman Flail inland from GOLD Beach.

The cost of GOLD Beach; men from the Green Howards are laid to rest in a battlefield cemetery a few days after 6 June.

without pause towards St Gabriel. Files of captive Germans began to move down the dusty roads towards the beaches.[12]

The 7th Green Howards had meanwhile taken the road bridge across the River Seulles north of Creuilly and together with 4/7th Dragoon Guards Shermans had taken the village. By 1800 on D-Day both they and 5th East Yorks were holding a line from St Gabriel to south of Creuilly. A final attack went in at 2130 when all three battalions in 69 Brigade, supported by Sextons from 86th Field Regiment and support fire from 2nd Cheshires, cleared the hamlet of Brecy and across to Columbs. Here their D-Day came to an end having advanced 7 miles inland, but Hastings' prediction about it being a battle for each individual farm and village was already proving true.

As GOLD Beach covers a large area, this sector has been divided into two walks which could be completed over the course of a day or joined together to make one long, full-day walk.

Walk 7a: Jig Beach

STARTING POINT: Seafront car park, Rue Royal Hampshire, Asnelles

GPS: 49°20′35.4″N, 0°34′21.2″W

DURATION: 3.85km/2.4 miles

Park your vehicle in the car park on the seafront close to this section of Jig Beach; it is located on the far eastern side of the built-up area that overlooks the beach. Walk down onto the beach. This is the area where the 1st Dorsets landed on D-Day. The unusual hexagonal shaped gun position they encountered is now lying in the sand and the bunker here has collapsed and is gradually being reclaimed by the sea. The dominance of the high ground beyond is visible from here and the fields of fire up and down the beach clearly seen.

From here **proceed along** the beach; at high tide you can take a small path that runs along the edge of the houses. Follow this to the area of the dunes further up the beach on the left. **Stop.** This area overlooks where the 1st Hampshires landed and suffered such heavy casualties from the 88mm bunker ahead of you and the machine-gun positions in the dunes. This small stretch of beach became one of the deadliest strips of sand on any British D-Day landing ground.

Continue along the beach and then **go up the ramp** to the bunker. **Stop.** The bunker here – WN-37 – was well sited with a

The 50mm bunker that covered the beach where 1st Dorsets landed now being reclaimed by the sea.

The German 88mm bunker overlooking Gold Beach where the 1st Hampshires landed.

good field of fire straight down the beach and overlapped with the other bunkers' guns at the far end of the beach where you started. There are memorials on the beach, including one that assigns the final victory over the position but makes no mention of the role of the Assault Engineers' AVRE in attacking the bunker from the rear. The number of near misses on the bunker are evident as the concrete is pockmarked from shrapnel. There are also two Tobruk pits visible here; one back towards the dunes and another to the rear of the bunker.

Now **walk along** the seafront, passing on the left some of the buildings that were here on D-Day, all showing signs of battle damage. The Asylum was later demolished and never rebuilt, but the layout here is the same as in 1944 and it can be seen why no landing was made directly in front of this section – Item Beach – of the seafront. At the end of this boulevard are the bunkers of WN-38. The main casemate held a 50mm gun which could only fire away from Jig Beach rather than onto it, but behind there are Tobruk pits which housed mortars that could fire on both beaches. These bunkers, and others down the road beyond the seafront position, are on private land but can be viewed from the boundary fence.

Return along the seafront back to the main bunker and then walk across the car park to Rue du Debarquement and then take the **first left**, Rue The Dorset Regiment, and follow it as it becomes Rue Royal Hampshire Regiment and continue back to the car park and your vehicle.

Walk 7b: King Beach

STARTING POINT: Car park, Place de l'Amiral Byrd, Ver-sur-Mer

GPS: 49°20'11.8"N, 0°31'33.8"W

DURATION: 8.55km/5.3 miles

Park your vehicle outside the Musée America-GOLD Beach in the centre of Ver-sur-Mer. The name of this museum causes some confusion as there is no connection with the American landings on D-Day and actually relates to the first USA–France transatlantic flight which touched down here in 1927. The museum in fact has extensive displays relating to the landings on Jig and King Beaches, with many objects and photographs donated by veterans. It is open every day in July and August, and every day except Tuesday in May, June, September and October.

From the museum **go across** to Avenue Paul Poret and **turn right**. Take the **first left** onto Rue des Roquettes. Follow this until bunkers are visible to your right; here **go right** and follow a track to the bunkers. These are the remaining bunkers of the Mont Fleury Battery. They show the varied state of completion of the bunker complex by D-Day, with some casemates not finished. Direct hits from the naval gunfire are also visible. This site was captured by the 5th East Yorks, and was where CSM Hollis carried out the first of his brave actions which resulted in the award of the Victoria Cross. One of the bunkers is currently (2011) being turned into a house, the first time this has happened in

One of the completed bunkers at Mont Fleury.

Many bunkers like this at Mont Fleury were not finished by D-Day.

Normandy. Another large bunker is visible in Rue Hector Berlioz. In this street take the **first left** into Rue Claude Debussy. This new estate was not here in 1944 and the only building was the distinctive 'Lavatory Pan Villa', which is seen at the end of the street where it joins the main road. Here go onto Avenue Franklin Roosevelt and **turn left**. Cross over the D514 and follow a minor road downhill towards the beach. At the crossroads of tracks **stop**.

The small building on the right-hand corner of this junction is the old railway halt in what was known as Le Paistry Vert. This structure was here on D-Day right in the middle of the minefields and on the pre-D-Day aerial photographs it looked like it was a bunker. When CSM Stan Hollis landed here he fired at it with a Lewis gun from his landing craft and was surprised to discover later that it was 'only a Bloody tram stop'. Now known as the 'Hollis Hut', it was restored by the Green Howards Association and there is an information panel on the walls of it.

Walk down onto the beach to see the area where the 6th and 7th Green Howards landed, and beyond where 5th East Yorks came ashore. You can either walk along the beach or return to the Hollis Hut and **go left** onto Voie du Debarquement. From either route, join Rue du Corps du Garde and follow to the seafront and the large bunker that was part of WN-33. This contained an 88mm and was capable of firing in both directions. **Continue** along the seafront to a small square; a lifeguard station ahead on the sea wall is in fact another part of WN-33, a hexagonal bunker that housed a 50mm anti-tank gun on D-Day.

From the square **go south** on Avenue Colonel Harper to the D514. This is the area is known as 'Hertford Corner' as it has two memorials to Hertfordshire-related units. The Bedfordshire and Hertfordshire Regiment were beach masters here and guarded this section of GOLD Beach for the rest of the Normandy campaign. Across the road is a Sexton self-propelled gun painted in the colours of the 86th Field Regiment Royal Artillery, formed from the Hertfordshire Yeomanry. Directly opposite is a third memorial to all the Royal Artillery units of the 50th (Northumbrian) Division who served in Normandy.

From the rear of the Sexton memorial take Avenue 6 Juin and then **first left** into Rue de la Rivière. Further up take the **second right** onto Chemin de Voie and follow this uphill to the first

The Sexton that forms the memorial to 86th Field Regiment Royal Artillery.

crossroads, here **going left** and then **first right** up a track to where it joins a minor road, Rue des Stins. **Turn right** and follow this along the high ground into Ver-sur-Mer. **Turn left** in the village onto Chemin de la Venelle aux Lievres. Continue past the civil cemetery on your left and join a track going south out of the village. Follow the battle-damaged wall on your right until it ends and then **stop**.

This is where the 7th Green Howards formed up with the Churchill Crocodile troop from 141st Royal Armoured Corps as they began their assault on WN-32. The bunkers are visible ahead across the fields where a small tree-lined area is seen.

Thankfully, this proved a bloodless battle, but the potential for killing in these open fields, if the garrison at WN-32 had been determined, are evident. **Continue** along the track to the bunkers.

The WN-32 site is one of the forgotten bunker positions in Normandy. The four casemates held 150mm guns facing towards the join between GOLD Beach and JUNO Beach,

The bunkers at WN-32.

161

The bunkers at WN-32 are today among the most intact gun positions in Normandy.

but could be taken out of their bunkers to fire in any direction. They were linked by telephone and radio to a number of observation posts and the position was ringed with wire and mines. The size of its garrison was unknown before D-Day and why the battery was out of action when the Green Howards took it is still not clear, but it could have been a bloody fight if the Germans had not given in after the Crocodiles demonstrated their flame ability. The bunkers are in very good condition, but are on private property and this should be respected. An information panel showing an aerial view of the site is along the edge of the three enclosed bunkers.

Go past the bunkers, keeping them on your right, and at the next crossroads **turn right** onto Rue Marefontaine. Follow this back into the village, and where it meets the D112 there is a large building on your left. **Stop**. This farm complex was here in 1944 and its walls once clearly painted with road signs post-D-Day. The remains of those signs are still visible, but are quite faded. They directed traffic to the main assembly areas and dumps around Crépon and there are 50th Division Tactical Signs also visible on the walls.

Continue through the village on Rue de la Liberation towards the church and follow the D112 back to the northern part of Ver-sur-Mer and the car park in front of the Musée America-GOLD Beach.

ARROMANCHES WALK: D-DAY LIBERATION AND THE MULBERRY HARBOUR

HISTORICAL SECTION

Arromanches had been selected as a site for one of two artificial harbours to be built by the Allies in the early days of the Normandy landings. It was realised that any invasion could only succeed with the availability of port facilities so that supplies, equipment, ammunition along with more men and vehicles could be brought in. None of the beaches where the landings would take place had such facilities, and those at Arromanches itself, along with Courseulles, Ouistreham and Port-en-Bessin, were too small. Cherbourg was the nearest major port to the west and Le Havre to the east, but it would potentially be many weeks or months before these would be reached and there was no guarantee they would be captured intact. The solution was to take port facilities in

German guards overlooking the seafront at Arromanches, 1943.

Arromanches Walk

1. Arromanches Museum
2. 360 Cinema
3. Viewpoint
4. Observation bunker
5. Longues Battery

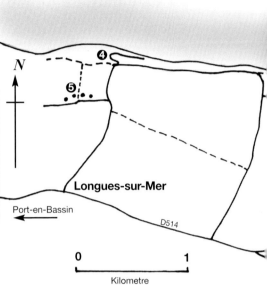

AA gun at the German gun
battery on the high ground
above Arromanches.

following the initial landings, build a port *in-situ* and supply the armies ashore from there.

The idea for an artificial harbour can be largely traced back to Winston Churchill who had first muted the proposal in the First World War, and from May 1942 the plan began to formulate in memorandums to the Combined Commanders planning the return to the European mainland. Churchill stressed that some design of pier would be needed on any landing area, which must be able to withstand bad weather and float up and down with the tide. He concluded to the planners, 'Don't argue the matter. The difficulties will argue for themselves.'[1] It was another year before the idea was discussed again and once it was accepted, as little as eight months remained until the actual landings would take place.

The proposed harbour facilities would be made up of a number of features. On all the landing beaches redundant ships known as 'Corncobs' would be brought over, lined up and sunk forming a breakwater where light shipping could then unload

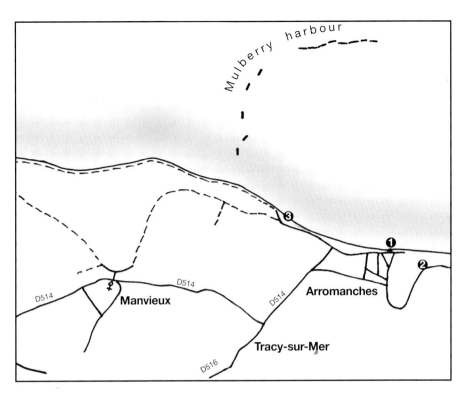

A section of the Mulberry harbour being constructed in London's docks.

supplies via smaller craft and DUKWs onto the beach. These were the 'Gooseberries' and it was planned to have all fine running by D+5. Two of the Gooseberries – at GOLD and OMAHA beaches – would then be expanded into a complete artificial harbour, each to be on a similar scale to Dover harbour in the UK. Extra breakwaters would be made by bringing in concrete caissons known as 'Phoenix' sections. These were huge

hollow concrete vessels which could be floated over, taps turned on inside allowing the sea-water in and then secured to the seabed with rubble; when it was decided rubble would be needed one officer came up with the idea of using rubble

A Phoenix section.

from Blitzed London – the concept being that the enemy may have destroyed buildings in our capital city but that rubble would then be used against them in the invasion of Europe.

Each harbour would have two entrances and within have berthing facilities for deep-water ships, besides berths for everything from landing craft to tugs. Inside the safety of the

Pontoon section of the Mulberry harbour.

Corncobs and Phoenixes small craft could then move around in all weathers transporting material from ship to shore. To assist in rapid unloading piers – 'Whales' – would be constructed with the floating roadways suggested by Churchill. Although they would be secured to the seabed, the engineering was developed in time to make them able to move up and down with the swell. Having these roadways meant that large numbers of tanks and vehicles could be quickly unloaded and sent inland. Outside the port for ships of especially large size, 'Bombardons' – large floating steel structures – would be placed allowing stores to be unloaded and brought into the harbour or onto the beach. Collectively, all these elements made up 'Mulberry', the name given to the harbour and there would be a Mulberry A at OMAHA Beach and Mulberry B at Arromanches, west of GOLD.

The D-Day plan was that all these elements would be in the Channel on the day of the landings and once the areas where the Mulberry harbours were going to be built were secure, the block ships would move in, the Phoenix sections sunk and the piers and other facilities put in place. Thus, on 6 June the vessels bringing everything that was needed patiently waited for events on the land to unfold. And while the landings went well that morning, before anything could be constructed on the British sector first Arromanches had to be taken. This was tasked to the men of the 1st Bn Hampshire Regiment. This unit had landed in the first wave on GOLD Beach and taken heavy casualties getting off the beach, including their commanding officer. Major Warren, one of the company commanders, had taken over and held an Orders Group with his remaining officers at a captured radar station east of Arromanches. His plan was simple, to hit the town from the rear while the Germans within were under fire. Warren called in naval gunfire from a destroyer, plus the self-propelled 25-pounders from 147th Field Regiment. D Company would make the assault, and B and C were to lay down covering fire from the high ground above the town. The battle was highly successful. D Company cleared the town against only slight resistance and twenty prisoners were taken at no loss to the Hampshires. By 2100 Arromanches was liberated; for the Hampshires D-Day had gone from tragedy to success.

With the town now in Allied hands it was hoped that work

on the Mulberry could begin. However, just to the west of Arromanches was a substantial German gun battery located close to the village of Longues-sur-Mer. This had survived the pre-D-Day bombardment and was still potentially active on D-Day. It, therefore, had to be neutralised before the construction of the artificial harbour could begin, otherwise it would be in a position to fire on it. This battery site consisted of four 152mm naval guns in casemates made from 600m3 of concrete to protect them from bombardments. None of the tons of bombs or Allied naval shells had affected the capability of the battery and on D-Day it had fired on both OMAHA and GOLD beaches. No British units were in reach of it by the close of D-Day, but on 7 June the 2nd Bn Devonshire Regiment, commanded by Lieutenant Colonel C.A.R. Neville, was called up to assault the position. They had landed on GOLD the day before and taken the village of Ryes, where they had dug in for the night. On the 7th they attacked Longues encountering no opposition from the garrison, capturing all the casemates and a large number of prisoners without any loss. They remained here until the next day when the course of battle took them to Port-en-Bessin.

Work finally began on Mulberry B late on D-Day as the Gooseberries were brought in. Next day explosives put in the sea and sunk on an even keel, Phoenix sections were put in place, rubble unloaded and work on the piers and Bombardons began. This work was completed by the Port Construction Companies of the Royal Engineers, who were able to open the first pier in the east (known as the 'LST Pier') by 14 June. Just two days later the breakwaters were half complete, two piers were now in operation but the roadways were not running as envisaged as bad weather had sunk five tows of Whale roadways and two Phoenix sections. On the following day the weather got progressively worse, building up to a major storm in the early hours of 19 June.

A raging gale on a lee shore is a seaman's nightmare. Ships and craft crowded into the shelter of the Gooseberry breakwaters and the Mulberry harbours but there was not enough room for them all. As huge waves broke in the shallow water off the land, ground tackle of heavier landing craft did not always hold and numbers were driven ashore; there, pounded by the surf, many broke their backs or were badly damaged. Rhino ferries were swept high up the beaches, reducing to matchwood small craft in their path. The shuttle service

Aerial view of the Mulberry harbour.

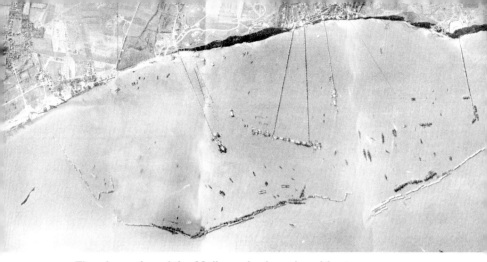

The sheer size of the Mulberry harbour is evident.

from England was suspended but craft which had already left for France when the storm arose arrived in the assault area to add to the congestion and increase the number that met with disaster. . . . When at last, on June the 22nd, the storm abated the whole invasion coast was strewn with wreckage. About eight hundred craft of all types were stranded, most of them heavily damaged and many entirely destroyed; on some beaches wrecked craft were piled on one another in dreadful confusion.[2]

Roadway section allowing tanks and vehicles to drive onto the shore.

One of the main piers.

Docking facilities for hospital ships were also an important part of the harbour.

After the storm the beach was strewn with debris.

At Arromanches the harbour had been damaged but generally had withstood the storm well; its shelter had saved many vital ships within. But at OMAHA Beach the weather had been at its worse and the placing of the breakwaters different than at Arromanches. Here Mulberry A was completely destroyed, so much so that all that could be done with the wreckage was to use it to repair the damage to Mulberry B at Arromanches. From a wider point of view, the storm had not only delayed the arrival of supplies, but also men at a vital point in operations. Up to 18 June on the British sector, for example, the daily average of men arriving had exceeded 15,700 men per day. Between 19 and 23 June this dropped to under 4,000, with the tonnage in stores dropping from 10,666 to 4,286 per day.

Mulberry B was gradually repaired and remained in British use until the autumn of 1944. As the Allied advance took the British Liberation Army out of the Normandy bridgehead into France, then Belgium and finally Holland, the line of supply still stretched all the way from Mulberry to wherever the British were fighting, which by the late summer was well over a

Allied personnel remained in the harbour until the end of the war. Here in 1945 supplies were still being brought ashore by landing craft.

hundred miles away. Cherbourg had been taken and found so damaged by the Germans it was unusable; the same was true at Le Havre. It was not until Antwerp was finally taken and re-opened as a port that the use of Mulberry gradually reduced, but it never properly closed and the amazing artificial port remained in use until VE Day.

Walk 8: At Arromanches

STARTING POINT: Car park, Arromanches Museum

GPS: 49°20′24.7″N, 0°37′16.0″W

DURATION: 14.1km/8.77 miles

This walks gives the walker a good idea of the size and scope of the Mulberry harbour, and can be extended to take a pleasant and picturesque coastal walk over to the Longues Battery, one of the best preserved German gun batteries in Normandy where the guns are still in place.

Start in the car park of the Arromanches museum. This museum (www.musee-arromanches.fr) tells the story of the Mulberry harbour and has a unique model of it, made in the

173

On the first anniversary of D-Day a ceremony was held on the beach at Arromanches.

A section of the original roadway is now on display in Arromanches as a memorial to the Mulberry harbour.

Sections of the harbour became tourist attractions as early as 1946.

1950s by a British railway modelling company. It is an excellent way to start this walk. From the museum walk into Rue du Six Juin 1944 and **go left**, going **straight across** at the next junction and follow the route uphill. For now ignore the memorials you see as these will be visited later in the walk. Just past a Sherman tank follow the track ahead up onto the cliff tops above the town. Here there are superb views over where the Mulberry harbour was located and the remaining sections of it are clearly visible. There is also a viewing platform here, and a memorial to the Royal Engineers, who did such important work in the building and maintenance of the harbour. Close by is the Arromanches 360 Cinema (www.arromanches360.com); this is unique in Normandy and is a 360-degree film about the Battle of Normandy and well worth a visit.

Sections of the harbour remain on the beach today.

At low tide it is possible to walk out to some of the Phoenix sections close to Asnelles.

From the cinema follow the path downhill and then **right** into Rue Charles Laurent and to the car park where the Sherman tank is located. This M4 Sherman was given to the town as a permanent memorial to the fighting here in 1944. Retrace your route back down towards the town but just before the museum **turn right** and immediately **stop**. There is a roadway section of the Mulberry harbour on display here and a memorial to Major Alan Beckitt, the 'architect of Mulberry harbour'. From here **continue**; you can go down onto the beach if it is low tide and walk below the sea wall, or walk along the sea wall keeping the town on your left. Either way, you will get a good view of the remains of the harbour and if on the beach be able to walk up to some of the sections here. If on the beach, **continue** to the next ramp, and on the sea wall continue past the next ramp and follow the path on the sea wall to the jetty. Here **go left** and walk

The fire-control bunker at the Longues Battery.

to a crossroads; here **go right** onto Rue des Freres Victor.

Stay on this route uphill. Further up there is a German bunker on the right, and again there are good views of the Mulberry remains from this route. The road ends a coastal path then appears on the **right**. Follow this path for the next few miles as it weaves its way along the cliff tops, taking care not to walk too close to the edge. Eventually, this path meets a minor road. **Take** this road and follow it running parallel to the cliffs; eventually it reaches the site of the Longues Battery.

Following this route you start at the Observation Bunker that was the eyes of the battery. If you have seen *The Longest Day* it will be familiar as the site was used as a location in that production. The bunker can be fully explored and then a path followed to the four gun casemates that retain their original firepower. There is also a small visitors' centre/shop here with toilets. From the car park at the shop follow the D104 towards Longues but before reaching the village take the **first left** down a minor unmarked road. Follow this across the fields to a crossroads of tracks and **go left** back towards the cliffs, then take the **second right**. Go down this minor road to the village of Manvieux and **go left** onto Rue de l'Eglise. Stay on this until it becomes Rue La Perruque and follow it back towards the cliffs. At a fork in the track **go right** and stay on this back down into Arromanches. In the town follow the main road back into the centre and the car park at Arromanches museum.

Unique in Normandy, the main casemates still have their original armament.

Area Nine

OMAHA BEACH WALK: 'BLOODY OMAHA'

HISTORICAL SECTION

**Major General
Leonard T. Gerow
commanded US V Corps.**

O MAHA Beach has arguably become the most iconic of the D-Day landing areas. From its early portrayal in films like *The Longest Day* to a point where it achieved almost legendary status in *Saving Private Ryan* the fighting here has attracted much interest, and, to a degree, much controversy. OMAHA

The 29th Division Landings on OMAHA Beach.
National Archives

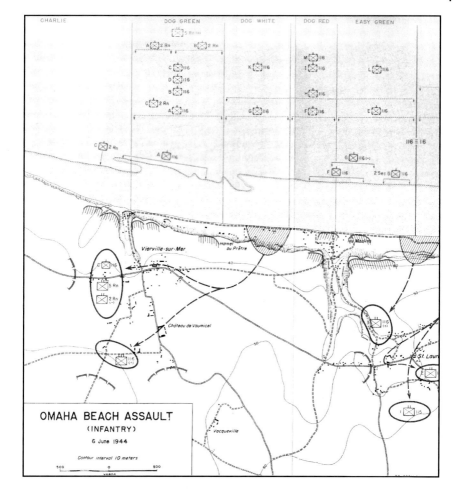

OMAHA BEACH ASSAULT
(INFANTRY)
6 June 1944

Contour interval 10 meters

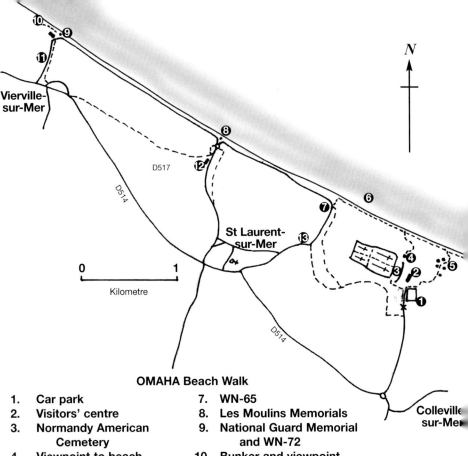

OMAHA Beach Walk

1.	Car park	7.	WN-65
2.	Visitors' centre	8.	Les Moulins Memorials
3.	Normandy American Cemetery	9.	National Guard Memorial and WN-72
4.	Viewpoint to beach	10.	Bunker and viewpoint
5.	WN-62	11.	Mulberry roadway section
6.	Site of beach defences (2011)	12.	Omaha Beach Museum
		13.	Site of airfield

Beach was where D-Day went seriously wrong, where casualties were at their highest – more men died on OMAHA than all the Commonwealth beaches put together – but where the bravery and tenacity of individuals overcame adversity. Bloody OMAHA it was, tragic its losses certainly were, but for the American Second World War generation it came to symbolise all that USA gave in the war.

OMAHA Beach covers a wide area from Vierville-sur-Mer in the west across to Colleville-sur-Mer to the east, a distance of nearly 4½ miles. The beach was unlike all other D-Day locations in that it did not immediately lead to an urbanised area with good roads. Instead, the beach was dominated by a high bluff,

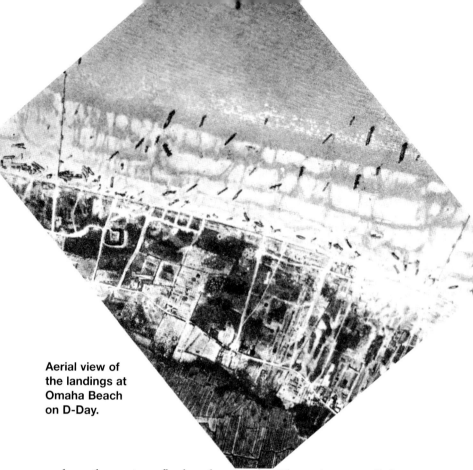

Aerial view of
the landings at
Omaha Beach
on D-Day.

and on the eastern flanks, sheer rocks. The only way off the beach was via four 'draws' – minor roads set in a gully that led up off the beach area to a lateral inland road. Once the beach was in Allied hands, the plan was to improve the road exits to allow the huge amount of men and traffic that would follow to exploit the advance inland. While far from ideal, OMAHA had been selected because it offered the only landing area between the Cotentin peninsula where the rest of the American forces would land and GOLD Beach, the right flank of the British landings. It also provided a suitable location to build a second Mulberry harbour, so that American troops could be properly resupplied post-D-Day.

Two infantry divisions were detailed to land here at H Hour; the 1st Division to the east and 29th Division in the west. Both were part of Major General Leonard T. Gerow's V Corps. Their objective was to secure OMAHA Beach, link up with the British on the left just north of Bayeux and meet up with the airborne forces around Carentan and ground forces that had landed on Utah Beach. This was part of the overall strategy to take the Cotentin peninsula and push on to Cherbourg so that a deepwater port could be captured. The major potential threat to the landings was a gun battery at Pointe du Hoc, further supported by others close to Grandcamp-Maisy. These needed to be neutralised to ensure success on OMAHA and as objectives were allocated to American Ranger units (see the Pointe du Hoc Walk, p. 205).

The two OMAHA divisions were very different. The 1st was part of the American regular army and had a long tradition of fighting, and indeed had been in action in both North Africa and Sicily. Its unit commanders were experienced combat veterans who had taken part in amphibious operations, and many of its men had been in action several times. The 29th Division, in contrast, had never seen combat. It was a National Guard division with men recruited in specific geographic areas, much like the Territorial Army system in the British Army. From towns and cities in Maryland, the District of Columbia and Virginia, men had joined up together, trained together and now were about to go to war together. Although the division was 'raw', like many British formations with no front-line experience, it had undergone extensive battle training and amphibious warfare training prior to Overlord. It was also felt that the common bond between the men because of where the division had been recruited gave it excellent *esprit de corps*.

On paper OMAHA Beach was not wide enough to land two divisions side by side. However, there was a necessity to do so and as much faith had been placed in the ability of the pre-D-Day bombardment to take out the major defences that this was not considered much of an issue. The beach was therefore divided into two divisional areas with four narrow sub-sectors – Dog Green to Easy Green – where the 29th would come in between the Vierville and Les Moulins draws, and wider sectors – Easy Red to Fox Red – where 1st Division would assault between St Laurent and above a hamlet called Le Grand Hameau. Supporting them were ships from two Naval Task Forces and Sherman DD tanks from two different armoured battalions. As on the British beaches, the key to breaching the defences of the Atlantic Wall were engineers, and on OMAHA a

Special Engineer Task Force commanded by Colonel John O'Neill was supported by two Engineer Special Brigades. These men would clear the mines, cut lanes in the barbed wire, neutralise any remaining bunkers and make the beach suitable for heavy traffic to be unloaded. They would then set about modifying the draws so they offered better exits from the beach; for this task they had Sherman bulldozer tanks and also engineer bulldozers. Unlike the British beaches, there were no AVREs or 'Funnies' – in fact, the only such vehicle used by the Americans was the DD tank.

Opposing the assault troops were German units from the 352nd Infantry Division commanded by General Dietrich Kraiss, a formation responsible for a long stretch of coastline from the Cotentin area to Asnelles. Kraiss had divided his coastline into three defensive areas. The first between Carentan and Grandcamp was held by the 914th Grenadier Regiment supported by an artillery battalion and men from an *Ost Battalion*. The second sector was between Grandcamp and Colleville-sur-Mer and held by the 916th Grenadier Regiment, with artillery from two different battalions. The final sector was from Colleville to Asnelles and here the 726th Grenadier Regiment manned the bunkers, with an artillery battalion offering fire support. Prior to D-Day, in a rare example of Allied intelligence failure, it was believed this stretch of coast was held by the same division as on the British sectors and that the 352nd was well inland near St Lo. As such the intelligence briefings for both American divisions detailed to land at OMAHA indicated that no more than a thousand men defended the whole beach, with a handful of units up to 3 hours away. In fact, many more times that number were available, and all close to the coastline.

The German defences at OMAHA made full use of the terrain. The high bluffs above the beach offered both good vantage points for the artillery battalion observers and also for sighting anti-tank guns and machine-gun positions. On the area where the landings were planned to take place there were fifteen Weiderstandnest (WN-60–WN-74) equipped with anti-tank weapons ranging in calibre from 47mm to 88mm, along with 20mm flak positions and numerous machine-gun positions. The majority of these were equipped with the older MG34, which could fire anything up to 1,200 rounds a minute depending on which model it was and whether it was mounted on a tripod, bipod or fixed position. Estimates for the number of machine guns vary, but it is commonly accepted that at least 85 weapons were available to the defenders, meaning that it was possible to direct something like a 100,000 rounds a minute down on to the beach. In addition, there were fifteen mortar positions and on nine of the bunkers turrets from redundant French tanks were fitted. With the superb fields of fire, all of them overlapping, OMAHA offered a considerable obstacle to any landings. Add to that minefields, anti-tank ditches and barbed wire, plus the artillery support to the rear with guns up to 150mm, like all D-Day beaches it would be no walk over.

In the final hours leading up to D-Day these defences were bombed from the air, and finally hit by naval gun fire from both American and British ships firing shells up to 14in calibre. The landings were timed to take place an hour before the British assault, with only 30 minutes of daylight accurately to direct the naval bombardment before the first landing craft hit the beaches. All the assault vessels were launched at 11 miles from the beach to stop them being hit by shore fire, which resulted in a long final approach in very rough seas, making things even tougher for the troops inside. The weather was poor with rain and wind, and a sea swell of several metres. A decision was also made to launch all the DD tanks at 6,000yd from the beach, the greatest distance they were released on D-Day. Dozens of Shermans were thrown into the rough seas, as waves beat against their canvas sides, signalling the start of their journey to support the infantry landings.

The 352nd Division reported that they could see Allied shipping at 0502, and orders went in to the German gun batteries behind OMAHA Beach to take on targets at sea. By 0550 the Allied naval bombardment was in full swing, with shells dropping all along the landing area, and 6 minutes later the final air bombardment began. Like all of the British beaches, this preliminary fire proved largely ineffective. It was difficult to co-ordinate accurately and some targets were very small, while others avoided detection in the half-light. The aerial bombardment was often way off the mark and the final part of the bombardment took place with a 'run-in shoot' of 105mm M7 Priests firing from LSTs (Landing Ship Tanks) as they approached the beach and rockets from Landing Craft Tank (Rocket)s. While the German troops under this terrible rain of

Troops come ashore at OMAHA in a hailstorm of fire.

steel were pushed to the limit of their endurance, the majority of their weapons remained intact as the American landing craft made the final approach.

The two assaulting regiments were the 116th Infantry Regiment from 29th Division on the right, commanded by Colonel Charles D.W. Canham, and the 16th on the left, from 1st Division, commanded by Colonel George A. Taylor. Both these regiments, as was standard practice in the American Army, had been divided into Regimental Combat Teams (RCT). These were all-arms formations combining infantry, engineers and support weapons such as mortars and bazookas. But before these men would land American Engineers from Gap Assault Teams were detailed to land to clear paths through the minefields and wire and mark them for the follow-up waves; they had as little as 30 minutes to achieve this. On British beaches these men would have been assisted by armoured vehicles; on OMAHA there were none, as there were no Funnies. The DD tanks, meant to support them, had launched so far out they had now floundered. The historian of the 741st Tank Bn wrote that,

185

on the order, the tanks rolled gracefully into the rough sea and many
of them sank immediately, carrying many men to watery graves. The
more fortunate were able to leave their sinking tanks and swim about
until rescued . . . Only one platoon of B Company beached, none of
C Company . . . The Tanks that landed carried out their missions . . .
[but] smooth operation was hampered by the dead bodies which lay
about all over the beach. Frequently the crews had to pull a few
bodies from their path, and proceed.[1]

In total some twenty-seven of the twenty-nine tanks launched at
6,000yd sank. Just three tanks made it in from LCTs but all
became casualties on the beach.

This meant these combat engineers landed on their own facing
the whole cacophony of firepower that remained on OMAHA
Beach. The official history recalled their problems.

Men burdened with equipment and explosives were excellent targets
for enemy fire as they unloaded in water often several feet deep. Of
16 doers only 6 got to the beach in working condition, and 3 of these
were immediately disabled by artillery hits. Much equipment,
including nearly all buoys and poles for marking lanes, was lost or
destroyed before it could be used. Eight navy personnel of Team 11
were dragging the preloaded rubber boat off their LCM [Landing
Craft Mechanised] when an artillery shell burst just above the load
of explosives and set off the primacord. One of the eight survived.
Another shell hit the LCM of Team 14, detonating explosives on the
deck and killing all navy personnel. Team 15 was pulling in its
rubber boat through the surf when a mortar scored a direct hit and
touched to the explosives, killing three men and wounding four.
Support Team F came in about 0700. A first shell hit the ramp,
throwing three men into the water. As the vessel drifted of out of
control, another hit squarely on the bow, killing 15 of the team. Only
five army personnel from this craft reached shore. Despite such
disasters and under continued intense fire, the engineers got to work
on obstacles wherever they landed and with whatever equipment and
explosives they could salvage. Some of the teams arriving a few
minutes late found the rapidly advancing tide already into the lower
obstacles. Infantry units landing behind schedule or delayed in
starting up the beach came through the demolition parties as they
worked, and thereby impeded their progress. One of the three doers
left in operation was prevented from manoeuvring freely by riflemen
who tried to find shelter behind it from the intense fire. As a final
handicap, there were instances where teams had fixed their charges,
were ready to blow their lane, and were prevented by the fact that

infantry were passing through or were taking cover in the obstacles. When Team 7 was set to fire, an LCVP [Landing Craft, Vehicle, Personnel] came crashing into the obstacles, smashed through the timbers, and set off seven mines; the charge could not be blown. In another case, vehicles passed through the prepared area and caused misfire by cutting the primacord fuse linking the charges. A naval officer, about to pull the twin-junction igniters to explode his charge, was hit by a piece of shrapnel that cut off his finger and the two fuses. The charge laid by Team 12 went off but at heavy cost. Their preparations completed for a 30-yard gap, the team was just leaving the area to take cover when a mortar shell struck the primacord. The premature explosion killed and wounded 19 engineers and some infantry nearby.

In net result, the demolition task force blew six complete gaps through all bands of obstacles, and three partial gaps. Of the six, only two were in the 116th's half of the beach, and four were on Easy Red, a fact which may have influenced later landing chances. Owing to the loss of equipment, only one of the gaps could be marked, and this diminished their value under high-water conditions. Their first effort made, the demolition teams joined the other assault forces on the shingle or sea wall and waited for the next low tide to resume their work. Casualties for the Special Engineer Task Force, including navy personnel, ran to 41 percent for D Day, most of them suffered in the first half-hour.[2]

Wave after wave is brought in.

As the work of the remaining engineers was still on-going the first wave of infantry came ashore. The weather had blown many landing craft off course, and many crews were about to put their loads down in the wrong part of the beach. This meant that the RCTs were immediately broken up, with vital equipment landing some distance from where it was needed, for example. A typical assault team looked like this,

Each LCVP carried an average of 31 men and an officer. The 116th assault craft were loaded so that the first to land would be a section leader and 5 riflemen armed with M-1s and carrying 96 rounds of ammunition. Following was a wire-cutting team of 4 men, armed with rifles; 2 carried large 'search-nose' cutters, and 2 a smaller type. Behind these in the craft, loaded so as to land in proper order were: 2 BAR [Browning Automatic Rifle] teams of 2 men each, carrying 900 rounds per gun; 2 bazooka teams, totalling 4 men, the assistants armed with carbines; a mortar team of 4 men, with a 60-mm mortar and 15 to 20 rounds; a flame-thrower crew of 2 men; and, finally, 5 demolition men with pole and pack charges of TNT. A medic and the assistant section leader sat at the stern. Everybody wore assault jackets, with large pockets and built-in packs on the back; each man carried, in addition to personal weapons and special equipment, a gas mask, 5 grenades (the riflemen and wire-cutters also had 4 smoke grenades), a half-pound block of TNT with primacord fuse, and 6 one third rations (3 Ks and 3 Ds). All clothing was impregnated against gas. The men wore life preservers (2 per man in 16th Infantry units), and equipment and weapons of the 16th were fastened to life preservers so that they could be floated in.[3]

As a coherent force, this array of firepower and equipment would mean that the RCTs had a good chance of overcoming the predicted opposition. The Americans landing knew the enemy they faced was second-rate, comprising large numbers of ethnic, non-German troops, and that their weapons and defences had been shattered by the pre-H Hour bombardment. But the enemy had survived. His defences were intact and his weapons were ready. Second-rate the Grenadiers may have been compared to the average Allied soldier, but they had practised time and again at repelling an invader and now they were about to do it for real.

As the ramps in the first wave went down all hell broke loose. Machine guns fired from the bluffs. Guns from the WNs opened up on landing craft. Artillery shells dropped in the sand

The landing craft make journey after journey.

and surf, directed by observers on the high ground. Men were cut down as they tried to get off the boats, others were scythed down before they even had a chance to move forward. Boats exploded in fireballs. The survivors went to ground, tucked up against the beach defences the assault engineers had tried to clear, many of them now surrounded by the bodies of the engineers who had died in the first moments of the battle. More waves landed, and the casualties mounted. The story of LCI 91 tells a typical tale of woe.

> The LCI was struck by artillery fire as it made a first attempt to get through the obstacles. Backing out, the craft came in again for a second try. Element 'C' was barely showing above the rising tide, and the LCI could not get past. The ramps were dropped in six feet of water. As some officers led the way off, an artillery shell (or rocket) hit the crowded forward deck and sent up a sheet of flame. Clothes burning, men jumped or fell off into the sea and tried to swim in under continued artillery fire. It is estimated that no personnel escaped from No. 1 compartment of the craft out of the 25 carried there. A few minutes later LCI 92 came into the same sector and suffered almost the same fate, an underwater explosion setting off the fuel tanks. The two craft burned for hours.[4]

OMAHA all too quickly turned from a coherent organised battle into a thousand small engagements; each one personal, each one unique. Here and there handfuls of men got forward into cover near the edge of the beach. On the 1st Division sector there was a rock face up against the bluff many sought cover against; photographs show men here without equipment and without weapons, shock visible on their faces. Further down men had crawled to a sand embankment and sought cover there, the open ground beyond to the base of the bluffs impassable due to mines, wire and heavy fire. On the 29 Division area there was precious little cover and the beaches swept by fire, the high tide of the advance marked by men close up against the sea wall. Officers trying to take command soon became casualties, and junior leaders soon followed them. Chaos does little justice to describe the conditions that prevailed in those early hours of the landing.

Under different circumstances tank support would have tipped the balance, but only a handful of DD tanks had made it to the shore, and while some had been landed close to shore from LCTs they had quickly come under fire and were knocked out or immobilised. It was clear to the men on the ground that it was going to be a battle of small groups of men looking for a weakness and exploiting it.

The outstanding fact about these first two hours of action is that despite heavy casualties, loss of equipment, disorganization, and all the other discouraging features of the landings, the assault troops did not stay pinned down behind the sea wall and embankment. At half-a-dozen or more points on the long stretch, they found the necessary drive to leave their cover and move out over the open beach flat toward the bluffs. Prevented by circumstance of mislandings from using carefully rehearsed tactics, they improvised assault methods to deal with what defences they found before them. In nearly every case where advance was attempted, it carried through the enemy beach defences. Some penetrations were made by units of company strength; some were made by intermingled sections of different companies; some were accomplished by groups of 20 or 30 men, unaware that any other assaults were under way. Even on such terrain as OMAHA Beach, the phenomenon of battlefield 'isolation' was a common occurrence, and units often failed to see what was going on 200 yards to their flanks on the open beach.[5]

Despite this isolation, gradually these individual efforts began to be joined up, and slowly but surely the defences began to fall. One of those who helped turn the fortunes of battle on OMAHA was Brigadier General Norman Cota. His party had landed an hour or so into operations.

> *Beginning at 0730, regimental command parties began to arrive. The main command group of the 116th RCT included Col. Charles D. W. Canham and General Cota. LCVP 71 came in on Dog White, bumping an obstacle and nudging the Teller mine until it dropped off, without exploding. Landing in three feet of water, the party lost one officer in getting across the exposed area. From the standpoint of influencing further operations, they could not have hit a better point in the 116th one. To their right and left, Company C and some 2nd Battalion elements were crowded against the embankment on a front of a few hundred yards, the main Ranger force was about to come into the same area, and enemy fire from the bluffs just ahead was masked by smoke and ineffective. The command group was well located to play a major role in the next phase of action.[6]*

Major General Norman Cota.

Cota is reputed to have said to his men 'Gentlemen, we are being killed on the beaches. Let us go inland and be killed.' Whatever was said his presence, along with the other officers of his command group, helped tip the balance,

> *Reorganization for assault was spurred by the presence of General Cota and the command group of the 116th Infantry . . . Exposed to enemy fire, which wounded Colonel Canham in the wrist, they walked up and down behind the crowded sea wall, urging officers and non-coms to 'jar men loose' and get moving.[7]*

Get moving they did. During the course of the rest of the day gradually WN after WN was overrun. Men advanced along the bluffs, neutralising machine-gun positions and trench systems. Clear from fire, engineers could then do the work they had trained for and clear lanes so the bulk of the survivors, tucked into cover, could move forward and exploit the situation. Battle after battle like this took place well into the late afternoon and by the early evening the last remaining resistance was inland close to the villages of St Laurent-sur-Mer and Colleville-sur-Mer. The battle for OMAHA beachhead was effectively over. It had nearly been a failure. The whole American timetable for D-Day was now seriously off kilter given that it had taken most of

The beach now secure, the follow-up waves arrive.

the day to get off the beach rather than a few hours. What had gone so wrong? Why had OMAHA been so bloody?

No enquiry was ever made into what had happened at OMAHA Beach, nor was it the subject of any congressional investigation as some of the American failures in Italy were post-war. It still remains the subject of great debate, but what must be stated is the eventual outcome of OMAHA was only possible because of the tenacity and bravery of those who were thrown onto the beach on D-Day. Lacking armour support, with no engineer vehicles and specialists scattered wide with only limited kit, heroism and initiative got the men off the beaches. But could it have been any different? Like all the British beaches, the defences had survived the pre-D-Day strikes intact. On the British beaches a combination of specialist equipment from the Funnies, greater availability of armour (with DD tanks being launched much closer to the beach) and engineers arriving at the same time as the armour meant that despite casualties and much opposition the defences could – and were – overcome. The American plan to land the engineers on their own, the lack of any serious armoured support and the lack of specialist equipment the British had certainly contributed to the problems and the casualties, but there is no doubt that the nature of the terrain at OMAHA – a defenders' paradise – helped tip the balance in the favour of the Germans. It is only when you stand on OMAHA Beach now and look back up to the bluffs that you can appreciate what a task was asked of the men here on D-Day. What of the losses? What did it cost to get off OMAHA Beach on D-Day? While certain aspects of the landings at OMAHA Beach remain a mystery, one of the greatest of them is the subject of casualties. The official history made the following observation in the post-war report,

> *Unit records for D Day are necessarily incomplete or fragmentary, and losses in men and materiel cannot be established in accurate detail. First estimates of casualties were high, with an inflated percentage of 'missing' as a result of the number of assault sections which were separated from their companies, sometimes for two or three days. On the basis of later, corrected returns, casualties for V*

The assault troops depleted, the men of the 2nd Division arrive to push inland.

Corps were in the neighbourhood of 3,000 killed, wounded, and missing. The two assaulting regimental combat teams (16th and 116th) lost about 1,000 men each. The highest proportionate losses were taken by units which landed in the first few hours, including engineers, tank troops, and artillery.

Whether by swamping at sea or by action at the beach, materiel losses were considerable, including twenty-six artillery pieces and over fifty tanks. No satisfactory over-all figures are available for vehicles and supplies; one unit, the 4042nd Quartermaster Truck Company, got ashore only thirteen out of thirty-five trucks (2½ ton), but this loss was much higher than the average. On the Navy side, a tentative estimate gives a total of about 50 landing craft and 10 larger vessels lost, with a much larger number of all types damaged. The principal cause for the difficulties of V Corps on D Day was the unexpected strength of the enemy at the assault beaches.[8]

Even seventy years after the event the full extent of the casualties is not known, but most historians now accept that certainly more American soldiers died on OMAHA Beach than all the other beaches put together, putting fatalities, therefore, at well over 2,000. The records of the American Battlefields and Monuments Commission, which manages the cemetery that overlooks the beach, only have records of those buried in its cemeteries, not those who were repatriated, so the more than 1,000 graves there bearing the date of 6 June 1944 will continue to represent but a fraction of the true story of the tragedy until more detailed research finally explains what D-Day cost the USA on 'Bloody OMAHA'.

Walk 9: On OMAHA Beach

STARTING POINT: Car park of the Normandy American Cemetery, St Laurent-sur-Mer

GPS: 49°21′28.3″N, 0°51′03.9″W

DURATION: 14.5km/9 miles

With stops at the cemetery, visitors' centre and one of the museums en route, this is a full-day walk. Food can be obtained at Les Moulins but it is easier to take some with you.

Leave your vehicle in the parking area of the cemetery (opening hours are 9am–6pm, 15 April–15 September, and 9am–5pm the rest of the year) and begin your tour at the visitors' centre. This can take up to an hour, and then afterwards explore the cemetery before actually starting the walk.

The visitors' centre at the Normandy American Cemetery.

The Normandy American Cemetery has become one of the most famous American war cemeteries, having been featured in the opening sequence of *Saving Private Ryan*. The site was dedicated in July 1956 and covers 172 acres. There are 9,386 graves here and a further 1,557 names inscribed on the memorial to the missing. Many believe that it is the largest American war cemetery in Europe; in fact, that is the Meuse-Argonne Cemetery, near Verdun from the First World War. However, the sheer scale of the American sacrifice is understood here with crosses seemingly going on into infinity. It is all the more sobering when you consider this is only part of the story; the American repatriated more than 60 per cent of their dead after the Second World War, a practice started after the previous world war.

An immediate post-war aerial photograph of the Normandy American Cemetery. (US National Archives)

American graves either take the form of a marble cross or Star of David in the case of Jewish servicemen. The name of the casualty is reproduced in full along with his rank, unit, division, state where he came from and date of death. No details of age are recorded, and it was decided that personal inscriptions would not be added in the same way as they were in Commonwealth cemeteries. In this way the graves are not as personal. The following Medal of Honour winners are buried here:

Technical Sergeant Frank Peregory (Block G, Row 21, Grave 7) 116th Infantry, 29th Division. He was killed on 14 June 1944 and the decoration was for bravery at Grandcamp-Maisy on 8 June. His citation reads:

On 8 June 1944, the 3ʳᵈ Battalion of the 116ᵗʰ Infantry was advancing on the strongly held German defenses at Grandcamp, France, when the leading elements were suddenly halted by decimating machinegun fire from a firmly entrenched enemy force on the high ground overlooking the town. After numerous attempts to neutralize the enemy position by supporting artillery and tank fire had proved ineffective, T/Sgt. Peregory, on his own initiative, advanced up the hill under withering fire, and worked his way to the crest where he discovered an entrenchment leading to the main enemy fortifications 200 yards away. Without hesitating, he leaped into the trench and moved toward the emplacement. Encountering a squad of enemy riflemen, he fearlessly attacked them with hand grenades and bayonet, killed 8 and forced 3 to surrender. Continuing along the trench, he single-handedly forced the surrender of 32 more riflemen, captured the machine gunners, and opened the way for the leading elements of the battalion to advance and secure its objective. The extraordinary gallantry and aggressiveness displayed by T/Sgt. Peregory are exemplary of the highest tradition of the armed forces.

First Lieutenant Jimmie W. Monteith Jr (Block I, Row 20, Grave 12) 116th Infantry, 29th Division. He was killed on 6 June 1944 and the medal was awarded posthumously for bravery that day. His citation reads:

For conspicuous gallantry and intrepidity above and beyond the call of duty on 6 June 1944, near Colleville-sur-Mer, France. 1st Lt. Monteith landed with the initial assault waves on the coast of France under heavy enemy fire. Without regard to his own personal safety he continually moved up and down the beach reorganizing

The sheer scale of the Normandy American Cemetery is staggering.

men for further assault. He then led the assault over a narrow protective ledge and across the flat, exposed terrain to the comparative safety of a cliff. Retracing his steps across the field to the beach, he moved over to where 2 tanks were buttoned up and blind under violent enemy artillery and machine gun fire. Completely exposed to the intense fire, 1st Lt. Monteith led the tanks on foot through a minefield and into firing positions. Under his direction several enemy positions were destroyed. He then rejoined his company and under his leadership his men captured an advantageous position on the hill. Supervising the defence of his newly won position against repeated vicious counterattacks, he continued to ignore his own personal safety, repeatedly crossing the 200 or 300 yards of open terrain under heavy fire to strengthen links in his defensive chain. When the enemy succeeded in completely surrounding 1st Lt. Monteith and his unit and while leading the fight out of the situation, 1st Lt. Monteith was killed by enemy fire. The courage, gallantry, and intrepid leadership displayed by 1st Lt. Monteith is worthy of emulation.

Brigadier General Theodore Roosevelt Jr (Plot D, Row 28, Grave 45)

Commanding 4th Division. He died of a heart attack on 12 July 1944. The medal was awarded for bravery in the Normandy campaign. The son of the President, his brother's grave from the First World War was moved so they could be buried side by side. His citation reads:

197

For gallantry and intrepidity at the risk of his life above and beyond the call of duty on 6 June 1944, in France. After 2 verbal requests to accompany the leading assault elements in the Normandy invasion had been denied, Brig. Gen. Roosevelt's written request for this mission was approved and he landed with the first wave of the forces assaulting the enemy-held beaches. He repeatedly led groups from the beach, over the seawall and established them inland. His valour, courage, and presence in the very front of the attack and his complete unconcern at being under heavy fire inspired the troops to heights of enthusiasm and self-sacrifice. Although the enemy had the beach under constant direct fire, Brig. Gen. Roosevelt moved from one locality to another, rallying men around him, directed and personally led them against the enemy. Under his seasoned, precise, calm, and unfaltering leadership, assault troops reduced beach strong points and rapidly moved inland with minimum casualties. He thus contributed substantially to the successful establishment of the beachhead in France.

Other interesting graves include:

Two brothers who inspired *Saving Private Ryan* (Block F, Row 15, Graves 11 and 12)
Second Lieutenant Preston Niland 22nd Infantry and Sergeant Robert Niland 505th Parachute Infantry Regiment (PIR). Robert was killed on D-Day and Preston on 7 June. A third brother was thought killed in the Pacific, so the fourth was allowed home. However, the brother in the Pacific actually survived the war. It was their story that largely inspired the script writers of *Saving Private Ryan*.

Father and son (Block E, Row 20, Graves 19 and 20)
Colonel Ollie Reed, 115th Infantry died on 30 July 1944 and his son First Lieutenant Ollie Reed Jr of the 163rd Infantry had died earlier on 6 July. Colonel Reed was from Kansas and had served in the First World War, becoming a regular army officer in the inter-war period. His son died in Italy and the Colonel's wife requested that his body be brought here for burial so father and son could rest side by side.

Leave the cemetery on a minor road and follow it to where a **grass path** heads off towards an obelisk memorial. This leads you into an area where the remains of German trenches are visible along with concrete Tobruk pits. The defences in this area are all part of WN-62 which overlooked Fox Green beach where men from both the 16th and 116th Regiments landed, having become mixed up due to the tides. The potential fields of fire from this position are easy to comprehend. The bunkers here housed anti-tank weapons, there were machine-gun positions and some of the Tobruks contained mortars. The memorial commemorates the losses of the 1st Division in the opening phase of the Normandy campaign until 24 July 1944 and lists all those who died during that period. Medal of Honour winners are picked out in gold lettering.

Memorial to the 1st Division overlooking the beach where they landed.

From here **walk down** to the beach. Each bunker can be visited or the well-trodden path can be followed. On one of the bunkers is a memorial to the US Engineer units which took part in the assault in this area. From here go out onto the beach and **stop** and look back.

From this part of the beach looking back up to the bluffs it is possible to comprehend the enormous task facing the American troops who landed here on D-Day, and the great

The defences above the beach are still visible, including many trenches and dugouts.

American Engineers Memorial; without teams of Engineers, breaking the defences would have been impossible.

The sandbank on the edge of the beach where many troops sheltered, pinned down by machine-gun fire.

The winter tide of 2011 exposed a handful of Rommel's Asparagus, once part of the beach defences.

advantage the German defenders had. Throughout the walk stop and look back up the beach like this, as it will certainly reinforce the point about how terrain influences battles.

Continue along the beach. At high tide it may be necessary to walk close to the sand embankment where many men sheltered, if not, do not forget to inspect it as erosion is gradually making it disappear. Beyond it is the marshland once strewn with mines and barbed wire. About a kilometre down the beach **go across** the sand dunes where there is a path cut through; follow this across a small wooden footbridge to a car-park area below one of the bluffs and at the entrance to the Easy-1 Exit or draw.

The bunker here is part of the WN-65 defences and still houses the original anti-tank gun used on D-Day. Men from M/116th Infantry Regiment landed on the beach below the bunker but remained pinned down until later in the morning when naval gunfire scored a direct hit on the bunker (damage still visible) and a mixed unit of infantry, engineers

German bunker at WN-65 overlooking the beach at Omaha and still housing the original armament.

and signallers assaulted the position and forced the remaining Germans to surrender. The bunker now has a number of memorials and the interior can be visited. The stairs to the left of the bunker mark an older route off the beach for American

A more recent memorial on the beach commemorating the American sacrifice here on D-Day.

troops in the follow-up waves after D-Day; one of the most famous of Normandy photographs was taken here and can be seen on an information panel nearby. Going up the steps and looking back again demonstrates the advantage the defenders had from the bluffs.

From the bunker **walk downhill** towards the houses and into Rue de la 2eme Division US. Follow this until it reaches the beach area again. Here you are overlooking Easy Green where parts of F/116th and G/116th Infantry landed. Either continue along the path by the road or drop down onto the beach. **Continue** until you reach the Battle of Normandy Memorial at Les Moulins.

Les Moulins was protected on both sides of the draw, to the west by WN-68 and to the east WN-66. Officially known as Dog-3 Exit, it was one of the planned routes off the beach but on D-Day was the scene of bloodshed as men from the 116th Infantry tried to get inland. Tanks from 743rd Tank Bn had been disembarked directly onto the beach rather than launched at sea and it became one of the few occasions where tanks were able to assist the scattered parties of infantry and engineers eventually to overrun the defences, although some tanks became casualties from guns in the bunkers. However, it wasn't until the evening that the exit was finally secure after some bitter fighting in the bunkers and trenches atop the bluff.

Continue along the beach. Further up on the left is a marker stone set back from the road marking the site of the first American cemetery in France. It was one that was closed post-war and the graves either repatriated or removed to the Normandy American Cemetery.

Again **continue** until you reach the main National Guard Memorial at the far end of the beach. This commemorates the National Guard units of the 29th Division and is sited on top of one of the anti-tank bunkers of WN-72. Its field of fire is clearly visible. There are several other bunkers in the area, and one of the last easily visible pieces of the Mulberry harbour that was built here and later destroyed in the storms. Beyond the Mulberry section a track goes uphill to another bunker which is worth walking to as again it shows the fields of fire from the defences here. On a clear day the entire extent of OMAHA Beach can be seen from here.

Returning to the area of WN-72, follow the minor road to the

Marker commemorating the first American cemetery 'then and now'.

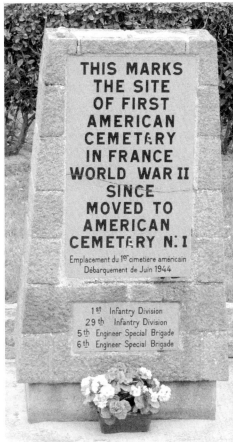

THIS MARKS
THE SITE
OF FIRST
AMERICAN
CEMETERY
IN FRANCE
WORLD WAR II
SINCE
MOVED TO
AMERICAN
CEMETERY N. I

Emplacement du 1er cimetière américain
Débarquement de Juin 1944

1 st   Infantry Division
29 th   Infantry Division
5 th   Engineer Special Brigade
6 th   Engineer Special Brigade

left uphill. On this part of the route a memorial to the 29th Division and another to the Rangers will be seen, as well as some sections of a Mulberry roadway section that belong to a local museum. Stay on the minor road (Rue de la Mer) into Hamel-au-Prêtre. Turn **second left** into Rue Paveé (D514) and stay left before taking the **first left** into Rue du Hamel-au-Prêtre. This is then followed along the top of the bluffs and there are good views towards the beach. There are a few tracks that lead to the edge of the cliffs that offer a better view, but private property should be respected at all times. Further along the track becomes Rue du 6 Juin 1944, **follow** this downhill

View from a German bunker on the far end of Omaha Beach showing the incredible fields of fire the Germans enjoyed.

back to the Les Moulins area. At the roundabout take Rue Desire Lemiere and then **first right** onto Chemin de la Fresnaie. Follow this to where it joins the D517 and into St Laurent. Go through the village on Rue du Val. American troops did not reach this area until quite late on D-Day and there was still some German resistance in the area from the shattered units of 352nd Division. Continue out of the village and at a junction with a Normandy stone house on the left go **straight on**. This leads to an area where a memorial stone is visible. **Stop.**

This is on the bluffs above WN-65 and marks the site of one of the first American provisional airfields. This sort of infrastructure was vital to the success of D-Day and work began on this airfield, A-21, on 8 June, with the first Dakota transport landing here at 1800 the next day. The airfield was used to bring in supplies, evacuate wounded and provide an emergency landing ground for fighters and small bombers. There is an information panel showing contemporary aerial views of the site.

At the memorial take the **right-hand** minor road and go downhill. At the end **turn right** and at the end of this section **turn left** and follow the path through the trees. This brings you to the southern boundary of the Normandy American Cemetery and joins up with the paths in the cemetery returning you to the car park and your vehicle.

Area Ten

POINTE DU HOC WALK: THE 2ND RANGERS, 6–8 JUNE 1944

HISTORICAL SECTION

As part of the Atlantic Wall the Germans believed in defence in depth; place weapons and bunkers on the beach to smash an invader as they landed but also back up those positions with sizeable artillery further away from the coast or in a flank position able to fire into nearby potential landing grounds. The Allied pre-D-Day planners focused on a number of bunker complexes containing artillery units that would pose a special threat to the landings. On the American sector one of these was at a coastal location called Pointe du Hoc, east of the seaside town of Grandcamp.

The position at Pointe du Hoc was strongly protected from attack by sea. Between Grandcamp and the OMAHA sector, the flat Norman tableland terminates abruptly in rocky cliffs. At Pointe du Hoc, these are 85 to 100 feet high, sheer to overhanging; below them is a narrow strip of beach, without the slightest cover for assaulting troops. Aerial photographs indicated what was later confirmed by French civilians: that the enemy regarded the position as nearly impregnable from seaward attack and were more concerned with defending it against an enemy coming from inland. The battery was part of a self-contained fortress area, mined and wired on the landward side. Its flanks were protected by two supporting smaller positions mounting machine guns and, on the west, an antiaircraft gun. These positions were sited to put enfilade fire on the beaches under the Point, and to aid its defence against any inland attack. Enemy troops at Pointe du Hoc were estimated at 125 infantry and eighty-five artillerymen, included in the sector of enemy coastal defences, from the Vire to the Orne, held by 716th Infantrie Division. This unit contained a high percentage of non-German troops, and was regarded as of limited fighting value. Elements of the 716th Infantry Division held the sector from Vierville to Grandcamp, in which, because of the continuous stretch of cliffs, coastal strong points were widely spaced. Those nearest Pointe du Hoc were one mile distant on the west and two miles to the east. The Germans had made no preparations to defend this part of the coast in depth. The 716th Infantry Division was stretched thinly along 30

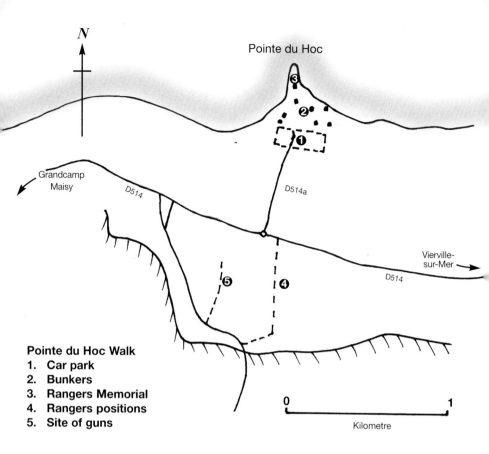

N

Pointe du Hoc

❸

❷

❶

Grandcamp
Maisy

D514

D514a

Vierville-
sur-Mer →

D514

❺

❹

Pointe du Hoc Walk
1. **Car park**
2. **Bunkers**
3. **Rangers Memorial**
4. **Rangers positions**
5. **Site of guns**

0 ———————————— 1

Kilometre

*miles of shore; behind it, but believed ten to twelve hours away, the
352nd Infantry Division in the St-Lô-Caumont area was the nearest
mobile reserve.*[1]

As all the American airborne troops were already allocated to
operations around Ste-Mère-Eglise, a Ranger Group, attached to
the 116th Infantry that was detailed to land on OMAHA Beach,
was given the task of taking on this formidable position. In
overall command was Lieutenant Colonel James E. Rudder,
with the group comprising men from 2nd Rangers and 5th
Rangers, the latter commanded by Lieutenant Colonel Max F.
Schneider. Rudder's men were to make the assault on the
coastal battery, while Schneider's were off-shore and would
await the success signal before moving in. In total some 225
Rangers would be put ashore on the narrow shingle beach
beneath the cliffs, ladder and rope their way up and neutralise
the battery site. Prior to D-Day Pointe du Hoc came under

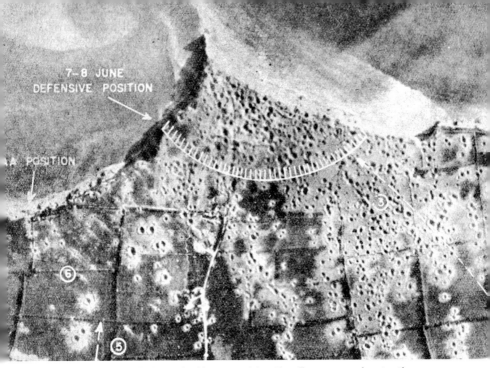

7–8 JUNE
DEFENSIVE POSITION

A POSITION

Aerial view of Pointe du Hoc used by the Rangers prior to the assault. (US National Archives)

heavy aerial bombardment with bombers of the Ninth US Air Force carrying out bombing runs and in the final hours destruction rained down from the 14in guns of USS *Texas* and a final strafe by eighteen medium bombers just twenty minutes before H Hour.

On 6 June the weather affected operations here, like other locations,

> *The leading group of nine surviving LCAs kept good formation, in a double column ready to fan out as they neared shore. Unfortunately, the guide craft lost its bearings as the coast line came in sight, and headed straight for Pointe de la Percée, three miles east of the target. When Colonel Rudder, in the lead LCA, realized the error he intervened and turned the column westward. But the damage had been done. The mistake cost more than 30 minutes in reaching Pointe du Hoc; instead of landing at H Hour, the first Ranger craft touched down about H+38, a delay that determined the whole course of action at the Point for the next two days. The main Ranger flotilla, eight companies strong, was following in from the transports, watching anxiously for the signal of success at Pointe du Hoc (two successive flares shot by 60-mm mortars). By 0700, if no*

207

message or signal had come, Colonel Schneider's force was scheduled to adopt the alternate plan of action and land at the Vierville beach. They waited ten minutes beyond the time limit and then received by radio the code word TILT, prearranged signal to follow the alternative plan. So Colonel Schneider turned in toward Vierville, where the 5th Rangers and A and B of the 2nd landed at 0745. Pending the outcome at OMAHA Beach, and the success of Colonel Schneider's force in fighting cross country to the Point, Colonel Rudder's three companies would fight alone.

The error in direction had further consequences. The correction headed Colonel Rudder's column of LCAs back toward Pointe du Hoc, but now on a westerly course, roughly paralleling the cliffs and only a few hundred yards offshore. The flotilla thus had to run the gauntlet of fire from German strong points along three miles of coast. Fortunately these were few, and their fire was wild and intermittent. The only serious casualty was a DUKW, hit by 20-mm fire as it neared the target area. Five of the nine men aboard were killed or wounded.[2]

This delay proved fortuitous for the defenders; by the time the Rangers began their ascent of the cliffs some 40 minutes had passed since the pre-H Hour bombardment had come to an end. The Germans could calmly take aim, unmolested by hostile file, and open up on the Rangers. An after action report for each boat landing the Rangers was compiled for the American official history,

LCA 861. Carrying a boat team of Company E, commanded by 1st Lt. Theodore E. Lapres, Jr., this craft grounded about 25 yards from the bottom of the cliff. Three or four Germans were standing on the cliff edge, shooting down at the craft. Rangers near the stern took these enemy under fire and drove them out of sight. At the instant of touchdown the rear pair of rockets was fired, then the other two pairs in succession. All the ropes fell short of the cliff edge, as a result of being thoroughly soaked. In some cases not more than half the length of rope or ladder was lifted from the containing box.

As the Rangers crossed the strip of cratered sand, grenades were thrown down from above them, or rolled over the cliff edge. These were of the 'potato-masher' type, with heavy concussion effects but small fragmentation. They caused two casualties. The hand-rockets were carried ashore, and the first one was fired at 15 yards from the cliff. It went over the top and caught. Pfc. Harry W. Roberts started up the hand-line, bracing his feet against the 80-degree slope. He made about 25 feet; the rope slipped or was cut, and Roberts slithered down. The second rocket was fired and the grapnel caught. Roberts went up again, made the top (he estimated his climbing time at 40 seconds), and pulled into a small cratered niche just under the edge. As he arrived, the rope was cut. Roberts tied it to a picket. This pulled out under the weight of the next man, and the rope fell off the cliff, marooning Roberts. However, a twenty-foot mound of clay knocked off the cliff enabled Roberts' team to get far enough up the side to throw him a rope. This time he lay across it, and five men, including Lieutenant Lapres, came up. Roberts had not yet seen an enemy and had not been under fire. Without waiting for further arrivals, the six Rangers started for their objective, the heavily constructed OP at the north tip of the fortified area. About ten minutes had elapsed since touchdown.

Just after Lapres' group got up, a heavy explosion occurred above the rest of 861's team, waiting their turn on the rope. Pfc. Paul L. Medeiros was half buried under debris from the cliff. None of the men knew what caused the explosion, whether a naval shell, or the detonation of a German mine of a peculiar type found later at one or two places along the cliff edge. The enemy had hung naval shells (200-mm or larger) over the edge, attached by wire to a pull-type firing device and fitted with a short-delay time fuze. The explosion had no effect on the escalade. Medeiros and four more Rangers came up quickly, found Roberts' party already gone and out of sight, and followed from the cliff edge toward the same objective.

LCA 862. This craft, carrying 15 Rangers and NSFC personnel, landed about 100 yards left of the flank LCA. The men had no trouble in disembarking, but once on the sand they found themselves exposed to machine-gun fire from eastward of the landing area. One man was killed and one wounded by this fire; two more injured by grenade fragments.

The forward pair of rockets had been fired immediately on touchdown, followed by all four others together. One plain and two toggle ropes reached the top, but one toggle rope pulled out. Tech. 5 Victor J. Aguzzi, 1st Lt. Joseph E. Leagans (commanding the team), and S/Sgt. Joseph J. Cleaves went up the two remaining ropes, arrived at the top almost together, and fell into a convenient shell hole just beyond the edge. There they paused only long enough for two more men to join; then, following standard Ranger tactics, the five moved off without waiting for the rest of the team, who came up a few minutes later.

LCA 888. Colonel Rudder's craft, first to hit the beach, had 15 men of Company E and 6 headquarters personnel, including Lt. J.

W. Eikner, communications officer. A few enemy troops were seen on the cliff edge as the LCA neared shore, but, when Sgt. Dominick B. Boggetto shot one German off the edge with a BAR, the others disappeared. The Rangers had trouble in getting through the beach craters; neck deep in water, they found it hard to climb out because of the slick clay bottom. A few grenades came over the cliff without causing casualties.

The rockets were fired in series, at thirty-five yards from the cliff base. None of the waterlogged ropes reached the top. When two Rangers, best of the group at free-climbing, tried to work up the smashed cliff face without ropes, they were balked by the slippery clay surface, which gave way too easily to permit knife-holds. Bombs or shells had brought down a mass of wet clay from the cliff top, forming a mound thirty-five to forty feet high against the cliff. A sixteen-foot section of the extension ladder, with a toggle rope attached, was carried to the top of the mound and set up. A Ranger climbed the ladder, cut a foothold in the cliff, and stood in this to hold the ladder while a second man climbed it for another sixteen feet. The top man repeated the process, and this time Tech. 5 George J. Putzek reached the edge. Lying flat, with the ladder on his arms, he held on while a man below climbed the toggle rope, then the ladder.

From there on it was easy. As the first men up moved a few yards from the cliff edge to protect the climbers, they found plenty of cover in bomb craters, and no sign of an enemy. In fifteen minutes from landing, all the Company E men from LCA 888 were up and ready to move on. Colonel Rudder and headquarters personnel remained for the moment below, finding shelter from enfilade fire in a shallow cave at the bottom of the cliff. By 0725, 1st Lt. James W. Eikner had his equipment set up and flashed word by SCR 300 that Colonel Rudder's force had landed. Five minutes later he sent out the code word indicating 'men up the cliff'; the 'Roger' that receipted for this message, again on SCR 300, was Eikner's last communication of D Day on the Ranger command net. When he sent the message PRAISE THE LORD ('all men up cliff') at 0745, no response was forthcoming.

LCA 722. Twenty yards left of Colonel Rudder's craft, LCA 722 hit shore with IS Company E Rangers, five headquarters men, a Stars and Stripes photographer, and a Commando officer who had assisted the Rangers in training. Touchdown was made at the edge of a crater, and the men could not avoid it in debarking. Enemy grenades were ineffectual, and the craters and debris on the beach gave sufficient cover from enfilading fire from the left. The only casualty was Pfc. John J. Sillman, wounded three times as the craft *came in, hit twice on the beach, and destined to survive. A good deal of assorted equipment came on this craft, including the SCR 284, two pigeons, a 60-mm mortar with ammunition, and some demolitions. All were got ashore without loss, though it took maneuvering to avoid the deep water in the crater. Tech. 4 C. S. Parker and two other communications men hefted the big radio set on a pack board, and managed to get it in and working before the first climbers from 722 reached the top.*

The rockets had been fired just before landing. One ladder and one plain rope got up and held (LCA 722 had experienced no trouble with water, and the ropes were comparatively dry). The single rope lay in a slight crevice, but the ladder came down on an overhang where it seemed exposed to the flanking fire and would be hard to climb. Tech. 5 Edward P. Smith tried the plain rope and found he could easily 'walk it up.' On top three or four minutes after landing, he saw a group of Germans to his right throwing grenades over the cliff. Sgt. Hayward A. Robey joined Smith with a BAR. Robey lay in a shallow niche at the cliff edge and sprayed the grenadiers with forty or fifty rounds, fast fire. Three of the enemy dropped and the rest disappeared into shelters. Pfc. Frank H. Peterson, lightly wounded on the beach by a grenade, joined up and the three Rangers went off on their mission without waiting for the next climbers.

The mortar section in this boat team remained below, according to plan, with the purpose of setting up their 60-mm on the beach to deliver supporting fires. But the beach was too exposed to make this practicable, and time was consumed in getting ammunition from the one surviving supply craft. About 0745 the mortar team went on top without having yet fired.

LCA 668. Company D's craft had been scheduled to land on the west side of the Point. As a result of the change in angle of approach, the two surviving LCAs came in to the left of Company E, and in the center of the Ranger line.

LCA 668 grounded short of the beach strip, as a result of boulders knocked from the cliff by bombardment. The men had to swim in about twenty feet. While 1st Sgt. Leonard G. Lomell was bringing in a box of rope and a hand-projector rocket, he was wounded in the side by a machine-gun bullet but reached shore and kept going. Despite the unusual distance from the cliff, and the very wet ropes, three rockets had carried the cliff edge with a toggle rope and the two rope ladders. However, the grapnels on the ladders just made the top; since the lead rope connecting grapnels with the top of the ladders was 40 feet long, the Rangers had, in effect, two plain ropes and a toggle. Sergeant Lomell put his best climber on the toggle while he tried one of the ladders. All ropes were on an overhang, and only the toggle line proved practicable. Even on it, climbing would be slow, so Lomell called for the extension ladders. Picking a spot high on the talus, his men found that one 16-foot section added to a 20-foot section reached the top of the vertical stretch, beyond which a slide of debris had reduced the slope enough to make it negotiable without ropes. Two men had got up by the toggle rope; the rest used the ladder and made the top quickly. Grenades caused some annoyance until the first men up could cover the rest of the party. Twelve men moved off from the edge with Sergeant Lomell and 1st Lt. George F. Kerchner.

LCA 858. Shipping enough water all the way in to keep the Rangers busy, this craft nevertheless kept up fairly well and was only a minute or two behind the others at the beach. The men were put out into a crater and went over their heads in muddy water. Despite the wetting, a bazooka was the only piece of equipment put out of action. Three men were hit by machine-gun fire from the east flank.

The rockets were fired in series, the plain ropes first. All the ropes were wet, and only one hand-line got over the cliff. It lay in a crevice that would give some protection from enemy flanking fire, but the direct approach to the foot of the rope was exposed. The Company D Rangers worked their way to the rope through the piles of debris at the cliff base. While one man helped the wounded get to Colonel Rudder's CP, where the medics had set up, all the party went up this one rope and found it not too hard going. They could get footholds in the cliff face, and a big crater reduced the steepness of the climb near the top. The group was up within 15 minutes. As in most other cases, the first few men on top had moved off together, and the boat team did not operate as a unit after the escalade.

LCA 887. As a result of Company D's unscheduled landing in the center of the line of craft, the three LCAs carrying Company F were crowded eastward, all of them touching down beyond the area originally assigned them. Few of the Rangers realized this at the time.

LCA 887 had not been much bothered by either water or enemy action on the trip in. The craft grounded five yards out from dry beach, and the shorter men got a ducking in the inevitable crater. No equipment trouble resulted; even Sgt. William L. Petty's BAR, wet here and muddied later when he slipped on the cliff, fired perfectly when first needed. Some enemy fire, including automatic weapons, came from either flank. Two Rangers were wounded.

Just before hitting the beach the two forward rockets were fired.

Only one of the plain lines carried, and 1st Lt. Robert C. Arman, commanding the team, figured the heavier ropes had no chance. So, all four of the mounted rockets, together with the boxes carrying toggle ropes and ladders, were taken out on the sand – a matter of ten minutes' heavy work, while the coxswain of the LCA did a notable job of holding the craft in at the beach edge. When the rockets were set up for firing, the lead wire for making the firing connection was missing. Tech/Sgt. John I. Cripps fired all four in turn by touching the short connection, three feet from the rocket base, with his 'hot-box'. Each time, the flashback blinded Cripps and blew sand and mud all over him. The other Rangers saw him clean his eyes, shake his head, and go after the next rocket: 'he was the hell-of-a-looking mess'. But all the ropes went up, and made it possible for the party to make the top. Sergeant Petty and some other expert climbers had already tried the plain rope and failed; it was on a straight fall, requiring hand-over-hand work with no footholds possible, and the men had trouble with their muddy hands and clothes on the wet rope.

Sergeant Petty started up one of the ladders, got thirty feet up, and then slid all the way back on the cliff face when the grapnel pulled out. Tech. 5 Carl Winsch was going up the other ladder when fire from somewhere on the flanks began to chip the cliff all around him. Petty went up after Winsch, and found him, unwounded, in a shell hole at the top. Here Petty waited for two more Rangers and then they set out for their objective.

LCA 884. This craft, the target for considerable enemy fire from cliff positions on the way to the Point, had replied with its Lewis guns and the BARs of the Rangers. Touchdown was made on the edge of a shell hole, in water shoulder-high. Three Rangers were hit by fire coming from the left flank. When rockets were fired in series, front to rear, four got over the cliff, but every rope lay in such position as to be fully exposed to the continuing enemy small-arms fire. Moreover, the Rangers were so muddled in getting through the craters on the beach that the plain ropes would have been unusable after the first climber went up. The only rope ladder that reached the top was caught below on beach boulders and hung at an awkward angle. Several men tried the other ropes without success, and Pvt. William E. Anderson got only part way up in his attempt at free-climbing. 1st Lt. Jacob J. Hill finally took the group over to the left, where they used the ladders of 883's boat team.

LCA 883. Last in the column of approach, this craft was last to reach shore, nearly 300 yards left of its planned position and considerably beyond the edge of the main fortified area on Pointe du

American Air Force bombers softening up the gun battery site prior to D-Day. (US National Archives)

Hoc. Just to their left, a jut in the cliff protected the boat team from the flanking fire that caused so much trouble for the other landing parties. They made a dry landing, and had a perfect score with the six rockets. This gave an opportunity to use the climbing assignments on a full schedule, using every rope. Nevertheless the going was hard, even on the ladders. 1st Lt. Richard A. Wintz, on a plain rope, found it impossible to get any footholds on the slippery cliff. The wet and muddy rope made it difficult for hand-over-hand pulling, and at the top Wintz was 'never so tired in his life'. He found six men together and started them out immediately.[3]

Within thirty minutes of the landings around thirty to forty Rangers out of 190 had come ashore. With the German defenders on the cliffs neutralised the survivors were faced with a landscape that would not have looked out of place in the previous war; the pre-D-Day bombardments had turned the battery site into a moonscape of craters. Rudder wondered if it

214

was still possible to achieve his objectives given the now small size of his party, but with the exception of the OP, which stubbornly held out, clearing the bunkers only took minutes as little opposition was encountered. It was a surprise, but as they entered the artillery casemates he and his Rangers were in for an even greater shock.

> One party after another reached its allotted emplacement, to make the same discovery: the open gun positions were pulverized, the casemates were heavily damaged, but there was no sign of the guns or of artillery equipment. Evidently, the 155s had been removed from the Point before the period of major bombardments. The advance groups moved on inland toward the assembly area.[4]

What had happened to the guns? Some recent accounts claim that Rudder knew they were not there when they landed, but the contemporary accounts clearly point to the fact that they were eventually discovered by accident.

> About 0900, a two-man patrol from D went down the double-hedgerowed lane that ran south from the highway near Company D's outpost. About 250 yards along the lane, Sergeant Lomell and S/Sgt. Jack E. Kuhn walked into a camouflaged gun position; there, set up in battery, were five of the enemy 155s missing from the Point. They were in position to fire toward Utah Beach, but could easily have been switched for use against OMAHA. Piles of ammunition were at hand, points on the shells and charges ready, but there was no indication of recent firing. Not a German was in sight, and occasional sniper fire from a distance could hardly be intended as a defence of the battery. So effective was the camouflage that Lomell and Kuhn, though they could later spot the guns from the highway, had seen nothing until they were right in the position.
> With Kuhn covering him against possible defenders, Sergeant Lomell went into the battery and set off thermite grenades in the recoil mechanism of two guns, effectively disabling them. After bashing in the sights, of a third gun, he went back for more grenades. Before he could return, another patrol from Company E had finished the job. This patrol, led by S/Sgt. Frank A. Rupinski, had come through the fields and (like Lomell and Kuhn) were in the gun position before they saw it. Failing to notice the fact that some disabling work had already been done, Rupinski's patrol dropped a thermite grenade down each barrel, and removed some of the sights. After throwing grenades into the powder charges and starting a fire, the patrol decided the guns were out of action and withdrew. A

runner was sent off at once to the Point, bearing word that the missing guns, primary objective at the Point, had been found and neutralized.

Just why the German guns were thus left completely undefended and unused is still a mystery. One theory, based on the fact that some artillerymen were captured that day on the Point, was that bombardment caught them there in quarters, and they were unable to get back to their position. All that can be stated with assurance is that the Germans were put off balance and disorganized by the combined effects of bombardment and assault, to such an extent that they never used the most dangerous battery near the assault beaches but left it in condition to be destroyed by weak patrols.[5]

With the guns finally neutralised, the Rangers secondary task was to move south and secure the highway so that when American forces broke out of the OMAHA beachhead the main road towards Carentan was already in Allied hands. Following the securing of

The American flag is draped on the cliffs after the Rangers had taken Pointe du Hoc. (US National Archives)

the Battery site, Rudder began to send men down to the highway to secure a position that could be defended. The force of sixty Rangers were joined by a handful of Paratroopers from 101st Airborne who had been dropped wide and patrols were sent out to try and seek out where the enemy was located. Confusion reigned on both sides,

Typical of the way men on both sides were cut off and isolated during the first two days was a capture within the Ranger lines. About noon Sergeant Petty came back to the CP to get a rifle for one of his men. Just as he arrived, Sgt. James R. Alexander fired his BAR back toward the highway at two Germans who appeared by a gate, halfway down the lane. One German fell, and Petty and Alexander went over to examine the body, three other Rangers tagging along for no particular reason. Petty was sitting astride the gate, looking at the dead German, when somebody yelled 'Kamerad' from the ditch bordering the lane. Three Germans were coming out of the ditch. Sgt Walter J. Borowski fired some shots into the hedgerow on the chance that there might be more men hiding. Two more Germans came out. Then the hedgerow was searched in earnest, but without further results. Two of the prisoners, a captain and a noncom, said they had had a machine gun, which the Rangers were unable to find. Altogether, about forty prisoners were taken in by Ranger patrols and outposts, to be grouped under guard in the field near the CP.[6]

Positions were quickly established. A roadblock was made on the Carentan road by the remaining men of 'D' Company, and men of E and F Company established defences in the *bocage* south of the road towards some farm buildings and with good fields of fire, and put an advanced outpost further out to spot for any potential contact with the Germans. At one stage a large German patrol passed by the twenty or so men of 'D' Company at the roadblock; a force much bigger than they could have taken on. Thankfully for the Rangers, the force was unaware of the men in the hedgerows and passed on by.

The first real test came that evening. Rudder had decided to continue to guard the main road in case men from the 29th Division arrived – there was no radio contact outside of the Pointe du Hoc positions and Rudder had no idea of the slaughter at OMAHA – but realised the 'D' Company roadblock position was weak, so moved them into the hedgerows to extend the defences there. The first contact with the Germans was made at 2330,

*the Rangers posted in front of the D-E corner were startled by a
general outburst of whistles and shouts, close by on the orchard
slope. Enemy fire opened immediately and in considerable volume.
Sgt Michael J. Branley and Pfc Robert D. Carty, in position west of
the corner, saw tracer fire from a machine gun to their right and only
twenty-five yards from Company D's side of the angle. South of the
corner, in Company E's outpost, the men spotted another machine
gun to the west, about fifty yards from Company E's defensive line.
Neither outpost had seen or heard the enemy approach through the
orchard. At the angle, and along E's front, the Rangers returned the
enemy fire at once, the BARs firing in full bursts. Carty and Branley
started back toward the corner to get better firing positions; Carty
was killed by a grenade, and his companion, hit in the shoulder by a
bullet, managed to crawl to the hedgerow.*

*In the Company E outpost, Corporal Thompson and Hornhardt
were almost walked over by a group of Germans who came suddenly
around a hump in the north-south hedgerow dividing the orchard.
Thompson saw their silhouettes against the sky, so the Rangers got
in their fire first at point-blank range and knocked down three of the
enemy. The others went flat and threw grenades, one of them
exploding in Thompson's face and cutting him badly. He gave his
BAR to Hornhardt and they started back for the corner.*

*Only a few minutes after the firing began, an immense sheet of
flame shot up over to the west, near the position of the abandoned
German guns. (The Rangers' guess was that, somehow, more
powder charges had been set off in the ammunition dump.) The
orchard slopes were fully lit up, and many Germans could be seen
outlined against the glare. The flare died almost at once, and the
firing ended at the same time. It is possible that the powder explosion
had disconcerted the Germans and ended their effort, but more
probably the attack was only a preliminary probe by combat patrols,
trying to locate Ranger positions by drawing their fire.[7]*

The next attack came in at 0100 on 7 June, and this time much
stronger with a greater use of grenades by the Germans, and in
one case the Germans were seen throwing mortar bombs by
hand as improvised grenades. Positions on the right flank were
overrun, but the Germans again withdrew into the darkness
until the final attack two hours later. On this occasion the mortar
fire supporting it was even heavier, and more positions overrun.
The Command Post in the middle of E and F Companies spotted
Germans only yards away and engaged them on the track. But
gradually the position was becoming untenable,

As the volume of enemy fire built up again from south and west, indicating a new rush was at hand, hasty and informal measures were taken to pass the word around for withdrawal back to the highway and the Point. Some Rangers failed to get the notice and were temporarily left behind. Petty and Robey were told to bring up the rear and cover the withdrawal with their BARs. Non-commissioned officers tried hurriedly to round up their men. Once started, movement was fast. S/Sgt. Richard N. Hathaway of the 5th Rangers had been posted halfway back to the highway, along the lane. His first notice of what was happening came when men ran by toward the north. Hathaway stuck his head through the hedgerow and shouted 'Hey! What's up? Where you going?' The nearest man stopped running, put his rifle in Hathaway's face, and demanded the password. Hathaway was so rattled that he could just remember the word in time. Told 'the Germans are right behind us get out quick to the Point!' he collected part of his group (he couldn't find some, but they came in later), and went north. There could be no question of bringing back the prisoners.

As the parties arrived at the blacktop, there was no sign of any pursuit, and an effort was made to reorganize those Rangers at hand and to see that none were left. A hasty check-up showed that the Company F men were nearly all there, but only a scattering of E and none from D. Lieutenant Arman figured that the Germans might have infiltrated between the highway and the Point, so sent one party over to the east and then into the Point across fields.[8]

Rudder believed that his force in the hedgerows had been pretty much destroyed in the fighting, and with less than ninety men in the positions around the battery site he decided to dig in and stay put until the men from OMAHA Beach did arrive. He was able to use naval gunfire to protect his positions, and some re-enforcements were landed on the afternoon of the 7th at the foot of the cliffs, along with food and ammunition. On 8 June friendly troops were spotted less than a thousand yards away and finally Rudder and his Ranger force were relieved after two days at Pointe du Hoc.

Walk 10: At Pointe du Hoc

STARTING POINT: Car park, Pointe du Hoc battlefield site

GPS: 49°23'39.0"N, 0°59'18.7"W

DURATION: 5.72km/3.6 miles

This is a short walk where most of your time will be spent at Pointe du Hoc itself. Park your vehicle in the car park, which is well signposted from the D514. Start your tour at the visitors' centre and then walk to the information panels that were installed in 2011. From here there is no set route around the site; you can follow the well-trodden pathways, go in all the bunkers, climb up onto the viewing platforms on top of the casemates and walk to the Observation Bunker, which was restored and re-opened in June 2011. For many years prior to this it was closed as the cliffs were collapsing in front of it; a multi-million dollar project organised by the American government has preserved the site and made it accessible in a way that has not been possible for some time. Although care must be taken at the edges, it is worth peeking down to get a sense of what an accomplishment it was for Rudder's Rangers to get up them on D-Day under fire from the Germans at the top.

When the site has been properly visited (allow at least ninety minutes), return to the car park and follow the access road back to the roundabout on the D514. Here **go left** and then take the **first right** onto a track going south from the D514. After about 300m, **stop**. This was where the Rangers dug in and held positions in the second half of D-Day with Fox Company on the left and Easy Company on the right, and Rudder's Command Post in the middle where the track is. An outpost was placed at the far end of the track.

From here **continue** and follow the track round to the right through to where it meets a minor road. **Turn right** and walk to a farm on the left. Here, take a track **opposite** and walk up for about 300m to where hedgerows can be seen left and right. This was the site where the German guns that should have been in the bunkers were discovered by a Ranger patrol and finally neutralised.

Return to the minor road and turn **right**. Follow the minor

POINTE DU HOC RANGER MEMORIAL

Right: Entrance to the renovated battlefield site.

Below: The bomb-scarred landscape is evident here.

Bottom: Rangers Memorial on the fire-control bunker.

road back to the D514. Here **go right** and stay on the left-hand side of the D514 (a busy road) to the roundabout and **turn left** back to the car park and your vehicle.

Pointe du Hoc today.

One of the gun casemates that proved empty on D-Day.

One of the guns that had been removed by the Germans and taken to a position inland where it was later put out of action by the Rangers.

Bocage lane leading to the Rangers' positions south of Pointe du Hoc.

UTAH BEACH WALK: THE 4TH INFANTRY AND 101ST (AIRBORNE) DIVISIONS ON D-DAY

HISTORICAL SECTION

UTAH Beach was the most western beachhead selected for the Overlord operations. The landings here by American troops were part of the wider plan to land in the Cotentin peninsula and advance on the port of Cherbourg; capturing it would give the Allies deep-water port facilities. The Atlantic Wall on the eastern side of this peninsula where the landings would take place was well defended, but an area around the dunes at Varreville was selected. The beaches here were sandy but solid, there was a low sea wall and some dunes, and while it was well defended, it was nothing outside the capabilities of the forces available for Overlord.

The German defenders were from a mixture of *Grenadier* and *Fusilier* battalions backed up with assault guns and engineers from two infantry divisions, and an airlanding division, supported by battalions from the *6. Fallschirmjäger Regiment* (Paratroops). Facing them in the landings were American infantry from 4th Division, backed up by armoured troops. Landing within the peninsula would be units from two American airborne divisions, 82nd and 101st, with the 101st Airborne landing nearest to UTAH Beach to secure the vital positions between Ste-Mère-Eglise and the coast.

The seaborne landings at UTAH Beach assembled off the French coast in the early hours of 6 June. Just out of range of German shore batteries, as the vessels gathered transport aircraft passed over carrying the airborne troops to their DZs. A little later at 0430 two troops from the 4th and 24th Cavalry Squadrons landed at the Îles St Marcouf to neutralise German positions there as it was feared they would interfere with the landings at UTAH.

Corporal Harvey S. Olsen and Private Thomas C. Killeran of Troop A, with Sergeant John S. Zanders and Corporal Melvin F. Kinzie of Troop B, each armed only with a knife, swam ashore to mark the beaches for the landing crafts. They became the first seaborne

American soldiers to land on French soil on D Day. As the troops dashed from their landing craft they were met with silence. The Germans had evacuated the islands but they did leave them heavily mined.[1]

Dawn arrived just before 0600 and in the next ten minutes more than 4,400 bombs rained down on the German defences at Tare Green and Uncle Red Beaches at Varreville where the troops were going to land. Later reports showed that this pre-H Hour bombardment had been quite effective, but a strange quirk of fate would mean that despite the damage done, the bombardment would not have any effect on the success or failure of the landings about to happen. The first troops approached the beach,

> *The first troops to reach shore were from the 2nd Battalion, 8th Infantry. The 1st Battalion landed a few minutes later. Both came ashore considerably south of the designated beaches. The 2nd Battalion should have hit Uncle Red Beach opposite Exit 3. The 1st Battalion was supposed to land directly opposite the strong point at les Dunes de Varreville. The landings, however, were made astride Exit 2 about 2,000 yards south.*
>
> *It is difficult to pinpoint the cause for this error. Both Red Beach control vessels had been lost, and one of the Green Beach control vessels had gone back to bring in the LCTs carrying DD amphibious tanks. Guiding the initial assault waves to the proper beaches was therefore the sole responsibility of one control vessel. The possibility of error was increased by the strong tidal current as well as by the beach drenching administered by naval fire support craft, which threw up a tremendous cloud of smoke, dust, and fine sand, obscuring the beach for many minutes just prior to and after the jump-off from the line of departure.*
>
> *Potentially this error was very serious, for it might have caused great confusion. In fact it did not. The original plans, in which each assault section had a specific mission, could not be carried out in detail, of course. Brig Gen Theodore Roosevelt, Jr., assistant commander of the 4th*

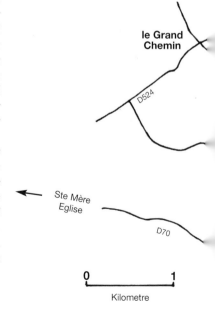

le Grand Chemin

D524

Ste Mère Eglise

D70

0   1
Kilometre

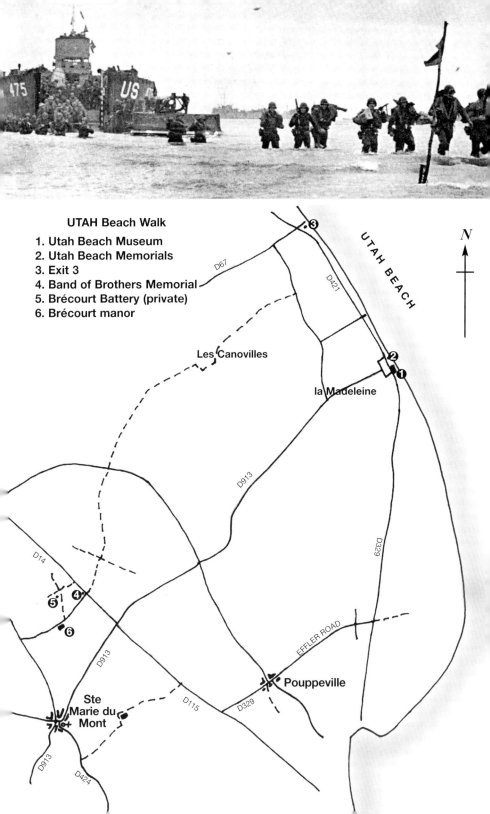

UTAH Beach Walk

1. Utah Beach Museum
2. Utah Beach Memorials
3. Exit 3
4. Band of Brothers Memorial
5. Brécourt Battery (private)
6. Brécourt manor

N

UTAH BEACH

D67

D421

③

Les Canovilles

la Madeleine

D913

D329

D14

④

⑤

⑥

EFFLER ROAD

D913

Pouppeville

D115

D329

Ste
Marie du
Mont

D913

D424

②

①

Division, had volunteered to coordinate the initial attack on the beach strong points until the arrival of the regimental commander, Colonel Van Fleet, and had landed with Company E. When it was realized that the landings had been made at the wrong place, he personally made a reconnaissance of the area immediately to the rear of the beach to locate the causeways which were to be used for the advance inland. He then returned to the point of landing, contacted the commanders of the two battalions, Lt Cols Conrad C. Simmons and Carlton O. MacNeely, and coordinated the attack on the enemy positions confronting them. These impromptu plans worked with complete success and little confusion. The errors in landing actually proved fortunate. Not only was the beach farther south less thickly obstructed, but the enemy shore defences were also less formidable than those opposite the intended landing beaches.[2]

Men from the 4th Division landing at Utah Beach.

With a successful landing and the defences breached, the work to clear the beach for the follow-up waves began, and was completed in an hour. More troops poured in, along with armour and supporting mortars and artillery. The units of 4th Division then began the task of reaching their D-Day objectives and gradually cleared the inland German defences, with one element of 8th Infantry making the first link-up with airborne troops at Pouppeville. These events were in complete contrast to those across the estuary at OMAHA Beach,

> *The relative ease with which the assault on UTAH Beach was accomplished was surprising even to the attackers, and gave the lie to the touted impregnability of the Atlantic Wall. The 4th Division's losses for D Day were astonishingly low. The 8th and 22nd Infantry Regiments, which landed before noon, suffered a total of 118 casualties on D Day, twelve of them fatalities. The division as a whole suffered only 197 casualties during the day, and these included sixty men missing through the loss (at sea) of part of Battery B, 29th Field Artillery Battalion. Not less noteworthy than the small losses was the speed of the landings. With the exception of one field artillery battalion (the 20th) the entire 4th Division had landed in the first fifteen hours . . . A total of over 20,000 troops and 1,700 vehicles reached UTAH Beach by the end of 6 June.*[3]

While the Task Force heading for UTAH Beach had been assembling, the men of 101st Airborne Division had already began the battle for the peninsula. Some 432 C47 transport aircraft carried 6,600 troops into Normandy in those early hours of 6 June. In addition, gliders would bring in men from Glider Infantry and some of the heavier equipment. The 101st Airborne's D-Day drop was less than successful, however,

> *Paratroop echelons approached the Cotentin from the west and made their landfall in the vicinity of les Pieux . . . Formations were tight until reaching the coast, but from the coast to the Merderet cloud banks loosened the formations, and east of the Merderet flak scattered them further. In general the division did not have a good drop . . . About 1,500 troops were either killed or captured and approximately 60 percent of the equipment dropped was lost when the bundles fell into swamps or into fields covered by enemy fire. Only a fraction of the division's organized strength could initially be employed on the planned missions, and many of the missions carried out were undertaken by mixed groups which did not correspond with original assignments.*[4]

The beach secure, the follow-up waves arrive.

One of the great tragedies was that many airborne troops were mistakenly dropped into the sea, or the nearby estuary or into flooded areas. Just a few inches of water for a heavily laden airborne soldier meant certain death, and many disappeared into the marshes and flooded zones. The 101st Airborne's D-Day, therefore, became a series of scattered battles rather than one coherent one. With small group of airborne men scattered far and wide, often without leaders, it is a testimony to their training and bravery that so many attempted to put into operation tasks they had trained for prior to the drop.

One objective that had initially missed the attention of airborne troops was the German gun battery located in the hedgerows close to a large farm complex known as Brécourt Manor. There was mixed information on the battery, and what type of guns were firing from it, but on D-Day guns were known to be firing from positions here onto the landings at UTAH Beach. Survivors of Easy Company, 2nd Bn 506th PIR were given the task of silencing it. The company had lost its commander in the drop and was now led by 26-year-old Richard 'Dick' Winters, a former college student from Pennsylvania. Winters only had a handful of men at his disposal, and most accounts put it at around thirteen airborne troopers. But he quickly formulated a plan and went in.

Winters positioned two .30 calibre machine guns to cover the attack and coming in from the north-east, he led his team down the hedgerow from gun pit to gun pit. The attack surprised the gunners, but they had their own machine gun teams close by and these soon opened fire. However, Winters' men quickly overwhelmed the first three guns and destroyed them with explosives before ten re-enforcements arrived from Dog Company and took on the final gun. By this time, enemy fire had increased and Winters took his party out. Casualties in his own company had been one man killed and one wounded, with two dead and one wounded from Dog Company. The Brécourt Manor Gun Battery had been silenced.

For Winters this was one of several actions on D-Day and in subsequent days in Normandy. It was a small-unit action that does not feature in the American official history, despite the fact that Winters was interviewed about it after the war. However, he appears to have downplayed the whole event, which could explain it. At the time the bravery and initiative of the men involved was indeed recognised as Dick Winters was awarded a Distinguished Service Cross, and three men the Silver Star, nine the Bronze Star and three the Purple Heart. Almost seventy years later, it is arguably the most famous American airborne action of D-Day and the tactics used by Winters and his men are still studied at West Point to this day.

For the 101st Airborne,

a hard fight had been fought on D Day . . . a fight that had not gone entirely according to plan and had cost heavy casualties. Not one

Airborne supply drop near Ste Marie du Mont.

battle but fifteen or twenty separate engagements had been fought . . . Initial dispersion was further aggravated by the Normandy terrain; the hedgerows made it difficult to assemble and still more difficult to coordinate the manoeuvre of units. Some units were completely unaware of others, fighting only a few hundred yards away. The groups were usually mixed, and men strangers to their leaders fought for objectives to which they had not been assigned. Still, the airborne operation was in general a success. Small groups of parachutists took advantage of a surprised and temporarily disorganized enemy to seize many of the vital objectives quickly.

When D Day ended, the 101st Airborne Division had accomplished the most important of its initial missions. General Taylor had estimated at noontime that, despite the errors of the drop, the tactical situation of his division was sound. The way had been cleared for the movement of the seaborne forces inland . . . Yet here, as elsewhere on D Day, the weakness of the American forces was more than offset by the almost total lack of aggressiveness on the part of the enemy. Positions which tactically should have required battalions for defence could be and were held by small improvised forces which had to worry more about cover from artillery and mortar fire than about counterattack. Probably the weakest feature of the whole situation at the close of D Day was the lack of communication. This had plagued the activities of most of the battalions during the day. At night, though it was only the southern forces that remained out of contact, the southern flank was precisely the most seriously threatened portion of the division sector . . . Of the 6,600 men of the 101st Division dropped on the morning of D Day, only 2,500 men were working together at the end of the day.[5]

Walk 11: In the UTAH Beach Area

STARTING POINT: Car park in front of UTAH Beach Museum

GPS: 49°24′54.0″N, 1°10′31.1″W

DURATION: 17.1km/10.6 miles

Although the area where the landings on UTAH Beach was small, the ground over which 101st Airborne operated on D-Day was wide, and as such this walk covers the ground around the beachhead and focuses on the 101st Airborne around Ste-Marie-du-Mont.

Start the walk at the excellent UTAH Beach Museum

The Utah Beach Museum.

(www.utah-beach.com). This museum re-opened in June 2011 with new displays telling the story of American troops in the landings and the role of the airborne. At least ninety minutes should be put aside for the museum before walking down onto the beach and seeing where the troops landed before walking up onto the sand dunes where the memorials are located. There are memorials to the 4th Division, the 90th Division (who landed in the D-Day follow-up) and a more recent one to the

Beach defences are still visible at Utah Beach.

American Navy. At low tide it is possible to walk along the shoreline, but it is easier to go from the memorials and a minor road that runs parallel to the sea. Stay on this until it meets a major road junction with sand dunes ahead. **Stop**.

This is the start of Exit 3 just north of the original Tare Green where the landings should have taken place on D-Day. This was the site marked 'Dunes de Varreville' on the D-Day intelligence maps and the bunkers ahead were part of WN-106, sometimes also called WN-7. This consisted of bunkers, two 50mm guns, one 47mm and a field gun in a bunker; traces of the bunkers can be explored in the dunes. The site was captured by men from 4th Division but close to it Lieutenant Colonel Robert Cole of 502nd PIR led a bayonet charge on D-Day, inflicting seventy-five casualties on the Germans in this area.

At the junction **go left** onto Exit 3, named Blair Road after Private First Class J. Blair, who died here on 10 June 1944 while serving with a Quartermaster unit. Follow this for a short way and then take the **first left** onto another minor road. On this road take the **first right** onto a track (marked on some maps as Le Grand Hard) which you follow across the fields until it meets a minor road. Here go **straight across** and continue straight ahead until this route meets the D14 at Le Grand Chemin. **Walk across** to the memorial overlooking a field on the other side of the road. **Stop**.

This is a memorial to the Easy Company attack on the Brécourt Manor Gun Battery. The gun site was across the field behind the tree line and Richard Winters' attack came in from your right towards the tree line. After D-Day an American hospital was later set up in this field. The field cannot be entered and respect for private property should be shown.

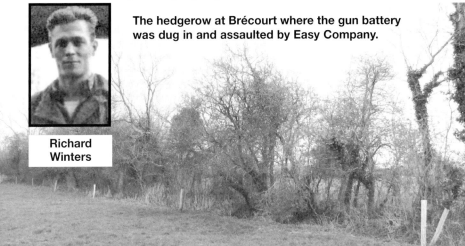

The hedgerow at Brécourt where the gun battery was dug in and assaulted by Easy Company.

Richard Winters

The Band of Brothers Memorial at Brécourt.

The distinctive church at Ste Marie du Mont.

The 'Liberty Way' marker at Ste Marie du Mont. Men from Easy Company were photographed here on D-Day. The First World War Poilu statue behind had been removed during the war.

Continue along the minor road to the left of the memorial signposted to Brécourt. Further up on the left a large Normandy stone farm complex can be seen. These are the buildings known as Brécourt Manor and the gun battery site was to the right, on the other side of the hedgerows. This is a working farm and a family home, and private property and this should be respected at all times.

Continue on this road past the farm and at the next junction **turn left** onto the D424 and follow it into Ste-Marie-du-Mont. Ste-Marie-du-Mont was the first major village inland from UTAH and prior to D-Day the Germans had troops based here and an OP in the church tower, which was linked to gun sites nearby, including Brécourt, by fixed telephone line as well as radio. Around the village more than 400 aircraft dropped the men from 101st Airborne in the early hours of D-Day and many small-unit actions were fought in the fields and hedgerows here. It was eventually liberated by men from the 501st and 506th PIR on D-Day. Today, the village has a number of cafés and shops, and also two good museums. One tells the story of the American operations here in 1944 and the other looks at the subject of the occupation of Normandy. The church is also open and worth exploring; bullet impact marks are noticeable in several places and on certain days the church tower is open allowing excellent views across the battlefields.

From the main square take the road to the south-east, Rue du Thouays. Follow this out of the village to the first junction and then **go left** onto Rue du Mont. Follow this through an area where a retirement home is located and continue to where it meets the D115. **Go right** and then **first left** onto the D329 and follow this into Pouppeville. The village of Pouppeville was where the 2nd Bn 8th Infantry Regiment met with men from the 3rd Bn 501st PIR, marking the first link-up between seaborne and airborne troops in the American sector on D-Day.

Continue through the village. You are now on Effler Road, and will see the road memorial on the right; it is named after Private First Class A.A. Effler. Effler was a nineteen-year-old from North Carolina who served with 531 Engineer Shore Regiment and died at UTAH Beach on 14 June 1944. Continue and go **straight across** at the first junction and then **left** at the second onto MacGowan Road, Rue Ferme du Mur. Private First Class W.E. MacGowan served with the 531st Engineer Shore

Regiment and died near here on D-Day, 6 June 1944. This later becomes Ham Road which is named after Private Otis A. Ham, a Mississippi man who served with the same unit as MacGowan. He was mortally wounded here and later died in the UK on 10 June. He is buried at Cambridge American Cemetery. **Follow** this route back to the UTAH Beach Museum and your vehicle.

The lanes around Utah Beach were named after men who died in the area and today these are perpetuated with permanent markers.

Area Twelve

AIRBORNE WALK: STE-MÈRE-EGLISE–LA FIÈRE – 82ND AIRBORNE ACTIONS ON D-DAY

The American 82nd Airborne Division on D-Day was tasked with dropping in the area west of Ste-Mère-Eglise. This veteran unit had fought in Sicily and Italy and on 6 June its major task was to secure the bridges and routes running west to east towards Ste-Mère-Eglise. This area had been flooded by the Germans to restrict the Allied ability to land gliders and airborne troops, and limit any invader using set roads and bridges. The Germans planned to control events by holding these bridges, but on D-Day things did not go quite to plan, for all concerned.

Eisenhower talking to American airborne personnel before the D-Day drop.

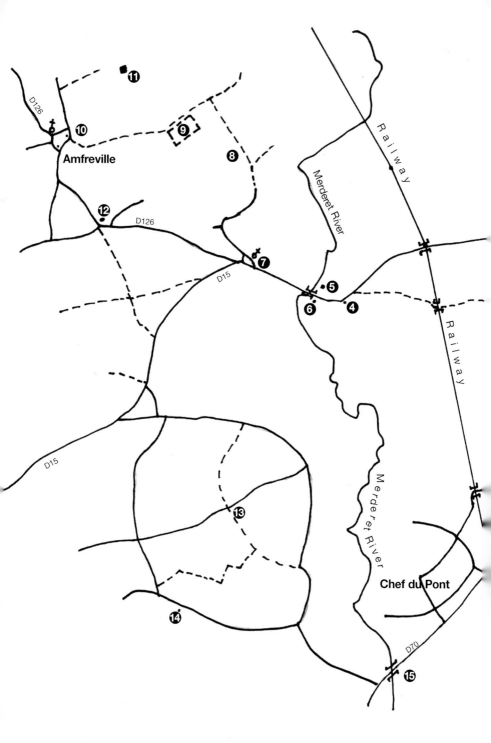

Amfreville

Chef du Pont

Merderet River

Merderet River

Railway

Railway

D126

D126

D15

D15

D70

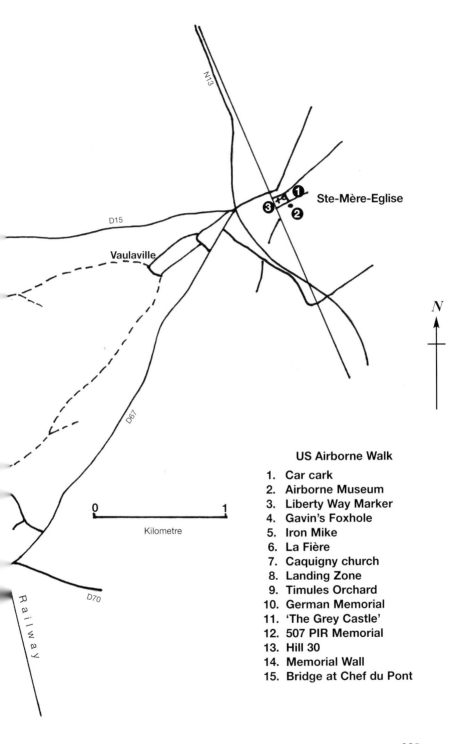

Ste-Mère-Eglise

US Airborne Walk

1. Car cark
2. Airborne Museum
3. Liberty Way Marker
4. Gavin's Foxhole
5. Iron Mike
6. La Fière
7. Caquigny church
8. Landing Zone
9. Timules Orchard
10. German Memorial
11. 'The Grey Castle'
12. 507 PIR Memorial
13. Hill 30
14. Memorial Wall
15. Bridge at Chef du Pont

For a number of reasons, the night drop of 5/6 June went badly wrong for the majority of the American airborne troops and men and units were scattered right across the landscape around Ste-Mère-Eglise. This certainly was the case west of Ste-Mère-Eglise, where the units charged with taking and holding the vital bridge leading to the causeway at La Fière dropped over a very wide area. But faithful to their training, many men were able to work out where they had landed, and estimate a route to their objective.

> By the middle of the morning 500 to 600 men of miscellaneous units had gathered at la Fière, which was one of the two known crossings of the Merderet in the 82nd Airborne Division zone. The la Fière crossing was an exposed narrow causeway raised a few feet above the river flats and extending 400 to 500 yards from the bridge over the main river channel to the gently rising hedgerow country of the west shore.
>
> Two of the first groups on the scene, portions of Company A of the 505th and a group mostly of the 507th Parachute Infantry under Lt. John H. Wisner, had tried to rush the bridge in the early morning but were repulsed by machine gun fire. When General Gavin arrived, he decided to split the la Fière force and sent seventy-five men south to reconnoitre another crossing. Later, receiving word that the bridge at Chef-du-Pont was undefended, he took another seventy-five men himself to try to get across there. The groups remaining at la Fière made no progress for several hours. Then General Ridgway, who had landed by parachute with the 505th, ordered Col. Roy Lindquist, the commanding officer of the 508th Parachute Infantry, to organize the miscellaneous groups and take the bridge.[1]

By the close of D-Day the position was in American hands, and while efforts had been made to get across the causeway and link up with those west of the flooded area, these had been repulsed. The men dug in and expected a counter-attack. They did not have long to wait as on 7 June the Germans made their move.

> While the 82nd Airborne Division had thus consolidated its base, its principal D Day assignment – the establishing of bridgeheads across the Merderet – came no nearer accomplishment. On the contrary, during the morning of 7 June it was touch and go whether a determined enemy counterattack might not break the division's hold on the east bank of the river. At about 0800 the attack of elements of

Aerial view of La Fière causeway. (US National Archives)

*the enemy 1057th Regiment began to form against the American la
Fière position. Mortar and machine gun fire ranged in, chiefly on
Company A, 505th Parachute Infantry, which was dug in to the
right of the bridge. An hour or so later four Renault tanks led a
German infantry advance across the bridge. The lead tank was
disabled by either bazooka fire or a shell from a 57mm. anti-tank gun
that was supporting Company A. Although this checked the
advance, the German infantry took advantage of the cover furnished
by the knocked-out tank and some burned-out vehicles, which the
American defenders had pulled onto the causeway during the night,
to open a critical fire fight at close range. At the same time German
mortar shells fell in increasing numbers among Company A's
foxholes. The American platoon immediately to the right of the
bridge was especially hard hit and eventually reduced to but fifteen
men. These men, however, encouraged by the heroic leadership of
Sgt. William D. Owens and by the presence in the thick of the
fighting of division officers, including General Ridgway, held their
line. The fight was halted at last by a German request for a half-
hour's truce to remove the wounded. When the half hour expired, the
enemy did not return to the attack. A count of Company A revealed
that almost half of its combat effectives had fallen in the defence,
either killed or seriously wounded.*[2]

The business end of the defence of the bridge against this
armoured attack had been the responsibility of two bazooka
teams which were dug in either side of the eastern part of the
bridge. In one of the positions to the left of the road was Marcus
Heim of 505th PIR.

*When we arrived at the bridge, men were placed down the pathway
to the right and to the left of the Manor House and out buildings.*

241

The four bazooka men included: Lenold Peterson, and myself, John Bolderson and Gordon Pryne. Peterson and I took up positions on the Manor House side facing Cauquigny, below the driveway. There was a concrete telephone pole just in front of us and we dug in behind it. We knew that when the Germans started the attack with their tanks, we would have to get out of our foxhole and reveal our position to get a better view of the tanks. Bolderson and Pryne were on the right side of the road just below the pathway. I do not remember how many paratroopers were around us, all I saw was a machine gun set up in the Manor House yard. On the right side down the pathway a few riflemen took up positions.

There was a 57mm cannon up the road in back of us along with

One of the captured French tanks used by the Germans, knocked out on the causeway. (US National Archives)

another machine gun. We carried anti-tank mines and bazooka rockets from the landing area. These mines were placed across the causeway about fifty or sixty feet on the other side of the bridge. There was a broken down German truck by the Manor House, which we pushed and dragged across the bridge and placed it across the causeway. All that afternoon the Germans kept shelling our position, and the rumour was that the Germans were going to counter attack. Around 5:00 in the afternoon the Germans started the attack. Two tanks with infantry on each side and in the rear following them was a third tank with more infantry following it. As the lead tank started around the curve in the road the tank commander stood up in the turret to take a look and from our left the machine gun let loose a burst and killed the commander. At the same time the bazookas, 57mm and everything else we had were firing at the Germans and they in turn were shooting at us with cannons, mortars, machine guns and rifle fire. Lenold Peterson and I (the loader), in the forward position got out of the foxhole and stood behind the telephone pole so we could get a better shot at the tanks. We had to hold our fire until the last minute because some of the tree branches along the causeway were blocking our view. The first tank was hit and started to turn sideways and at the same time was swinging the turret around and firing at us. We had just moved forward around the cement telephone pole when a German shell hit it and we had to jump out of the way to avoid being hit as it was falling. I was hoping that Bolderson and Pryne were also firing at the tanks for with all that was happening in front of us there was not time to look around to see what others were doing. We kept firing at the first tank until it was put out of action and on fire. The second tank came up and pushed the first tank out of the way. We moved forward toward the second tank and fired at it as fast as I could load the rockets in the bazooka. We kept firing at the second tank and we hit it in the turret where it is connected to the body, also in the track and with another hit it also went up in flames. Peterson and I were almost out of rockets, and the third tank was still moving. Peterson asked me to go back across the road and see if Bolderson had any extra rockets. I ran across the road and with all the crossfire I still find it hard to believe I made it to the other side in one piece. When I got to the other side I found one dead soldier and Bolderson and Pryne were gone. Their bazooka was lying on the ground and it was damaged by what I thought were bullet holes. Not finding Bolderson or Pryne I presumed that either one or both were injured. I found the rockets they left and then had to return across the road to where I left Peterson. The Germans were still firing at us and I was lucky again,

I returned without being hit. Peterson and I put the new found rockets to use on the third tank. After that one was put out of action the Germans pulled back to Cauquigny and continued shelling us for the rest of the night. They also tried two other counter attacks on our position, which also failed.

During the battles, one does not have time to look around to see how others are doing. We were told that when we took up our position by the bridge that we have to hold it at all cost until the men from the beach arrived, for if the Germans broke through they would have a good chance of going all the way to the beach. Our job was to be in the forward position by the La Fière Bridge with our bazooka to stop any German tanks from advancing over the bridge and onto Ste Mere-Eglise and the beaches. This we accomplished all the while the Germans were continuously firing everything they had at us. After I went across the road and found more rockets for the bazooka and returned, the third tank was put out of action and the Germans retreated. When the Germans pulled back, we looked around did not see anyone, we than moved back to our foxhole. Looking back up the road toward Ste Mere-Eglise, we saw that the 57mm cannon and the machine gun were destroyed. Looking down the pathway across from the Manor House we could not see any of our men. We were thinking that we were all alone and that maybe we should move from here, then someone came and told us to hold our position and he would find more men to place around us for the Germans may try again to breach our lines. We found out later, of the few that were holding the bridge at this time, most were either killed or wounded. Why we were not injured or killed only the good Lord knows.[3]

The bridge had held and would remain held until the relieving troops arrived from UTAH Beach on 9 June and the final attack across the causeway was made.

While the fight for the bridge was going on, across the marshes – unknown to Heim and his comrades – was a group of men from the 82nd surrounded in an orchard. Lieutenant Colonel Charles Timmes, 2nd Bn 507th PIR, had dropped in and like many that night, found that his men had been widely scattered. He gathered up those he could find, and sent some probing attacks towards Amfreville, close to where he had landed. This proved to be too strongly held for his force so he withdrew them to a position he could defend, a nearby orchard, linked up with men from 508th PIR and dug in. With no radio communications – none of his radios had survived the drop – he was unable to ascertain what was happening elsewhere, so he sent patrols out. One of these under First Lieutenant Levy got to the causeway between Cauquigny and La Fière. While they initially found it clear, they were forced back as the Germans arrived and so Timmes decided to hang on with around 150 men, machine guns and a 57mm gun. Over the course of the next few days his men beat off attack after attack; at once stage they were outnumbered by at least four to one. On 8 June an attack by men of the 325th Glider Infantry Regiment between Timmes' position and the chateau to the north known as

Colonel Charles Timmes.

'The Grey Castle' broke down, and the survivors withdrew into Timmes' position. They held out until late the following day when the battle of the La Fière causeway was over and men from the other side of the marshes finally linked up with these isolated airborne troops.

Further to the south-west another isolated group of 82nd men were in a bitter struggle to hold on to the high ground at Hill 30,

Elements of the 508th, amounting to about two companies of men under command of Lt. Col. Thomas J. B. Shanley, commanding officer of the 2nd Battalion, were the most important of at least four groups of paratroopers who assembled west of the Merderet but who for the most part, being forced to fight for survival, could contribute little toward carrying out planned missions. Dropped near Picauville, Colonel Shanley gathered a small force of paratroopers – too small to proceed with his mission of destroying the Douve bridge at Pont l'Abbé. He tried during the day to join other groups in the vicinity with whom he had radio contact, but under constant enemy pressure he was unable to effect a junction until late in the day. It had then become apparent to him that he was engaged with an enemy force of at least battalion strength, and he decided to withdraw to the battalion assembly area on Hill 30. In fact, the Germans, elements of the 1057. Regiment, had been pushing eastward in this area most of the day under orders to counterattack

245

in order to wipe out American parachutists west of the Merderet. Colonel Shanley's resistance undoubtedly helped save the forces at la Fière and Chef-du-Pont. Once he was firmly established on Hill 30, he formed a valuable outpost against continuing German attacks and a few days later would be in position to contribute substantially to establishing the Merderet bridgehead. For Colonel Shanley's success three enlisted men have received a large share of the credit. They were Cpl. Ernest T. Roberts, Pvt. Otto K. Zwingman, and Pvt. John A. Lockwood who, while on outpost duty in buildings at Haut Gueutteville, observed the forming of a German counterattack by an estimated battalion of infantry with tank support. They stayed at their posts holding off the enemy attack for two hours and allowing the main body of Shanley's force to establish an all-around defence at Hill 30.[4]

Thomas Shanley was a regular army officer who had transferred to the airborne on its formation. He had fought with the unit in Sicily and Italy and used his men here in a model example of a defensive action. In the end they held on for three days. The whole regiment was recognised with a unit citation which read,

The 508th Parachute Infantry is cited for outstanding performance of duty in action against the enemy between 6 and 9 June 1944 during the invasion of France. The Regiment landed by parachute shortly after 0200 hours, 6 June 1944. Intense anti-aircraft and machine-gun fire was directed against the approaching planes and parachutist drops. Enemy mobile anti airborne landing groups immediately engaged assembled elements of the Regiment and reinforced their opposition with heavily supported reserve units. Elements of the Regiment seized Hill 30, in the wedge between the Merderet and Douve Rivers, and fought vastly superior enemy forces for three days. From this position, they continually threatened German units moving in from the west, as well as the enemy forces opposing the crossing of our troops over the Merderet near La Fière and Chef du Pont. They likewise denied the enemy opportunities to throw reinforcements to the east where they could oppose the beach landings – the courage and devotion to duty shown by members of the 508th Parachute Infantry are worthy of emulation and reflect the highest traditions of the Army of the United States.[5]

While these are just three examples of what men of 82nd Airborne did on D-Day, they give a good flavour of how a scattered unit fought small but cohesive battles in the key areas where they knew the vital objectives were. These small-unit actions also testify to the character and bravery of these airborne troops, cut off from the big picture but determined to hold on until relieved.

Walk 12: In the Airborne Area

STARTING POINT: Car park, in front of the church at Ste-Mère-Eglise

GPS: 49°24'30.6"N, 1°18'57.8"W

DURATION: 20.1km/12.5 miles

This is a full-day walk and as there are few bars or cafés in this area you are advised to take a packed lunch with you. There are plenty of places in Ste-Mère-Eglise to get food, including a couple of sandwich bars. Park your vehicle in the car park next to the church in the centre of Ste-Mère-Eglise. Start your visit at the church.

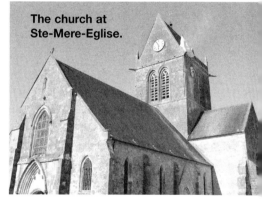

The church at Ste-Mere-Eglise.

The church at Ste-Mère-Eglise largely became famous following *The Longest Day* film in the 1960s. During the airborne drop in the early hours of D-Day some of the buildings in the square were damaged and caught fire. The local populace had been mustered and under the eyes of the German occupiers were putting the fire out. At this point men from 82nd Airborne were mistakenly dropped into the town. At least one man fell into the fire and perished, his explosive charges detonating in the heat. Others were cut down as they dropped into the square and while the image of airborne troops hanging dead from the lamp posts in the town was a little overplayed in the film, it certainly happened. One man, Private John Steele, became entangled on the church spire. He had to feign death when the Germans spotted him and opened fire. Steele was a thirty-one-year-old barber from Illinois who had dropped into Normandy with the 505th PIR. He was later brought down from the church tower and was captured and held by the Germans until his unit took Ste-Mère-Eglise later in the day, when he was released. He returned to Normandy in later years and became quite famous following his story being told in the film. The town placed a life-size model of Steele on the church tower, still hanging by a parachute, which can be seen for many miles around. Inside the church there are stained glass windows commemorating the airborne troops on D-Day and a commemorative service is held here each year.

The Airborne Museum close to the main square is also worth visiting before you start the walk. It has many large exhibits relating to the fighting around Ste-Mère-Eglise, much of the personal material donated by veterans. The museum is open every day and more information is available on their website (www.airborne-museum.org).

From the church walk across the square into Rue General de Gaulle and **turn right**. On your right is a Normandy memorial and a 0km marker which indicates the start of this section of the 'Liberty Way', running from Normandy to the Ardennes. This route is marked by similar stones along its length. At the next main junction **go left** onto the D16, Rue de Verdun. Follow this out of the town and where the road forks beyond the bridge **go right** onto the D15. Then take the **next left** onto Chemin d'Hiersac and follow this past the houses out in the countryside. At the next main junction of this minor road **go right** and follow it roughly westwards towards the railway line. Walking in this area will give you a good sense of the nature of the terrain the men of 82nd Airborne dropped into on D-Day. **Go over** the railway bridge and follow the next stretch of the minor road to the D15. At this junction **go left**. Almost immediately on your left is a chained-off hole. **Stop**. This is General Gavin's Foxhole. Brigadier General James 'Slim Jim' Gavin was Deputy Commander of the 82nd Airborne and had parachuted in during the early hours of D-Day in the area west of Ste-Mère-Eglise. Coming across the marshes he had found men dug in on their objective near the bridge at La Fière and set up his command post on this spot. Whether this is his actual foxhole is hard to say, but it certainly is in an area where he operated; right in the midst of battle, commanding his men from the front.

Continue along the D15 to the bridge area at La Fière. This is the area where a bitter struggle took place on D-Day and the following days as this vital site was first captured and then held by men of 82nd Airborne. Numerous decorations were awarded for bravery, and the road at the bridge is now named after Marcus Heim, in recognition of his bravery here in 1944. Today, the La Fière site is dominated by the fine bronze sculpture, 'Iron Mike', which looks out across the bridge and battlefield where so many fought and fell. There is also a very good orientation table next to the statue, which visually explains what took place here on D-Day. Across the road is the La Fière Battlefield B&B where the owners always welcome visitors and you can buy books and postcards.

From the bridge **go straight across** on the D15 and across the road that was the causeway in 1944 where the German column and tanks were knocked out. This is a busy road, so stay left on the verge. On the far side take the **first right**. There is an information panel immediately on your right, and after looking at this walk to the church. The Cauquigny church remained in no-man's-land' on D-Day, and it is known the Germans used the wall here as cover to fire

Iron Mike Memorial at La Fière.

The La Fière Battlefield B&B, a building that featured in the fighting here in June 1944.

The bridge at the start of the La Fière causeway.

on the airborne troops across the flooded marshes where the green fields are now. On 8 June a group from 325th Glider Infantry Regiment tried to get through here but were thrown back by the Germans. The next day a second attack came in from glider troops under Captain John Sauls and troops from 507th PIR under Captain Robert Rae. This attack started from La Fière and became the battle of the causeway. Supported by tanks that had come up from UTAH, the men struggled to get across the narrow road and into the area of the church. As the attack seemed to falter, Rae led ninety men in a rush across the causeway and with tank support overran the Germans and the position was taken. The causeway was now free for traffic and men to cross unhindered by German fire. Both Sauls and Rae were decorated for their bravery here on 9 June, and there is a memorial on the church to those who fought here along with one glider veteran who regularly returned to the area.

Cauquigny church.

From the church continue on the minor road in front

250

(Rue du Hameau aux Brix) and at the next junction **go right**. The farm buildings here give a good picture of the sort of structures in this area that both sides used in the fighting here in 1944. **Continue** past the houses and follow the minor road out in the fields. This area has gates that need to be opened and closed (cattle are in the area), but it is a recognised walking route so none of the gates will be locked. The area of fields you will walk though now was where many of the 82nd Airborne gliders landed on D-Day. This being soft ground, in the autumn and winter the marks made where gliders came in are often visible. Continue along the track until you reach a T-junction. Here **go left**, through another gate, and into a *bocage* sunken lane. Further up on the left is a memorial. **Stop**.

This memorial site commemorates the battle for Timmes Orchard. Colonel Charles Timmes held on here in the orchard from D-Day until 9 June with a mixed force of men from 325th GIR, and 507th and 508th PIRs until they linked up with other units from 82nd Airborne following the battle for La Fière causeway. From the memorial **continue along** the track and follow it into the outskirts of Amfreville. Here the track joins Rue de la Rosiere. A plaque on a building on the left indicates

Timmes Orchard Memorial.

this barn was used by the Germans as a field hospital in June 1944, with a tented hospital opposite where German nurses worked. It treated both Americans and Germans wounded on D-Day and in the period that followed.

Turn right here and at the next junction **stop**. The tree-lined road ahead is a private road to what the airborne troops called 'The Grey Castle', a chateau visible across the fields. Many of the German attacks came from here and this area was controlled by them for several days following the landings. The building on your right was used to interrogate prisoners and a plaque on the wall remembers one of them, First Lieutenant Walter Chris Heisler of 507th PIR.

Here **go left** and follow the road to the church. The Germans used the tower of this church as an OP until directed naval gunfire brought it down on 8 June. The shell came from an American battleship anchored off UTAH Beach. At the church **go left** onto the D126 and follow it out of the village to the 507th PIR Memorial site in Rue du Moulin. This commemorates the men of this unit, widely scattered on D-Day, who fought in a number of engagements here on 6 June and the following days. The unit lost more than 300 dead in Normandy.

From the memorial **go right** on the D130, Rue des Helpiquets, and immediately **turn left** onto a track in front of a Norman farm complex. Follow this track, going **straight across** at the first junction until it reaches the D15. Again, this route gives you an insight into the terrain and how it could be used by both sides for ambushes and defence. At the main road **turn right** and then take the **first left** into Gueutteville. On this road **go left** and then **first right** and then **left**. Follow this minor road out of Gueutteville and then take the first track on the **right**. This then leads to a crossroads of tracks at the summit of Hill 30. **Stop**.

Hill 30 is high ground, but looking around this area the close nature of the terrain with tree-lined sunken lanes and *bocage* hedgerows indicates what a defenders' paradise it is. This is where

507 PIR Memorial at Amfreville.

Lieutenant Colonel Shanley and his men of 508th PIR held out against attack after attack until relieved. A road sign is all that marks this part of the battlefield today.

Memorial plaque at the crossroads on Hill 30.

From the junction follow the minor road south-west (going **right** from where you emerged from the tree-lined track), at the next junction **go left** and at the end **left** again into a small hamlet. Continue and further up on the right is a fascinating decorated memorial wall made by a local to the men from 82nd Airborne who fought in this area. After the hamlet, take the **first right** and follow this road to the D70. Here **go left** to the road bridge. Just beyond it is a memorial. **Stop**.

This bridge at Chef du Pont was just as important as the bridge guarding the causeway at La Fière. The ground beyond the river was flooded in 1944, and the road you have just walked down from the hamlet was a causeway, as in the other location. Men from the 508th PIR took the eastern side of the bridge on D-Day,

the attempt to cross at Chef-du-Pont about two miles south had reached a temporary deadlock, as a relatively small number of Germans dug in along the causeway tenaciously resisted all efforts

Memorial wall near Hill 30.

to dislodge them. Late in the afternoon, after most of the paratroopers had been recalled to strengthen the la Fière position, the under-strength platoon left at Chef-du-Pont under Capt. Roy E. Creek was threatened with annihilation by an enemy counterattack. Under heavy direct fire from a field piece on the opposite bank and threatened by German infantry forming for attack on the south, Creek's position seemed desperate. At that moment a glider bearing an antitank gun landed fortuitously in the area. With this gun the enemy was held off while about a hundred paratroopers, in response to Creek's plea for reinforcements, came down from la Fière. The reinforcements gave Creek strength enough to beat off the Germans, clear the east bank, and finally cross the river and dig in. This position, however, did not amount to a bridgehead and Creek's tenuous hold on the west end of the causeway would have meant little but for the action of the 508th Parachute Infantry west of the river.[6]

That action was the fight for the ground around Hill 30, visited earlier in the walk.

From the bridge **continue** into Chef du Pont and take the **first left** onto Rue de la Cooperative. Take the **second right** down a tree-lined minor road and at the end follow this route round to the right past a farm complex. Follow this through the countryside and past some houses on the right to where it runs parallel to the railway line. **Cross over** the railway on the bridge and on the other side take the **left fork**. Stay on this as it weaves through the *bocage*. At the first junction **go left** and stay on this minor road – keep on going at every junction – until you reach a farm complex on your left. Here take Chemin de Vaulaville and continue to the D15. **Go right** and then **left** and follow the D15 back into the centre of Ste-Mère-Eglise and the car park in front of the church, and your vehicle.

A good follow-up visit to this walk is the Dead Man's Corner Museum (www.paratrooper-museum.org) at nearby Ste Comte du Mont. It houses an unrivalled collection of American airborne uniforms and equipment.

APPENDIX

D-DAY CEMETERIES IN NORMANDY

This section details information on military cemeteries with a D-Day connection not mentioned in the main text. For the British cemeteries only those with a significant number of D-Day burials or a D-Day connection are listed.

BAYEUX WAR CEMETERY

Burials: British 3,935, Canadian 181, Australian 17, New Zealand 8, South African 1, Polish 25, France 3, Czech 2, Italian 2, Russian 7, German 466, unidentified 1.

Location: The cemetery lies on the south-west side of the main ring road around the city of Bayeux. It is about 100m from the junction with the D5 to Littry, and almost opposite the Museum of the Battle of Normandy, which is well signposted throughout the Bayeux area.

Bayeux was entered by British patrols on 6 June 1944, but was formally liberated the next day. Charles de Gaulle established his first seat of government here until Paris was liberated, and it became the main staging post for the British Army in Normandy with supply depots, medical facilities and rest centres. The streets of Bayeux were too narrow for most

Burying the dead at Bayeux, 1945.

military vehicles, and so in June 1944 the Royal Engineers and Pioneer Corps constructed a ring road round Bayeux to make the flow of traffic more smooth; the ring road is still in use seventy years later, although it is now maintained by the French authorities!

Bayeux War Cemetery is the largest British military cemetery of the Second World War in France; the original graves here were of soldiers who died of wounds in the military hospitals at Bayeux. Both during and after the Second World War graves were moved in from all over the Normandy battlefields, as the Graves Registration Units headquarters were here and they had active teams searching the Normandy battlefield for isolated burials, and later they closed and moved many small battlefield cemeteries.

As the largest British cemetery in Normandy, Bayeux gives a good cross section of the sort of men and units that took part in operations on D-Day and later. Every day of the Normandy campaign from 6 June to the breakout is represented on the graves. Every rank from brigadier downwards is in evidence; aside from the brigadier there are eleven colonels, giving an indication of the heavy losses sustained in senior officers in Normandy. With so many graves, and so many names and stories, it is difficult to select some, but for those who like to know a little of the men buried in a huge city of the dead like Bayeux the following serve as some good examples.

Bayeux War Cemetery, 1946. (Ken Smith)

Senior Officer: Brigadier John Cecil Currie was a regular soldier whose career had started in the First World War. He had been commissioned in the Royal Artillery in 1914, served on the Western Front, been decorated with the Military Cross and post-war served in Iraq. He commanded armoured troops in Persia and later played a heroic part in the battle of El Alamein and commanded 4th Armoured Brigade in Normandy until he was killed by shell fire on 26 June 1944.

Normandy VC: Corporal Sidney Bates VC was serving with the Norfolks when he took part in action at Sourdeval in August 1944, which resulted in the posthumous award of the Victoria Cross. From Camberwell, in London, Bates was badly wounded in the action, dying of his wounds the next day. His citation reads:

> *In North-West Europe on 6th August, 1944, the position held by a battalion of the Royal Norfolk Regiment near Sourdeval was heavily attacked. Corporal Bates was commanding a forward section of the left forward company which suffered some casualties, so he decided to move the remnants of his section to an alternative position from which he could better counter the enemy thrust. As the threat to this position became desperate, Corporal Bates seized a light machine-gun and charged, firing from the hip. He was almost immediately wounded and fell, but he got up and advanced again, though mortar bombs were falling all round him. He was hit a second time and more seriously wounded, but he went forward undaunted, firing constantly till the enemy started to fall back before him. Hit for the third time, he fell, but continued firing until his strength failed him. By then the enemy had withdrawn and Corporal Bates, by his supreme gallantry and self-sacrifice, had personally saved a critical situation. He died shortly afterwards of the wounds he had received.*

Poignant Inscriptions: With the establishment of permanent cemeteries after the First World War, headstones replaced wooden crosses and a space was reserved on the headstone for a personal inscription. Controversy followed when the families were forced to pay for the inscription, a policy eventually abandoned by the time of the Second World War. As no payment was required, although families could make a donation, the majority of graves have personal inscriptions and some are very touching, giving a brief glimpse into the loss some families suffered. A handful of examples for Bayeux are:

An aerial photograph of Bayeux War Cemetery, late 1940s.

Gunner Joseph Ferneyhough (I-C-8), 116th Field Regiment Royal Artillery, 30 July 1944, aged 26. Son of Frank and Margretta Ferneyhough, of Hanley, Stoke-on-Trent; husband of Harriett Ferneyhough, of Hanley.

'Only those who have loved & lost know war's bitter cost.'

Lieutenant William Herbert James McIlroy (X-L-16), 5th East Yorkshires, 6 June 1944, aged 22. Son of James Alexander Crossett McIlroy and Margaret Cecilia McIlroy, of Westbury Park, Bristol.

'He gave the greatest gift of all, his unfinished life.'

Sergeant Gordon Maitland Pickford (XII-A-4), 49th Reconnaissance Regiment, died 16 August 1944, aged 34. Son of Frederick Albert and Agnes Mary Pickford; husband of Ivy Alice Winifred Pickford, of Egham, Surrey.

'A Grenadier Guard Drummer who blew silver bugle at Menin Gate Ypres 1929.'

Private Bernard Percy Joseph Alexander (XIV-K-18), Kensington Regiment, died 18 June 1944, aged 24. Son of Robert George and Irene Winifred Alexander, of Eastcote, Middlesex.

'A Scouts promise fulfilled, to do my duty to God and the King. God bless you.'

Bayeux Memorial to the Missing.

Beny-sur-Mer Canadian War Cemetery

Burials: Canadian 2,043, British 4, French 1.

Location: The cemetery is reached from Courseulles-sur-Mer by taking the D79 to Caen. Or conversely, take the D79 from Caen to Courseulles-sur-Mer. At a crossroads of the D79 and D35 to Beny-sur-Mer, follow signs to Reviers. The cemetery is about a kilometre from here, and can be seen on high ground alongside the road.

Beny-sur-Mer Canadian War Cemetery.

The Canadian 3rd Division landed at JUNO Beach on 6 June 1944, and then fought their way inland. The objective was Caen, but this was not reached when the Canadians encountered battle groups from the *716. Division* and *21. Panzer Division*, and later the *12. SS Hitlerjugend Division*. Heavy casualties were suffered in the fighting inland from JUNO and are reflected in the burials here. Of the total, nearly 300 graves bear the date 6 June 1944.

Because of the volunteer nature of Canadian units, large Canadian families joined the army in the same way as had happened a generation before in the First World War. It is therefore perhaps not surprising that among the burials here are nine pairs of brothers, a record for a cemetery of the Second World War. Incredibly, one family had a triple bereavement in Normandy. This was unknown in the British Army, as the practice of placing men from one family together in a unit had largely been discontinued after the First World War. The brothers are:

Gunner Edward Blais, Royal Canadian Artillery, 13 July 1944, aged 28 (IX-H-1)

Rifleman Raymond Blais, Regina Rifle Regiment, 8 July 1944, aged 20 (XIII-G-3)

Trooper Kenneth Boyd, 7th Recce Regiment, 9 July 1944, aged 21 (XI-A-3)

Lieutenant Nairn Boyd, 27th Armored Regiment, 8 July 1944, aged 26 (XI-E-2)

Rifleman Gordon Branton, Regina Rifles Regiment, 6 June 1944, aged 24 (XI-E-16)

Rifleman Ronald Branton, Regina Rifles Regiment, 8 July 1944, aged 28 (XI-E-15)

Private George Hadden, Canadian Scottish, 10 June 1944, aged 19 (XIII-B-14)

Rifleman James Hadden, Regina Rifles Regiment, 19 July 1944, aged 20 (XIV-F-14)

Private John Hobbins, Stormont Highlanders, 8 July 1944, aged 30 (VII-F-3)

Private Michael Hobbins, Stormont Highlanders, 8 July 1944, aged 23 (II-E-11)

Lance Corporal Frank Meakin, Royal Winnipeg Rifles, 8 June 1944, aged 20 (XVI-B-3)

Corporal George Meakin, Royal Winnipeg Rifles, 8 June 1944, aged 23 (XIV-F-10)

Rifleman John Skwarchuk, Royal Winnipeg Rifles, 4 July 1944, aged 28 (XII-C-15)

Trooper Metro Skwarchuk, Royal Winnipeg Rifles, 6 June 1944, aged 25 (I-G-16)

Private Owen Tadgell, North Nova Scotia Highlanders, 8 July 1944, aged 29 (XIV-A-16)

Signaller William Tadgell, Royal Canadian Signals, 29 June 1944, aged 24 (X-H-3)

Rifleman George White, Royal Winnipeg Rifles, 8 June 1944, aged 27 (VIII-B-4)

Rifleman Robert White, Royal Winnipeg Rifles, 8 June 1944, aged 24 (VIII-B-5)

Rifleman Albert Westlake, Queens Own Rifles, 11 June 1944, aged 26 (III-D-8)

Private George Westlake, Nova Scotia Highlanders, 7 June 1944 (VIII-Γ-12)

Rifleman Thomas Westlake, Queens Own Rifles, 11 June 1944, aged 33 (III-D-7)

LA DELIVRANDE WAR CEMETERY

Burials: British 927, Canadian 11, Australian 3, Polish 1, German 180, unidentified 1.

Location: Take the main road northwards from Caen, the D7 to Langrune-sur-Mer. After about 12km, the war cemetery will be found on the right of the road, a few hundred metres before reaching La Delivrande crossroads and its twin-spired church. There is parking to the rear of the cemetery, down a side road that leads to the town civil cemetery. It is recommended you park here.

La Delivrande War Cemetery.

The burials in La Delivrande War Cemetery mainly date from 6 June and the landings on SWORD Beach, particularly Oboe and Peter sectors. Others were brought in later from the battlefields between the coast and Caen. There are now 942 Commonwealth servicemen of the Second World War buried or commemorated in this cemetery. Of the burials, sixty-three are unidentified but there are special memorials to a number of casualties known to be buried among them.

There are five lieutenant colonels buried in the cemetery, among them Lieutenant Colonel Hugh Owen Seymour Herdon (VII-C-9) who commanded the 2nd Bn Royal Warwickshire Regiment. He led them ashore at SWORD Beach on D-Day and was killed in the Lebisy Woods the next day, aged 38 and leaving behind a wife in Hassocks in Sussex. Among the D-Day burials, the majority are from the 1st Suffolks and 1st Royal Norfolks, but there are airborne graves too, including a glider load of men from 7 Para who crash-landed in the wrong area, and Lance Corporal Fred Greenhalgh (V-C-4) of 'D' Company, 2nd Oxs & Bucks, who died when he was thrown from a glider on landing near Pegasus Bridge and drowned in the marshland. His grave was moved here after the war.

RYES WAR CEMETERY

Burials: British 630, Canadian 21, Australian 1, Polish 1, German 326.

Location: Leave Bayeux on the D12 to the east, following signs for Ouistreham; at the village of Sommervieu go straight on along the D112, and after 3km turn right on to the D87. After climbing high ground and following the road to the left, the

cemetery will be found on the left-hand side. There is a parking bay in front.

The cemetery was started on 8 June 1944, following the 50th (Northumbrian) Division landing on nearby GOLD Beach on D-Day, and reflects the fighting that took place in this area on 6 June 1944, and the subsequent advance beyond Bayeux; in fact, it was once referred to as a 'GOLD Beach Cemetery'. Rear eche-

Ryes War Cemetery.

lon troops who died on or near the beachhead following D-Day are also buried here, along with a large number of Navy and Merchant Navy personnel. Some soldiers buried here are recorded as having died of wounds, so it is likely there was an Advanced Dressing Station in Bazenville at some point.

Among the burials are two brothers buried side by side. Marine Robert Casson (IV-B-2) died with 45 Royal Marine Commando on D-Day aged 26, and his younger brother Joseph Casson (IV-B-1) died with 9th Durham Light Infantry three weeks later on 27 June, aged eighteen. They were the sons of David and Mary Ellen Casson, of Whitehaven, Cumberland.

GERMAN CEMETERY LA CAMBE

Burials: In total, there are 21,222 German soldiers commemorated at La Cambe, of which 207 unknown and 89 identified soldiers are buried in a *kamaradengraben* – or mass grave – below the central tumulus.

Location: Exit the N13 at La Cambe and go south to the roundabout on the D113. Here follow the signs to the cemetery; the route takes you along a minor road that runs parallel to the N13 and to a car park in front of the cemetery. Park here.

German Cemetery La Cambe.

The German war dead from the Normandy campaign were scattered over a wide area, many of them buried in isolated or field graves, or small battlefield cemeteries. In the years following the Second World War, the German War Graves Commission, *Volksbund Deutsche Kriegsgräberfürsorge*, decided to establish six main German cemeteries in the Normandy area, with the one of the largest at La Cambe. Work on this cemetery started in 1954 and during this period the remains of more than 12,000 German soldiers were moved in from 1,400 locations in the *departments* of Calvados and the Orne, covering a wide area of the Normandy battlefield; among them were many German soldiers who had died on 6 June 1944. The cemetery was finished in 1961, and inaugurated in September of that year. Since this date more than 700 soldiers have been found on the battlefield, and are now also buried here.

Since the mid-1990s there has been an information centre on the site. Here there is a permanent exhibition about the *Volksbund Deutsche Kriegsgräberfürsorge* and casualties can be checked on a computer-based database; there are also toilet facilities. The cemetery is open daily from 0800–1900. The information centre is open daily from 0800–1200 and 1300–1900. There is parking at the main entrance and the cemetery is found by following the signs from the N13 Caen–Cherbourg main road.

ACKNOWLEDGEMENTS

As always, my walking guides are a team effort when they are in the research phase. For walking the ground with me and much constructive input I would like to thank: Tony Carr, Gary Cooper, Owen Dadge, John Hayes-Fisher, Marc Hope, Peter Smith and Andrew Whittington. Geoff Sullivan and his fantastic Search Engine have also been invaluable, and members of WW2 Talk (www.ww2talk.com) have been helpful in answering some specific enquiries.

Since I have been guiding Second World War tours for Leger Holidays, as far back as 1998 now, I have been lucky to meet hundreds of Normandy veterans. Many have become good friends, and in recent years I've been fortunate to spend time on the battlefields of Normandy with whole groups of them. In particular, I would like to mention: Bert Barritt, Ken Bell, Gordon Collinson, Ken Cooke, Alan Harrison, Douglas Haw, Dennis Heydock, Cyril Howarth, Frank Lodge, Fred Patrick, Roy Robotham, Ken Smith and Arthur Wragg.

In Normandy I would like to thank Vivian and Rodolphe Roger for their kindness, help and friendship, and also Paul Woodadge and his wife Myriam. Mark Worthington at the Pegasus Memorial has been very kind on visits there and thanks also goes to his wife Nathalie, director of the Juno Centre; the heritage of the Second World War could not be in better hands at two of Normandy's best museum sites!

Finally, my family. My parents, and especially my father who compiled the unpublished 'Normandy Roll of Honour' in the early 1990s and took me on my first visit to the D-Day beaches. And of course to Kieron, Ed and Poppy who have spent more than a decade visiting Normandy and taking time out of family holidays to walk some ground or drive off to an isolated memorial. To them I say, as ever, *toujours*.

NOTES

PEGASUS BRIDGE WALK: 6TH AIRBORNE DIVISION AT BÉNOUVILLE

1. Intelligence papers in WO 171/1357.

2. Ibid.

3. T. Buck, *Normandy 1944* (Fields of Battle, 2004), p. 44.

4. Ibid., p. 47.

5. 2nd Oxfordshire & Buckinghamshire Light Infantry War Diary, WO 171/1357.

6. Ibid.

7. Buck, *Normandy 1944*, p. 52.

8. 2nd Oxfordshire & Buckinghamshire Light Infantry War Diary, WO 171/1357.

9. 'Story of 7 Bn. Light Infantry, The Parachute Regiment, 1943–1944', WO 223/18.

10. Ibid.

11. Ibid.

12. Ibid.

13. Ibid.

14. Ibid.

15. Ibid.

16. Ibid.

17. Ibid.

EASTERN FLANK WALK: THE MERVILLE BATTERY AND AMFREVILLE–BRÉVILLE

1. N. Barber, *The Day the Devils Dropped In* (Pen & Sword, 2002), p. 74.

2. No. 3 Commando War Diary, DEFE 2/38.

3. No. 6 Commando War Diary, DEFE 2/42.

4. Ibid.

5. Major E. Dean, *Up The Airborne: The History of the 12th Yorkshire Bn The Parachute Regiment*, available at www.pegasusarchive.org/normandy/rep12thBn.htm (accessed 10 February 2011).

6. H. St G. Saunders, *The Red Beret* (Michael Joseph, 1950), p. 201.

7. 5th Black Watch War Diary, WO 171/1266.

Commando Walk: The 1st Special Service Brigade on D-Day

1. M.C. McDougall, *Swiftly They Struck* (Odhams, 1954), p. 66.

2. From papers in the author's collection.

3. McDougall, *Swiftly They Struck*, pp. 76–77.

4. Ibid., p. 80.

5. Ibid., p. 83.

6. Ibid., pp. 88–89.

7. No. 6 Commando War Diary, WO 218/68.

8. From papers in the author's collection.

SWORD Beach Walk: 3rd Division on D-Day

1. N. Scarfe, *Assault Division* (Collins, 1947, repr. Spellmount, 2004), p. 64.

2. Ibid., p. 67.

3. Lieutenant Colonel Arthur Denis Bradford Cocks DSO, commanding 5th Assault Regiment Royal Engineers, 6 June 1944, aged 39. His body was recovered from the beach and taken back to the UK. He is buried in Frimlet (St Peter's) churchyard, Surrey.

4. Major John Frederick Harward, 1st South Lancashires. He died of wounds on 7 June 1944. He is buried in Hermanville War Cemetery.

5. Recommendations for Honours and Awards for Gallant and Distinguished Service (Army), WO 373/48.

6. WO 373.

7. WO 373.

8. WO 373.

9. Scarfe, *Assault Division*, p. 74.

10. P.R. Nightingale, *A History of the East Yorkshire Regiment (Duke of York's Own) in the War of 1939–1945* (n.p., 1952), p. 123.

11. WO 373.

12. Nightingale, *A History of the East Yorkshire Regiment*, p. 123.

13. 1st Suffolk War Diary, WO 171/1381.

14. From information supplied by Brian Guy.

15. 1st Suffolk War Diary, WO 171/1381.

16. Ibid.

17. Scarfe, *Assault Division*, p. 85.

JUNO BEACH: NAN BEACH WALK – INLAND TO TAILLEVILLE

1. Lieutenant Colonel D.B. Buell was awarded the DSO for bravery on 6 June 1944.

2. W.R. Bird, *North Shore* (Brunswick Press, 1983), p. 201.

3. Ibid., p. 202.

4. W.T. Barnard, *Queens Own Rifles of Canada* (Ontario Publishing Co., 1960), p. 194.

5. C.C. Martin, *Battle Diary* (Dundurn Press, 1994), p. 6.

6. Ibid., pp. 8–9.

7. 80th Assault Regiment RE War Diary, WO 171/1808.

8. G. Brown and T. Copp, *Look to Your Front: Regina Rifles* (Wilfred Laurier University Press, 2001), p. 32.

JUNO BEACH WALK: MIKE BEACH – THE FIGHT FOR COURSEULLES

1. C.P. Stacey, *The Victory Campaign* (Queen's Printer, Ottawa, 1960), p. 104.

2. 1st Hussars War Diary, WO 179/2989.

3. Ibid.

4. A. Brandon Conroy, *A History of the First Hussars Regiment 1856–1980* (self published, Canada, 1951), p. 52.

5. Recommendations for Honours and Awards for Gallant and Distinguished Service (Army) WO 373/48.

6. Ibid.

7. Ibid.

8. 1st Canadian Scottish War Diary, WO 179/2969.

9. Private C.H. Evans from Alberta, Canadian Scottish, 6 June 1944, buried Ryes War Cemetery (II-A-2) and Private W.E. Fahnri from Berne, Switzerland, Canadian Scottish, 6 June 1944, buried Ryes War Cemetery (II-A-1).

10. R. Roy, *Ready For The Fray: The History of the Canadian Scottish Regiment* (Evergreen Press, 1958), p. 226.

GOLD BEACH WALK: 50TH DIVISION ON D-DAY

1. D.S. Daniell, *The Royal Hampshire Regiment Volume Three: 1918–1954* (Gale & Polden, 1955), p. 216.

2. Ibid., pp. 216–217.

3. Ibid.

4. Ibid.

5. Ibid.

6. A.E.C. Bredin, *Three Assault Landings* (Gale & Polden, 1946), p. 52.

7. E.W. Clay, *The Path of the 50th: The Story of the 50th – Northumbrian – Division in the Second World War, 1939–1945* (Gale & Polden, 1950), p. 241.

8. R. Hastings, *An Undergraduate's War* (Bellhouse Publishing, 1997), p. 224.

9. Ibid., p. 227.

10. *London Gazette*, 15.8.44, pp. 3807–3808.

11. Hastings, *An Undergraduate's War*, p. 225.

12. Clay, *The Path of the 50th*, p. 243.

ARROMANCHES WALK: D-DAY LIBERATION AND THE MULBERRY HARBOUR

1. W.S. Churchill, *The Second World War* (Time, 1959), p. 214.

2. Major L.F. Ellis, *Victory in the West Volume I: The Battle of Normandy* (HMSO, 1962), p. 272.

OMAHA BEACH WALK: 'BLOODY OMAHA'

1. Anon, *741: D Day to VE Day* (n.p., n.d.).

2. Anon, OMAHA *Beachhead* (Historical Division, War Department, Washington, repr. 1984), pp. 42–43.

3. Ibid., p. 43.

4. Ibid., p. 56.

5. Ibid., p. 58.

6. Ibid., p. 53.

7. Ibid., p. 60.

8. Ibid., pp. 109–110.

POINTE DU HOC WALK: THE 2ND RANGERS, 6–8 JUNE

1. Anon, *Small Unit Actions* (Historical Division, War Department, Washington, repr. 1982), p. 2.

2. Ibid., p. 6.

3. Ibid., pp. 12–17.

4. Ibid., p. 21.

5. Ibid., pp. 29–33.

6. Ibid., p. 44.

7. Ibid., p. 53.

8. Ibid., pp. 58–59.

UTAH BEACH WALK: THE 4TH INFANTRY AND 101ST (AIRBORNE) DIVISIONS ON D-DAY

1. 4th Cavalry account from website http://www.25thida.com/4thcav.html (accessed 24 June 2011).

2. Anon, UTAH *Beach to Cherbourg* (Historical Division, War Department, Washington, 1948), pp. 45–47.

3. Ibid., p. 55.

4. Ibid., pp. 14–15.

5. Ibid., pp. 41–42.

AIRBORNE WALK: STE-MÈRE-EGLISE–LA FIÈRE – 82ND AIRBORNE ACTIONS ON D-DAY

1. G.A. Harrison, *Cross Channel Attack* (Historical Division, War Department, Washington, 1951), p. 291.

2. Ibid., pp. 346–347.

3. Heim account from http://www.thedropzone.org/europe/normandy/heim.html (accessed 10 June 2011).

4. Harrison, *Cross Channel Attack*, p. 293.

5. From documents in the author's papers.

6. Harrison, *Cross Channel Attack*, pp. 292–293.

INDEX